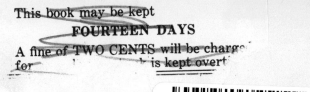

W9-AXF-046

THE RISE OF THE HOUSE OF
DUVEEN

JAMES
HENRY
DUVEEN

THE RISE OF THE
HOUSE OF
DUVEEN

NEW YORK
ALFRED A KNOPF
MCMEVII

L.C. catalog card number: 55-9282
© *James Henry Duveen, 1957*

THIS IS A BORZOI BOOK,
PUBLISHED BY ALFRED A. KNOPF, INC.

FIRST AMERICAN EDITION

AUTHOR'S NOTE

I HAVE PRESENTED *in this book the history of the Duveen family in the art-business down to the year 1939. I might be doing others an injustice if I did not categorically state that my history does not cover the present Duveen Brothers, Inc. and Duveen Art Galleries, operating in New York, or any other firm or gallery in any country operating under the name Duveen. I am not familiar with the principals or with their business and have not included them in this history of my family.*

CONTENTS

I	ORIGINS	3
II	THE PRODUCE MERCHANT	11
III	HIS OWN MASTER	26
IV	EGG-SHELL AND HAWTHORN	37
V	LONGING FOR LONDON	45
VI	BETSY DUVEEN	51
VII	HENRY J. DUVEEN'S ENTRY	61
VIII	OXFORD STREET	71
IX	ESTHER	78
X	INTERIOR DECORATION	87
XI	THE BREAK	93
XII	GEORGE SALTING	104
XIII	CHARLES DUVEEN	112

Contents

XIV   THE DUVEEN FORTUNE   120

XV   JOEL DUVEEN'S ILLNESS   125

XVI   OLD BOND STREET   131

XVII   EMBARRASSING VASES   137

XVIII   THE POMPADOUR CHAIRS   145

XIX   THE MONS FIGURE   160

XX   THE "DON QUICHOTTE" TAPESTRIES   170

XXI   THE MAZZARENTI COLLECTION   182

XXII   PIERPONT MORGAN   192

XXIII   THE ANTIQUE STAMPS   200

XXIV   ELEVEN REMBRANDTS   212

XXV   THE RODOLPHE KANN COLLECTION   228

XXVI   THE MAYERLING MYSTERY   237

XXVII   THE HAINAUER COLLECTION   251

XXVIII   OPEN WARFARE   257

XXIX   EXCAVATED TREASURE   267

XXX   BENJAMIN ALTMAN   279

XXXI   THE PASSING OF THE FOUNDER   289

INDEX   *follows page* 293

ILLUSTRATIONS

The Duveen Family, a Wedding Photograph

                          FACING PAGE   52

Sir Joseph Joel Duveen, the Founder of Duveen Brothers   53

James Henry Duveen   84

Nankin Vases, "Lange lyzen" Type   85

Hawthorn Jar, K'ang-hsi Period   180

Sèvres Vases   180

Gobelins Tapestry from a Boucher Design   181

Nankin Vase (the "Embarrassing Vase")   212

Famille noire Vase   212

"The Night Watch," by Rembrandt   213

THE RISE OF THE HOUSE OF
DUVEEN

DUVEEN GENEALOGY

*In this abbreviated genealogy the names that occur frequently
in the text are printed in heavy capitals.*

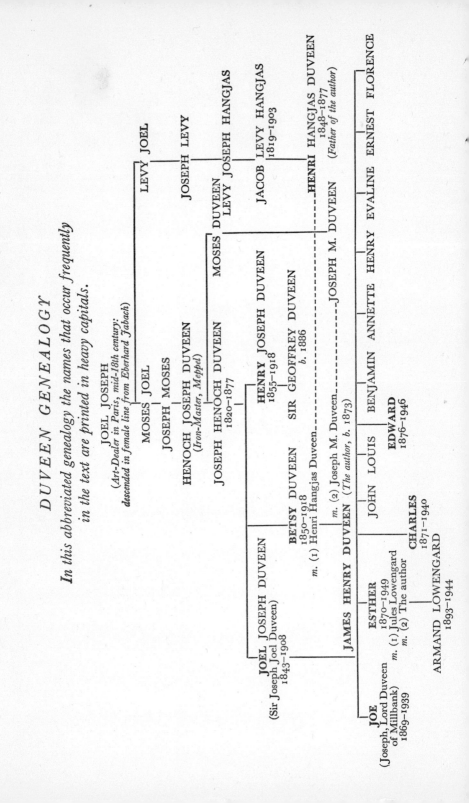

JOEL JOSEPH
*(Art-Dealer in Paris, mid-18th century:
descended in female line from Eberhard Jabach)*

LEVY JOEL

MOSES JOEL

JOSEPH MOSES

JOSEPH LEVY

HENOCH JOSEPH DUVEEN
(Iron-Master, Meppel)

JOSEPH HENOCH DUVEEN
1820–1877

MOSES DUVEEN
LEVY JOSEPH HANGJAS

JACOB LEVY HANGJAS
1819–1903

HENRI HANGJAS DUVEEN
1848–1877
(Father of the author)

JOEL JOSEPH DUVEEN
(Sir Joseph Joel Duveen)
1843–1908

BETSY DUVEEN
1850–1918
m. (1) Henri Hangjas Duveen

HENRY JOSEPH DUVEEN
1855–1918

SIR GEOFFREY DUVEEN
b. 1886

m. (2) Joseph M. Duveen
(The author, b. 1873)

JOSEPH M. DUVEEN

JAMES HENRY DUVEEN   JOHN LOUIS   BENJAMIN   ANNETTE   HENRY   EVALINE   ERNEST   FLORENCE

ESTHER
1870–1949
m. (1) Jules Lowengard
m. (2) The author

EDWARD
1876–1946

CHARLES
1871–1940

JOE
(Joseph, Lord Duveen
of Millbank)
1869–1939

ARMAND LOWENGARD
1893–1944

I

ORIGINS

THOUGH MANY REASONS have contributed to impel me to write this book, the chief one is the memory of my uncle Joel Joseph Duveen. On the death of my father at the untimely age of twenty-nine, when I was four years old, my uncle was appointed my guardian by the Dutch court. He took a constant interest in me as I grew up; and, seeing how much I admired his energy and brilliance, he loved to tell me his interesting experiences. I was an eager listener and made notes of all he told me. He frequently invited me to accompany him on long journeys, and I spent many holidays with him on the Continent; the most pleasurable and exciting parts of these travels with him were the stories of his early life and the reminiscences of his business career.

In 1908 King Edward VII bestowed a knighthood upon him, and he changed his name by letters patent to Joseph Joel Duveen (I shall call him in this book by his original first name, Joel). When the knighthood was announced the press published so many inaccurate statements about him that my uncle sent his son Edward to ask me to write his life story. The invitation opened up such vistas before me that I determined to do so. My cousin went on to tell me that my uncle wanted to see me at once and did not want his son Joe to know. We went straight away to his house, "The Elms," on Hampstead Heath; but we were not allowed to see him. Joe (later Lord Duveen) previously had been on bad terms with his father and the other members of his family. But during his father's last illness he gained ascendancy over him and assumed command. He prevented me from seeing my uncle, who died a few months later, on November 9, 1908. So ended my first intention of writing the life of Joel Duveen.

Nearly a quarter of a century later I began to write my own reminiscences, and in two books I included many of my uncle's stories. In April 1939, a little before Joe, then Lord Duveen of Millbank, died, my cousin Edward approached me again with the request that I write a history of the Duveen family in order to show how the real makers of the firm of Duveen Brothers [1] were not Joe, but his father and uncle, Joel and Henry Duveen. Edward was then a director of the London firm, and he offered to furnish me with much inside information. I accepted with enthusiasm and had written fifteen chapters when the Second World War broke out in the autumn and stopped my work.

In 1945 I wanted to resume work on the family history. Our furniture had been moved into the country and back again, and I found that during these moves the trunk containing my papers and the finished chapters had disappeared. I was too discouraged to make a fresh start.

A friend, however, sent me in 1954 a fascinating book, *Duveen*, by S. N. Behrman, a gifted American author, which I read with the greatest interest. In it he has produced a brilliant picture of Lord Duveen's character and methods, and he

[1] See Author's Note.

is to be congratulated on his successful portrait. But this exciting book is chiefly concerned with the period of Lord Duveen; and I am grateful to its author for inspiring me to take up my pen again and place on record the greatness of the older generation who, by more brilliant but less grandiose methods, created the firm Lord Duveen raised to a height that may never again be equalled.

I therefore began again, in spite of advanced age (I am now eighty-three), to set down my memories of a line of great and intrepid connoisseurs in art. In our careers the art treasures in which we dealt and the great figures who formed our clientele are more interesting than we are ourselves. For this reason I have tried to picture the characters of my family by their adventurous dealings rather than by long biographical sketches; the incidents related are authentic in all details except names, some of which have been disguised for obvious reasons.

Joel—Sir Joseph Joel Duveen—at the time of his death in 1908 had eight sons and four daughters living; it had been his ambition to have all his sons in the great firm that he had created. But his son Joe, an individualist in the Napoleonic mould, was determined to have neither rivals nor even any relatives close to the throne. By the time of his father's death he had driven four of his brothers out of the firm. Later he forced the other brothers also out of the partnership. Joel's younger brother Henry's only son, Geoffrey, who after a distinguished career at Oxford entered the firm, also found the atmosphere intolerable and left to achieve eminence, as Sir Geoffrey Duveen, in another sphere.

When Joe, then the famous Lord Duveen, died, the only members of the family who remained in the firm, and these as associates and not as partners, were his younger brother

5

Edward and his favourite nephew, Armand Lowengard, who was my wife's son by her first husband. He achieved the lonely eminence he had desired by bequeathing the whole of the stock of the great firm of Duveen Brothers to Armand Lowengard and two associates who had served him well for many years; so there were no more Duveens in the original firm when he died. Captain Lowengard had had his strength seriously impaired by grave wounds sustained during service in the First World War. When the Second World War broke out a few months after Lord Duveen's death, Armand again volunteered for service with the French Army, although he was now president of Duveen Brothers. The re-opening of the wounds sustained in the First World War and high blood-pressure caused his discharge after a few months; but he returned to occupied Paris and became a leading figure in the organization of the resistance movement. He was denounced to the Germans but escaped and eventually found his way to North Africa, and finally reached New York via Lisbon. Not long after his return high blood-pressure, aggravated by his war adventures, brought on an apoplectic seizure, and a year later another stroke ended his life. So, at the age of fifty-one, passed the only member of the Duveen family who remained in the great firm that was built up by the genius of the brothers Joel and Henry Duveen in the hope that their descendants would remain the Rothschilds of the art-dealing world.

With this explanation I can begin my story of the House of Duveen. It begins with the penniless son of a ruined iron-master in a small Dutch town and ends with the death of a man whose wealth was estimated at nine million pounds. This volume will tell the story of the rise of the firm and its prosperity and progress during the lifetime of its founders.

6

It is my intention, if I am spared, to complete the saga in another volume describing the period when Joe was the undisputed master.

The House of Duveen goes back a long way in the history of art-collecting, but, owing to the old Jewish prejudice against surnames, it was not until the enforcement of the Code Napoléon over a great part of the European continent that Jews were forced to adopt unchanging family names. Until then sons had merely added their father's proper name to their own proper name, with, at times, the word *"Ben"* (son) in between. Thus, Joel's son became Joseph Ben Joel, or simply Joseph Joel. The forced adoption of surnames made the confusion even worse, for whereas some chose their own new names, others who might be absent, or who refused to comply for religious reasons, were given them by the officials, who frequently used the occasion for bestowing ridiculous or even insulting names. In the case of my family, two great-grandsons of Joel Ben Joseph of Paris emigrated from Paris to Holland during the French Revolution, and they became in 1810, respectively, Henoch Joseph Duveen and Levy Joseph Hangjas. The former had chosen the name of du Vesne, after a French grandmother, and the latter had been "given" the name of Hangjas "by default." Both men dealt in antiques, but having had to flee practically penniless from France, they had to start again from the bottom. In spite of all these vicissitudes, the two families remained in touch, although Hangjas lived at The Hague and Duveen, after living for some years in northern Germany, finally settled down in the little town of Meppel in the north-east of Holland.

The French name du Vesne (which soon became the Dutch equivalent Duvane, written Duveen) was brought into the family by a girl who was descended from the great art-collector Eberhard Jabach, head of a rich family of merchant-bankers which had fled from Spain during one of the early persecutions of the Jews. They used their old business relations with the East to establish flourishing centres in Cologne, Paris, Leghorn, and the Netherlands. Eberhard Jabach was the greatest art-connoisseur and collector of his time, and he was the most important buyer at the sale of King Charles I's incomparable collection. The tradition is that when he returned from this sale he re-entered Paris at the head of a convoy of wagons loaded with artistic conquests, like a Roman victor at the head of a triumphal procession. Not many years later, he was forced by financial reverses to sell one hundred and ten pictures to Louis XIV, and this was the nucleus around which the famous Louvre collection was formed. Among these pictures were Giorgione's "Rustic Concert," "Holy Family with Saint Catherine," and "Saint Sebastian and Donor"; Titian's "Christ at Emmaus," "Entombment," and "Jupiter and Antiope"; Correggio's "Antiope"; Caravaggio's magnificent "Death of Mary"; and many others.

In 1664, at the founding of the French East India Company by Louis XIV's great minister, Loubet, Eberhard Jabach was appointed its director. In 1671 he was appointed director of the Manufacture Royale d'Aubusson (the famous tapestry works).

Eberhard died a rich banker. He was painted by many artists, but his best portrait is a Van Dyck, which once hung in the Hermitage, St. Petersburg. Another is the great family portrait painted by Charles Le Brun, court painter of Louis XIV, in which appears the little girl who was to marry du Vesne. Goethe wrote that the contemplation of this picture gave him his final inspiration to climb the heights of Parnassus. The Jabach family, which never entirely abandoned Cologne, produced many collectors who left great reputations in the annals of the ancient city. But the direct line died out, so that at the beginning of the nineteenth century the great family mansion was an almost abandoned show house. It was demolished in 1930, shortly after I had seen it.

Henoch Joseph, who in 1810 took the name Duveen from this descendant of Eberhard Jabach, took over a small but flourishing ironworks at Meppel in Holland, leaving one of his daughters to carry on the antique-business. She married the Ridder (Chevalier) van Esso, and it was from these two that Joel Duveen, while still a schoolboy, began to learn all about antique-dealing. The Hangjas branch of the family had settled at The Hague, and continued in the art-business. Several of their offspring intermarried with leading art-dealers, such as de Maan, van Schaak, and Fresco. Levy Fresco settled in London, where he and his descendants carried on his business in the little shop that is said to have served Charles Dickens as model for his *Old Curiosity Shop*. I remember this Levy Fresco and his three sons Leon, John, and Mike.

My grandfather, Jacob Levy Hangjas, was born in Haarlem in 1819. He and his two brothers were all antique-dealers, but my grandfather also dealt in old metals. He had two large warehouses for his wholesale antique-business, as well as a warehouse and wharf on the wide river Spaarne for the breaking up of steamers. Before I was ten years old I spent a good deal of time in the two warehouses where the old porcelain and pottery were stored, and it was in these warehouses that my uncle Joel Duveen made his first purchases. Jacob Hangjas had four sons and two daughters, all of whom, with the exception of the youngest daughter, Jeanette, became antique-dealers.

9

The branches of these two families were united again in their third generations when Henri Hangjas and Betsy Duveen (sister of *Joel* Joseph Duveen, who altered the order of his first names when he was created the first Sir *Joseph* Duveen) were married in 1872. I was their first child. As was customary in France, Belgium, and Holland in those days, my father added his wife's name to his own. He died in 1877 just after he had agreed to enter into partnership with his distant relative and brother-in-law, Joel Joseph Duveen. After a widowhood of six years, my mother, Betsy Hangjas-Duveen, married in 1883 her first cousin Joseph Duveen, a son of Duveens who lived in Zwolle.

Thus, when in 1911 I married my cousin Esther Duveen (widow of the leading Paris art-dealer, Jules Lowengard, and daughter of my uncle Joel Duveen) this was the family's third intermarriage in a century. We had been in love since childhood, but our parents had been quite determined that there should be no further intermarriage. Like a very remote ancestor and namesake, I also waited for my Rachel; but instead of seven years I waited for twenty.

II

THE PRODUCE MERCHANT

JOEL JOSEPH DUVEEN, who was to become the founder of Duveen Brothers,[1] dealers in works of art, London, Paris, and New York, was born in Meppel on April 30, 1843. His father, Joseph Henoch Duveen, was the son of the Henoch Duveen who left his father's antique-business to take over the ironworks. The family antique-business was continued by Henoch's sister and her husband, the Ridder van Esso.[2]

Joel's mother, Eva van Minden, was the highly educated only child of an East India merchant who had been ruined by Napoleon's Continental System. She was a very beautiful but rather delicate woman. Joel was her first-born; her next

---

[1] See Author's Note.

[2] *Ridder* is the Dutch for knight. The Ridder van Esso had earned his title in 1832 during the bombardment of the Citadel of Antwerp when this fortress was besieged by a French army. He had helped to save the life of his officer, the Count van Limburg Stirum, who had his foot smashed by an enemy bomb. Van Esso had been unable to carry this young giant out of danger, and so had covered the wounded man with his own body until a surgeon had joined him in carrying the officer to safety. Ultimately the Count's leg had to be amputated, and Van Esso received the Willems Kruis—the highest decoration in the Dutch Army, and carrying a knighthood.

child was a daughter, born three years after Joel. Four years after this, in 1850, my own mother was born; and after an interval of five years Eva Duveen gave birth to her last child, Henry Joseph Duveen, who ultimately was to become his elder brother's partner in the firm of Duveen Brothers. Unfortunately, this last confinement exhausted her weak constitution, and she remained an invalid until she died on August 22, 1864, at the age of fifty-two. My grandmother seems to have been loved by everyone who knew her, for her kindness and for her charity to the poor and suffering. When in 1936 I visited the family graves in the Meppel Jewish cemetery I read on her tombstone the Hebrew words "A Noble Woman."

While I was staying with my Uncle Joel at Bettws-y-Coed in September 1905 he told me the sad story of his mother's untimely death. "The early death of my mother," he began, "was a terrible blow. She had never recovered from her last childbirth, and although she was always cheerful in appearance, we knew that she was only pretending to feel better. I was twelve when Henry was born, and even before then I used to spend most of my spare time with my father's brother-in-law, Uncle the Ridder, and his wife. The beautiful things in the old family business began to attract me before I was six, and my aunt, who had grown up in the business, delighted in teaching me. As I grew older her husband also began to take an interest in teaching me styles and qualities. But I think that what really pleased him most was the telling of his adventures to an eager listener. Gradually I became so enamoured of the beautiful things that I began to hope that I would be able to become an antique-dealer, too. I left school shortly after I was sixteen, but by then my mother had become a permanent invalid, and my father spent most of his time with her, while I had to help with looking after the works. Shortly after a year there, I was able to manage the workmen, while my father gradually lost all interest in the works and spent most of his time by my poor mother's bedside. On the morning of her death my mother sent for me while my father was out, and when I came into the room she whispered: 'I am leaving you, my love. You are the eldest. Look after your father, and watch over your sisters and little brother.' She seemed very tired and remained silent for a time. Then, as if coming back from afar, she said: 'Bend your head, dear,' and as I did so she placed her hand on my head and gave me her last blessing. Then the nurse beckoned me to leave the room."

Uncle Joel, who was then sixty-two, had great difficulty in uttering these last words, and I looked away. After a moment's silence he rose and proposed a walk.

I was most anxious to hear more of his early history, but I did not broach the subject again until he did so himself two days later during a walk in the Lledr Valley.

"My father," he began, "was very intelligent and energetic, but everything was different after my mother's death. He had lost everything. He neglected the little works, and, remembering my mother's last words, I began to work seriously at what had been a hobby between school hours. Our foreman taught me all the intricacies of the work and how to get the best out of the men without ordering them about too much. When I left school I had more time to enjoy my other hobby: listening to my uncle, the Ridder, in his antique-shop or on the street bench by the side of his door. He had taken over the old-established business which the family had carried on for generations. He taught me a great deal about antiques.

"But as I grew older the management of the works fell more and more on me and, when I was twenty-two, I managed to secure for the firm the contract for the manufacture of part of the metric weights and measures which the Netherlands government required for the colonies. We worked hard for nearly three years on this job, and everything was ready to be judged when a government official came to inspect the work. He was extremely friendly, and he even stayed at our house during the several days it took him to make his inspection. The evening of the last day he showed me a fine gold watch that one of the other contractors had given him, but I did not dare to offer him a present. However, he was even more friendly when he left the next morning. A week later we received the official notice that our work had been rejected. This practically ruined the business. The irony of the whole thing is that later on the same weights and measures which we had to sell for old metal were accepted by the government without any changes, except the name "Joseph Duveen Meppel" was changed to the name of the firm that had bought them from us as old metal. My father decided to go to Amsterdam to start a small cotton-wool factory with the remainder of his fortune, but I refused to go with him. Holland had become too small for me. I wanted to go to England. My father called this madness, and he would have nothing to do with it. In my foolhardy self-reliance I told him that I would fight my own way and not trouble him for one penny.

"Until then the idea that I might have to leave home had never entered my head, and, as my father had never refused me anything I wanted, I had put nothing aside. So I went to see my Uncle Jaap, who was very fond of me, and he not only provided me with some money, but gave me a letter of introduction to old friends of his, Messrs. Dumouriez and Gotschalk of Hull, wholesale importers of Dutch produce.

"On arrival at Hull, I was received very kindly by my uncle's friends, but they were extremely disappointed to find that I knew very little English.

" 'What can we do with you?' exclaimed old Mr. Dumouriez. 'I don't see how we can use you.'

"I had burnt my boats and knew that I had to obtain employment at any cost, so I replied that I would do any work, even manual labour, for them until I knew sufficient English to be able to get into their business department. They were impressed by this, and they agreed to employ me as a *volontaire*, with weekly pocket-money of fifteen shillings. And that, my boy," said Uncle Joel with a laugh, "was my entry into big business in England!"

One evening a few days later he resumed his history. I had already written out that first part, and Uncle had been very pleased when I showed it to him.

"All right, my boy. Some day you'll write my life, and I'll give you this evening for another instalment." Aunt Rosetta had gone to bed, so he was able to continue without interruption until well after midnight.

"Let me see," he began, "where did we get to?"

"To your arrival in Hull and your appointment as *volontaire* by Dumouriez and Gotschalk at fifteen shillings a week."

"Yes, a princely income," he laughed, and then he began: "That first morning I feared that I had taken on something that I could not do. No one in the office understood a word of Dutch, and my first attempts at English were so bad that they only made me ridiculous. For some hours I wandered aimlessly around the firm's warehouse until I met the old foreman—a Dutchman from Friesland. Even he did not speak English properly, but his Frisian was not so far removed from the Yorkshire Anglo-Saxon. In fact, his dialect was nearly as difficult for me to follow as the 'English' of the Yorkshire-men. However, in a few minutes we became very friendly, and he offered to give me a few hours that evening to show me the stock. Towards the end of this inspection, I saw a large quantity of smoked hams lying about as if they had been abandoned. I asked him why such a quantity of good food was being neglected. He answered that this was a consign-ment of such poor quality that the firm did not care to offer it to their customers.

"This was a chance for making myself useful, and I asked old Jan whether these hams were still good enough to eat. When he told me that they were, I asked him if he would help me the next day—a Sunday—if I gave him ten shillings. He agreed, and early next morning we steeped the hams in a large tank of strong brine which Jan had prepared the previous evening. At eight o'clock that evening we began to take the hams out of the brine, and the whole job was finished in a few more hours. The hams looked really good, and the next morning I took two of them to Mr. Dumouriez. I told him what we had done, but he only remarked: 'We can't sell such poor quality to our customers.' I asked his permission for the lot to be put up for auction the next day, and then I got my first encouragement, for after a moment's frowning his expression changed and he said: 'All right, young man. That's not a bad idea.' The hams were duly included in the auction, described as a job-lot, and they fetched just over thirty pounds.

"Apart from having made a good beginning with my em-ployers, it also had the effect that old Jan and I became good friends. One day he had hinted something was wrong in the office, and when I pressed him he said he suspected that some of the younger men in the office were selling information to competitors, telling them our sources of supply and who were our customers. He felt sure that the loss of business during the last two years was due to this. He said, finally, that he suspected two rather fast young fellows who were spending much more money on drinks and theatres than they earned. He could not give me any proof, but I made up my mind that as soon as I knew sufficient English I would inquire into this dirty business. After a few weeks I thought that I knew enough for my purpose. By that time I also knew a good bit about the Hull produce-business. It was mostly a system of quick transit. The cargoes arrived from Holland and, when unloaded, most of the consignments were taken straight from the dock to the station to be forwarded to wholesalers and retailers all over England. In almost every case a clerk from the importer's office would merely remove or obliterate the Dutch sender's name and address—a precaution against retailers getting into direct contact with the Dutch firms. When the consignments arrived at the railway station, the new addresses would be attached and the consignments would be forwarded to their various destinations.

"It seemed clear to me that the cause of the leakages would be found at the dock or at the station. When I heard from Jan that a large number of consignments for Dumouriez and Gotschalk would be arriving early the next morning I got up at five and went to the dock. I had already paid several visits there, so I knew the lie of the land. I took up a convenient position for my watch, and after waiting for about half an hour, I saw a youth beginning to copy the addresses on various consignments. I realized that I was on the right track. When he had finished he strolled into a small shed where cups of hot tea were sold. I remained at my post, and about a quarter of an hour after the youth had entered the shed one of our young clerks came along. He began to obliterate our address, and while he was doing this, the first youth came out of the tea-shed. The two had some talk together. Then, on the point of parting, our man looked around and, judging the coast clear, handed a bit of paper to the younger one, who, in turn, put something into the hand of our clerk.

"I knew now all that I wanted to know, and when Mr. Dumouriez arrived at the office that morning I told him what I had suspected and what I had seen. Mr. Gotschalk was called in, and then the young clerk was sent for. He was questioned by both gentlemen and very soon cornered. He confessed to accepting bribes from four firms, all of which he named. The result was that this man and another clerk who had helped him to prepare the various lists were discharged. Moreover, the disclosure of the firms which had bribed the men was useful in the counter-measures which were taken.

"A few days after their interview with the bribed clerks my employers informed me that they had decided to allow me a salary of three pounds a week for making myself generally useful. I felt that this was just their way of recompensing me for what I had done and, as I did not like it, it suddenly occurred to me that I could do much more than make myself merely useful. In a flash I had my plan ready, so I said: 'Gentlemen, I think that I can do more than that if you will let me.' Without stopping, I told them that, if they would agree, I thought that I could recapture the whole of their lost trade and make many new customers. They were interested, so I explained further. I told them that if I could have a list of the names of customers who had left them to deal with other firms, and particularly of the type of goods they used to order, I felt sure these firms would come back if my plan was adopted.

"My employers were quite keen to go into the details, and I gave them my ideas. I told them that lists of all our import goods should be sent to those firms at the lowest possible prices, but that whatever they used regularly to order from Messrs. Dumouriez and Gotschalk before they had closed their accounts should be priced at net cost. The two old gentlemen agreed at once, but while I had been talking I had also been thinking, so I continued by telling them that I should also like to try to obtain lower quotations from our Dutch sources of supply.

"Mr. Gotschalk interrupted me with 'They would never agree to that.' However, I knew that my chiefs were very strong financially, and on this knowledge I based the rest of my plan. So I said: 'Gentlemen, I know that you always pay one month after delivery; but I think that if you offer to buy for immediate cash after the goods have been received and approved, and if I can promise them very much bigger orders if they make further reductions, you will be able to get all your lost customers back and to make new ones as well.'

" 'And how would you do that?' asked Mr. Gotschalk.

" 'By taking the lists with me to Holland tonight and going to see the Dutch sellers myself. I guarantee that I will return within a week with better quotations than you have ever had,' I replied.

" 'I think he is right,' said Mr. Gotschalk to his partner; but Mr. Dumouriez said: 'There is only one small difficulty about this plan. There is no boat out to Holland today, and it is too late to catch the Harwich boat. So, as tomorrow is Sunday, you could not get across until Monday night at the earliest.' I never gave in if I could help it, so I asked: 'If I can

find a way to get across, could you see to it that the necessary lists would be made out for me? The two old gentlemen looked at each other, and then Mr. Dumouriez observed: 'You are a madman, but I think you'll do it, and I'll
see to it that the lists will be ready for you within an hour.'

"I went straight away to the docks, and you can imagine
how happy I was when I heard from one of the gate-men that
a Dutch flat-bottomed fishing smack was going to sail for
Harlingen, the Frisian port on the Zuider Zee, two hundred
and thirty miles away, that afternoon. I ran all the way to the
quay-side. The whole family—man, wife, and a son—were
drinking coffee (the Dutch equivalent for a light lunch) on
deck, and in a moment we had arranged my passage—five
gulden (about eight shillings) for the voyage, and ten stivers
(pence) for each cooked meal. The skipper intended to sail
about four that afternoon, but at my request he agreed to sail
at one o'clock.

"I packed a few things for the journey and then called at
the office for the papers. After eating a hurried lunch, I was
on board the smack about half past twelve, and we sailed almost immediately. The weather was not good, for there was
a strong breeze blowing from the north; but it was not too bad
until we came near the mouth of the Humber, for then Skipper Willems had to take in a good bit of sail. The old-fashioned smack seemed to dance instead of float, and she heeled
over to such an extent that I thought she would capsize alto-
gether. I did not like the idea of going below, as I was afraid
that I would drown like a rat in a trap if she should turn turtle;
but the result was that I was drenched within a few minutes.
The crew—father, mother, and son—were protected by their
oilskins, but they were so busy dealing with the wild gusts that
they had no time to think of my comfort.

"After an hour of this, I came to the conclusion that Mr. Dumouriez had been right when he said that I was a madman; but just about dark the wind slackened, and then the skipper came over to me and told me that the wind was easing up and veering to the west, so that we could expect the ship to sail much more steadily. He was right, and shortly afterwards he came again and advised me to go below and to change my soaked things. He took me down into the *kajuit* that I would have to share with his son, and after lighting a small oil-lamp, told me that I could get into the hammock, as his son would bring another one for himself. I changed in a great hurry and hoisted myself into the hammock. This was the first time that I had had anything to do with this sort of swing, and when I tried to lie down the whole thing turned over and I was thrown down on the hard floor. Fortunately, the young man arrived and showed me how to master this kind of tumbling bed. He also brought a pot of hot coffee with some thick slices of bread covered with thin slices of smoked beef. After a really hearty meal, I managed to lie down in my net and I did not wake until about ten in the morning.

"As I came on deck the sun was shining, and I heard that we had had a strong, favourable breeze all night. The skipper hoped to make port that night about nine. I was treated to coffee again, this time with Dutch honey-cake, and at twelve we had the midday meal. It was the old-fashioned thick pea soup served in pewter bowls. In each bowl there was a pig's foot, a good piece of beef sausage, and various titbits of salted pork. I thoroughly enjoyed this old-style meal, made all the more pleasant by the thought that, in spite of the first bad hours, I would arrive at Harlingen without having lost a working hour, for in those days no Frisian would have talked about business on a Sunday.

21

"The next morning I was at it from eight o'clock, and from the very beginning I got what I wanted. The cash payments for much larger quantities, and the first-class reputation of Dumouriez and Gotschalk for fair dealing, worked miracles. So after two hard days' work in the various centres, I returned to Hull—this time via London and York—with a fine collection of offers at prices that would enable the firm to make good profits while beating all competitors both in price and quality. My chiefs were very pleased, and they proved it by raising my salary to six pounds a week."

For a moment my uncle sat back in his chair, beaming with pleasure at that memory of his first business success in England. Then he continued quite excitedly: "But this was nothing compared with the working of the campaign that I had planned on my return journey. I had the whole office working at those lists, and I studied the details so that I could attack our unfair competitors in their weakest spots. Every price-list which went out to the inland customers had a few specialties marked with red ink, and those items were quoted at our cost price plus nominal charges for freight. But this was the only thing to which the two old gentlemen demurred. I pointed out that this was throwing a sprat to catch a whale, and that my new system would do away with all advertising or sending special salesmen round with samples. The upshot was that Mr. Gotschalk smacked me on the shoulder and said: 'Go ahead, Duveen, I'm sure it will work!'

"Well, my boy," my uncle continued, "up till then the firm had not touched the western counties; but now I went right across with our campaign, and I begged them to let me go to Liverpool and Manchester myself. By this time my chiefs were willing to agree to anything I proposed, so I went, and came back in four days with orders that surpassed any which they had ever booked. Again the firm treated me generously, for although I had expected something of the sort, my salary was raised to sixty pounds a month. I was never at a loss for words, but this time I could not find anything to say for a few seconds; then I stuttered: 'Gentlemen, I can't accept this, it's too much.' 'We are the best judges of what is too little or too much, and we consider it right,' observed Mr. Dumouriez.

"I was overcome by their kindness and, on account of this generous treatment, I refused several offers of bigger salaries from competing firms who soon became aware of my success. Before the year was out, I was the best-paid employee in the Hull produce-business. I had repaid your grandfather the money which he had lent me, and I had made my own father happy with my success. He even admitted that I had done wisely by going to England."

I had heard as a child that my uncle Joel had begun in England by going into the produce-business, but I never had heard why he had left this business, so I asked him the reason.

"One day," he said, "a Dutchman whom I had once known in Holland came to me and proposed that I should go into partnership with him. He told me that he and another Dutchman had sufficient capital and that we would share the profits equally. Whereas I had refused to leave the firm for a larger salary, a partnership was a great temptation, and after a sleepless night I decided to approach my chiefs for a small partnership. I knew that I was well worth it and felt that they would consent. So the next morning I went to see them in their private office. At first I was rather embarrassed, but after some halting remarks, I explained the position to them. 'You see, gentlemen,' I said, 'I have been very happy here, and you have treated me more than generously; so when I was offered higher salaries and commission on the turnover by other firms, I refused, and I never even mentioned these offers to you. But a partnership is worth more to me than a large salary, for I should then feel that I was working for myself as well. From you I would accept a very small partnership instead of the one third which has been offered to me. Please, give me a partnership, I don't care how small, and you will see how I will work to deserve it.'

"At this point Mr. Dumouriez called out: 'Stop, Duveen,' and then he went on to say: 'I want to think this over and discuss it with Mr. Gotschalk, so we will leave it until tomorrow morning, and if we can agree on our decision by then we will let you have it.' I was puzzled by this curt reply from Mr. Dumouriez, and I had another bad night worrying about the matter. I was not very hopeful when on entering the private office the next morning I saw two very serious faces at the table. Mr. Dumouriez began by telling me that he and his partner had discussed the matter thoroughly and that they had come to the conclusion that they could not give me a partnership; but that they were willing to increase my salary as they had done several times before without my asking for a rise.

"When I asked him why they objected to me as a partner, Mr. Dumouriez reflected for a moment, and then said: 'Look here, Duveen, we have the greatest respect for your cleverness and your energy and we like you; but we are old men, and if we take you on as a junior partner you will be too strong for us. We should not be able to restrain you, and in a year's time you would be our master. And that, young man, is the reason that we are willing to do anything except give you this partnership.' And then," my uncle continued, "I made the greatest mistake I have ever made in my life, for if I had not been so eager to be my own master, I am certain that they would have given me a partnership in time and then I would have become the Pierpont Morgan of the world's produce-market instead of the head of what is, after all, only a retail business."

And at the time that he spoke these words Joel Duveen had just bought the Rodolphe Kann collection for one million pounds!

III

HIS OWN MASTER

ON THE EVENING that he left Messrs. Dumouriez and Gotschalk, Joel Duveen, who had been for some months in love with Rosetta Barnett, the daughter of a jeweller in Hull, proposed and was accepted. Her parents gladly gave their consent to the young man, for they knew him to be clever and successful, and the fact that he was now his own master had removed any hesitation which they might have had to giving their daughter to a man who had not yet made his way in the world. The only member of the family who objected to the match was the husband of an elder daughter of the Barnetts. He had taken a violent dislike to Joel, and it was through this man's influence that old Barnett had insisted on at least a year's engagement before the marriage should take place. However, the future looked very auspicious for the young lovers, and during the first few months business, too, was going all Joel's way. He managed to open up good connections all over England, and with his knowledge of the Dutch provision market, everything seemed set for really big business. But when it came to putting down money for the goods which had been received from Holland, Joel received his first shock. The partner who was to have supplied the money seemed not to have the large liquid capital of which he had spoken and which Joel knew to be absolutely essential for obtaining merchandise at the best prices. This led to difficulties with the Dutch sources of supply; instead of the turnover increasing, it began to fall off. This caused constant difficulties, and Joel, who was never a very patient man, threatened to leave. After this, money was forthcoming for some time; but when another couple of months had passed, Joel began to hear whispers about accommodation bills of exchange, and even about money-lending transactions. As this was against the terms of the contract, Joel faced his Dutch partner with these rumours, with the result that there was a violent quarrel, ending with Joel leaving the firm.

This had its repercussions in the Barnett family, where the son-in-law advised that the engagement between Duveen and Miss Rosetta should be broken off. Her brother Barney, however, took his friend's part, but any date for the wedding was left open until Duveen's circumstances should have improved sufficiently to warrant his being able to keep his wife properly.

This was a great blow to the young suitor, and his prospects of fulfilling this condition were now nebulous. The obvious course would have been to return to his old firm; but when I interrupted my uncle's narrative of this episode he said: "No, my boy; I had spoilt any chance of that at the end of my last talk with my old chiefs. Just before I left their room, Mr. Gotschalk warned me that the elder of my two prospective partners was practically insolvent. On hearing this, I took it to be a last rather unfair attempt to make me remain with them, and I betrayed this thought by smiling. Mr. Gotschalk noticed this, for he lost his temper and ended the interview with: 'All right, young man, remember the Dutch proverb that he who won't listen must suffer; but it will be no use coming back to us when it's too late!' "

The break between the partners occurred just before Easter, and Joel decided to go to Holland for a short holiday. But he hated to travel alone, so he begged his friend Barney Barnett to go with him. Accordingly, the two young men left for Holland, and on the Easter Sunday they visited my grandfather, Jacob Hangjas, in Haarlem. He was already living in the beautiful seventeenth-century corner house by the bridge over the Bakenesser Canal, the house where I spent the first nine years of my life.

He was a wholesale art-dealer, and he kept his stock in two large warehouses; but he was also a collector, and his house was furnished with fine specimens of antique furniture. Apart from the usual glass cabinets there were also several cabinets built into the walls of the old house. All were filled with titbits that my grandfather had chosen out of many thousands of pieces ever since, as a boy of fifteen, he began to deal in antiques. His wife, Anna de Misiers, daughter of a French Huguenot and a Dutch mother, also had an innate taste for beautiful things, and she had gathered a collection of small Chinese tear-bottles, Bow fruit-bearers, and old Chinese cups and saucers. The cabinet containing the porcelain was in the dining-room. During the meal young Barnett could not keep his eyes off it and kept on making admiring remarks to Joel. When, after the meal, they were alone for a moment he said: "Do you think that I could buy some of these cups and saucers? I could sell them like hot cakes in our shop."

"My uncle wouldn't sell anything out of that cabinet, but he is sure to have large quantities in his warehouses. How many would you like to buy?" asked Joel.

"A good-sized case full, if they are cheap."

28

Joel was never slow to see the possibilities, and he replied: "Look here, Barney, if you can sell these things like hot cakes, jewellers and antique-dealers all over England could do the same; so, instead of your buying one case, I will go halves with you in buying a dozen cases, and then we will sell them all over England." Young Barnett was always a very cautious business man, but his forceful friend convinced him by the power of his arguments, and Barnett agreed to give the proposition a try.

My grandfather, who when I was still a schoolboy told me his part in the business, took the two young men to his warehouses, and here, carried away by the sight of a whole enormous floor covered with thousands of matched cups and saucers —some in dozens and others in half-dozens—and encouraged by his uncle's offer to let them have the lot against three months' bills, Joel bought them all at half a gulden (tenpence) per cup and saucer. By now Barnett, excited by the low price, was as enthusiastic as his enterprising friend, and then my grandfather asked them to come to his other warehouse to see a large quantity of good-quality old delft jars, which he could sell on the same conditions at seventy-five cents (1s. 3d.) apiece. The whole lot was bought, and the deal came to just over two hundred pounds.

Joel insisted on taking a few dozen cups and saucers and half a dozen jars with him as samples. He sold most of the consignment to antique-dealers in Leeds, Manchester, Liverpool, and Chester before the goods were delivered in Hull. The profit was more than a thousand pounds and from then onwards the two young partners travelled regularly through Holland, accompanied by my own father, who, although only twenty years old at that time, was already a great expert with a good knowledge of the Continental markets. He continually insisted that the two partners try the more valuable types of Chinese porcelain; and when, after three journeys, their capital had reached five thousand pounds, he succeeded in taking them to old Boas-Berg of Amsterdam, at that time the greatest art-dealer in Holland—but here I must tell the story in my uncle's own words.

"Your father had tried for some time to persuade us to go in for the more expensive things; but, although I could rely on his knowledge, and was very sorely tempted to do so, Barney was too nervous to follow Henri's advice. However, one day we were walking through the Kalverstraat in Amsterdam and were on the point of passing Boas-Berg's shop, when Henri drew our attention to a lot of fine tall Nankin vases, standing almost tightly packed on shelves right round the shop. They were sets of five of the rare *"lange lyzen"* type (see illustration).[1]

" 'Strange,' said Henri, 'Boas-Berg has at last gone in for Nankin. He always called it kitchen-ware.'

"I could not resist the temptation, and I walked in, followed by your father and Barney; but I had heard a good deal about this Boas-Berg as a man of an extremely difficult character, very rich and charging high prices. I could not take my eyes off these glorious vases. I made up my mind to buy, no matter at what price. It was the first time that I felt this irresistible urge to possess. Old Boas-Berg saw my look, and remarked: 'Yes, they are very good,' and then added: 'The only blue-and-white I have ever bought.'

" 'I can do with some good sets. How much do you want for the perfect ones?' I asked. 'Perfect ones! Do you think that I deal in damaged pots?' the bad-tempered old man

[1] *"Lange lyzen"* is the name that was given by the seventeenth-century Dutch importers to the graceful, slender figures painted in Nankin-blue on a perfect white ground.

shouted. However, I pleaded ignorance of his rule, and then repeated my question as to price per set. 'Sixty pounds,' he growled.

"I caught the approving wink of your father, and set to work at once. I walked along the shelves. 'I take this, and this,' said I, pointing at the sets with the deepest blue; but when I had got to the tenth, Boas-Berg shouted: 'Stop! I won't sell any more today!'

"My wholesale methods had frightened the old man. He had never done business in that way. I wrote out a cheque, and his wife made out the receipt; but when we left he did not even shake hands with us. He loved his stock better than money.

"Barney was furious, but Henri intervened with: 'Joel, you have done the finest piece of business you could have done. You were picking the best of the lot, and if you take them to London you will sell them all at a big profit.'

" 'And how do you know?' asked Barney.

" 'Because I have only once had such a fine set, and I sold it at once to young Tooth of London,' replied Henri.

" 'And what did you pay?' asked my cautious partner.

" 'I paid fifty pounds and Tooth paid me a hundred and fifty pounds,' said Henri.

"I was very pleased with what Henri had told us, but I had so fallen in love with the vases, and was so excited, that I could hardly speak, for I felt that I had started dealing in the finer things. I knew then that I could trust my eyes for recognizing the finest qualities. So, as we were walking towards our hotel, I begged Henri to return to Boas-Berg and have the vases delivered at once to the hotel.

" 'Don't make a fool of yourself, Joel! The old man may get annoyed and cancel the deal,' exclaimed Barney. But

Henri told him that Boas-Berg never broke his word, and that he, Henri, could understand my feeling about these 'jewels,' as he called them.

"While Henri returned to Boas-Berg, I arranged for a large sitting-room, and in less than an hour we had our meal with the vases all around us on cabinets, tables, and even on the large oak sideboard. Henri and I had arranged them to the best advantage. It was a very clear day, and I have never forgotten the sight of those lovely blues lighting up that large room. And I must say that Barney was then as pleased as I had been. He, too, enjoyed them, and he became quite enthusiastic that he had entered the really big antique-business. He didn't even talk about our ready money being practically exhausted by the £500 cheque; but in spite of my excitement, I had not forgotten the business side, for it meant that we would not be able to make the journey to Friesland, where we had found lots of the cheaper things for which we had already a very large market in Yorkshire and Lancashire. However, I had the remedy at hand, and I asked Henri—who was receiving five per cent on everything we bought—whether, if we made it ten per cent for this journey, he could arrange with his father to finance the remainder of our buying trip.

"Henri was quite sure, and offered to go straight away to Haarlem and see about it. When Henri had left, Barney reproached me, saying that I had been too generous; but I pointed out that Henri knew more about qualities and values than we did, and ended up with: 'That's worth much more than the extra five per cent.' This ended the argument, and when Henri returned that evening with the news that he had made the arrangement with his father, we made our plans. The next morning we travelled across the Zuider Zee to Stavoren in Friesland. We bought our usual stock from the

Frisian dealers as well as a few very fine pieces and, as your father had promised, at very low prices."

I could see the smile on my uncle's face at these happy memories, and I risked asking him for more. "Uncle, did that fine set of Mr. Rae the banker [2] also come with that Boas-Berg lot?"

"Yes, my boy, it did, and by that hangs another story. I had made a good many customers in Liverpool for the pretty little things we used to bring over, and Mr. Rae, who was already one of my customers, had recommended me to several of his friends. One day he sent a Mr. Nichols, a Liverpool gentle-man, to my show-room at the Stork Hotel. He said to me that his wife had caught the 'blues,' and wanted to make her sitting-room beautiful with some of my Nankin porcelain. He was obviously very fond of his wife, and when I went to see the room Mrs. Nichols showed me round. She was an extremely beautiful young woman, about thirty-five or forty years younger than her husband. She told me that she had seen how beautiful Mrs. Rae had made her sitting-room with my blue-and-white, and she would like me to do the best I could for her. She also gave me to understand that her husband wanted her to have the best, and that she was very anxious for the things to be in place the next morning after breakfast. I was to take all the other china out of the room and out of the cabinets. I promised that it would be done; I saw that it would take nearly the whole of what I had brought with me to Liverpool. I made a list of what would be required, then I went to the hotel, packed the things, and the next morning at seven I was at the house. With the help of the butler and a maid, I removed all the Victorian trash. Before nine, I had

[2] Mr. Rae was a wealthy Liverpool banker, and if I remember rightly he founded The North & South Wales Bank.

made that room like a garden filled with azure flowers. When Mr. and Mrs. Nichols came in, the lady gave a little gasp of admiration, and the husband said: 'Well done, young man! It's very beautiful, but how much is this going to cost me?'

"I told him that the whole thing had been done in such a rush that I had not had time to look at my cost prices, but that I would work it out that morning and would put the prices as low as possible. 'All right,' he replied, 'Mr. Rae has told me that I can trust you about prices, so you send in your bill and I will send you the cheque.' I sent him the bill, which came to just over two thousand pounds, and I had made five hundred pounds profit. But I charged him less than I would have got from dealers at the usual prices."

"Why?" I asked.

"Because the finest profit you can make is to keep a customer," was the reply, oracular, but true.

A couple of minutes passed in silence, and I was just going to remind my uncle that he had not yet told me about Mr. Rae, when he began: "I almost forgot to tell you how Mr. Rae got the best one of those ten sets. When the cases with the *lange lyzen* vases arrived at Hull, they were sold for two hundred and fifty pounds per set almost as soon as they were unpacked, but I had put the best set aside for Mr. Rae. I knew that he would never accept the vases as a present for all his kindness to me, so I intended to let him have them at cost price.

"About a fortnight after my return from Holland, the cases from Friesland arrived in Hull, and I left for Liverpool to hold my first exhibition of really fine things. I took with me a railway truckful of trunks, and the next day we set out the whole collection in two big show-rooms at the Stork. Then I called on Mr. Rae at his bank, and he came with me at once.

34

"When we entered the first show-room, I took him straight to the glorious *lange lyzen* vases. He gasped at their beauty, and in my enthusiasm I told him that I had bought this set for him and that I wanted him to take it. 'It will cost you sixty pounds,' I added. But I forgot that I was talking to a banker and a Scot, a man who would neither let himself be disposed of nor dictated to. He turned away from the vases, and as he walked to the door, he said: 'All right, Duveen, but don't buy any more china for me without letting me know first.'

"I was always a quick thinker, but he had disappeared through the door before I guessed the cause: I was suspected of 'clever salesmanship.' I felt very hurt, and sent him the vases without another word. The next day I received his cheque for sixty pounds—also without another word. In a few days I had sold out at good prices, but my pleasure was spoiled, and I returned to Hull with that memory constantly rankling in my mind."

"Did you ever see Mr. Rae again?" I asked my uncle.

"Oh, yes. About a year after this unpleasant incident he came to see me while I was having a show in Liverpool. When he came in he said: 'It seems that you don't want to do any more business with me. You never come to tell me now when you are here, as you used to do.'

" 'Mr. Rae, to tell you the truth, I thought that you were annoyed with me when I made you buy those *lange lyzen* vases.' He laughed, and said: 'Oh, that's all right. In fact we all love them. They are the finest pieces in my collection.'

"We did a big deal that day and we remained great friends until his death. But some years after the only misunderstanding I ever had with Mr. Rae, he told me that, a few months after I had sold him those vases, the dealer Agnew made him an offer of five hundred pounds for them; but it had never

35

been a question of money with him—only a principle of remaining his own master. I realized that this was true; and a few years before his death I offered him fifteen hundred pounds for the set, but he loved the vases too well to accept even this big price."

IV

EGG-SHELL AND HAWTHORN

S HORTLY AFTER that first deal in the more expensive types
of Nankin porcelain, Duveen and Barnett crossed over to
Holland again. Cousin Henri took them on their usual tour
round Holland and Friesland, and this time he advised them
to buy some fine pieces of the coloured varieties of Oriental porcelain. They bought a large quantity of fine Nankin,
and a few pieces of *famille verte* and *famille rose;* but, as the
Dutch dealers were asking very high prices for the best of
these pieces, my father advised them to come to Belgium
with him, where he knew of some really fine pieces in the
possession of dealers.

They were on the point of starting for Antwerp when a
young dealer, a youth of eighteen named Hamburger (a
cousin of the famous Utrecht antique-dealers), arrived in
Haarlem from Alkmaar with the news that he had bought a
dozen "eight-border" egg-shell plates for 1,500 gulden (about
£125 in those days) from a farmer-woman in his neighbourhood. He had not been able to pay cash, but he had left 200
gulden on account.

As a boy of sixteen I had this story from Hamburger himself when I visited him at his little shop in Alkmaar, and I will tell the story in his own words. He had received me with open arms when my Uncle Bernhard told him who I was. He expressed his sorrow at my father's early death, and made me happy by saying that he was not only a great expert, but a man who was known as never breaking his word—and this was not a general trait of the art-dealers in those days. Then he added: "I'll tell you what he once did for me. One day when I was only eighteen years old, I was stopping at farms in my neighbourhood for bits of antiques when a farmer-woman told me that she had just inherited from an old aunt twelve very beautiful little East-Indian plates, as thin as the shell of an egg.[1] From her description I knew she was talking about *famille rose* egg-shell plates. She had heard that morning that the plates were at the notary's office in Amsterdam. On my asking her how soon I could see them she told me that someone who had gone to Amsterdam that morning had promised to bring them. She was sure that I should be able to see them the next morning. I went the next morning with two hundred gulden in my pocket. I recognized the famous eight-bordered egg-shell plates, one of which had not long before been sold for eight hundred gulden at the Brakke Grond, the famous auction rooms in Amsterdam.

"She wanted three thousand gulden for the plates. To make a long story short, I got them for fifteen hundred and paid her two hundred gulden on account, with the promise to bring the remainder within three days. I rushed off to Haarlem to offer the plates to your father. When I arrived at about five, I found them all at dinner. Your uncle Joly and his English partner were also there, and on my telling them about the

[1] All Oriental porcelain is called *Oost-Indiesch* in Holland.

38

business, your father agreed to pay me six hundred pounds if the plates were all perfect. He promised to come to Alkmaar before ten the next morning. As arranged, I met the three of them with a two-horse diligence at Alkmaar station, and we drove out to the farm. The woman had put the plates in 'the best room,' where there was plenty of light. Your father and your uncle were very excited, and almost ran to the table to look at the plates. Your father took one in his hands and turned to me. Then I got the biggest smack I have ever had in my life.

" 'Do you mean to tell me that you have bought these plates for fifteen hundred gulden from this poor woman?'

"In my surprise at this totally unexpected question, I could only nod; and then he went on: 'You ought to be ashamed of yourself for swindling a poor woman. Those plates are worth at least ten times that amount, and you know that she will get that if she sends them to the Brakke Grond.'

"I was furious," Hamburger continued, "and if I had been older I am sure I would have gone for him; but then the woman started on me. 'You mean hound, here is your dirty money. I won't let you have the plates now!'

"I was just going to refuse the money when I caught a wink from your father, and as by then my head was in a whirl, I accepted it.

"We all went out together, but just as I was going through the door the woman flew at me and demanded the receipt she had given me. By this time I was so dazed that I obeyed her without realizing I was losing all proof of the transaction; but I was only a boy, and I had been betrayed by a man whom I had trusted. For a moment I thought that your father wanted to buy the plates behind my back. However, the moment we were outside the farm yard, he said: 'I have saved your money, my boy. Those plates are Samson copies [2] and are not worth more than about twenty francs apiece.'

"As I still looked suspicious, he added: 'They belong to some crook who has planted them here.' And a few days later I found out that the late Bram Poons of The Hague had made the plant.

"Yes, my boy," Hamburger continued after a moment, "your father was not only a great connoisseur, but he had a great heart, and I shall remember his cleverness and his kind-ness to my dying day."

I was told this story early in 1890, and when I spoke about it to my Uncle Joel during my next visit to London, he re-membered the incident most vividly.

"Yes," he said, "that was the trip when we bought the haw-thorn ginger jar," and, of course, I wanted to hear this, too. Uncle, as usual, was willing, and he told me the story.

After that disappointment at Alkmaar they had gone to Antwerp, Brussels, Ghent, and Bruges. The supply was much smaller than in Holland, but they bought a few very fine pieces of the coloured varieties, apart from making business connections that became increasingly useful during the next quarter of a century.

My uncle and his partner intended to travel back to Lon-don via Antwerp, but at the last moment my father received a telegram from my grandfather with the message: RETURN IMMEDIATELY HAWTHORN. He showed the telegram to Joel, who inquired: "What does he mean by hawthorn?" Henri explained that this was the rarest and most beautiful of all Nankin porcelain vases. They had just time to catch the Brussels-Amsterdam express, and arrived early that afternoon at Haarlem. My grandfather was waiting for them at the sta-

[2] Samson, of Paris, imitators of old porcelain and pottery.

tion and he gave them the details: a hawthorn ginger jar of the very finest blue he had ever seen. It was in the country house of Dolle Piet (Mad Pete) between Leyden and Haar-lem. This notorious young nobleman, now dead for many years, was a baron whose title went back to the Middle Ages. He had run short of money and had decided to sell this vase. A small Leyden dealer had offered him a thousand gulden; but he had refused to sell until he had checked the real value with Henri.

Joel Duveen, who never allowed the grass to grow under his feet, chartered the fastest pair of horses in Haarlem and drove the whole party to the large mansion. The Baron re-ceived them at the head of the grand outer stairway, and in-vited them all to come first into the library for a drink with him; but Henri begged him to let them see the vase while the light was still good. The Baron had the vase brought in, and then my uncle beheld the most beautiful "jewel" he had ever seen. I will repeat the description I wrote many years ago about the discovery of three such vases in the pantry of a wealthy Dutch family near The Hague: "In June 1877 a very small antique-dealer at The Hague heard of some blue-and-white vases in the pantry of a great family mansion in The Hague wood. After some difficulty, the lady took him into the kitchens and he saw the vases. Above the sink stood the superb hawthorn vases, a poem in white and blue. His knowledge was not great, but something of their magic must have penetrated his brain. He did not know that he was in the presence of the masterpieces of that nameless Chinese artist who succeeded once (and once only) in reproducing a won-derful sight which he saw one day when fishing. An ice floe passed him on the sluggish waters of the Blue River (Yang-tze Kiang). It had come from the upper reaches, where win-

ter still held sway, and now, dwindling to its end, passed the
flower-strewn banks. Some blossoms of the prunus had fallen
on to the floe, while the reflection of the azure sky in the dark
ice made for them a deep, crackled background. It was a sight
to wrench the heart of an artist with ecstasy. For years he
strove to reproduce those unforgettable colours, and for years
he failed. Each time the firing-kiln had been too hot, giving the
blue on his porcelain too black a tint, or it had been too cool,
causing the rich blue to become grey.

"He had tried the famous Mohammedan cobalt and the
even more famous Ch'êng-Hua cobalt which had produced
the wondrous light blues of the fifteenth-century Ch'êng-Hua
reign. At long last, encouraged by the boy emperor, Shêng-
tsu, whose reign was called K'ang-hsi, he did discover the quality of cobalt he needed. It had been brought over to the imperial porcelain factory at Ching-tê Chên by an Arab merchant.
At once the boy emperor, who was then fourteen years old and
who reigned over China from 1662 to 1722, promised the
Arab great riches if only he would bring over a much larger
quantity. Two years later the merchant arrived with two hundred camels carrying a vast amount of the precious mineral,
and the artist could experiment on a large scale.

"Again came defeat after defeat, but one memorable day
he opened his kiln to find that he had succeeded beyond even
his wildest dreams. He had achieved the impossible! There in
front of him lay vases of a deep yet translucent blue that had
the almost miraculous quality of a marbled waviness. The colour seemed to throb, just as the sunlit sky had made to throb
those blue reflections on the ice floe. The white prunus sprays,
nervously drawn on this palpitating blue, had an effect almost
of lightning. Even in the semi-dark, or in artificial light, when
blue loses its strength, those vases dwarfed every other thing
of beauty and made it look ordinary. Never again did the

artist's ovens produce that marvellous colour, and this though tens of thousands of vases were made."

Joel Duveen, who had already heard from Henri that if the hawthorn vase was really the first quality it would be worth from £300 to £400, had taken the measure of the impulsive and uncontrollable young nobleman. "I realized," he told me, "that if I tried to consult your father, this madman would think that there was a conspiracy, and I was so carried away by this glorious thing that I answered before your father could speak. I said: 'Baron, this is the most beautiful piece of porcelain I have ever seen, and I have made up my mind to have it at any price. I will give you five thousand gulden, cash down!' And, in spite of Barney's groan, I added: 'And that is about eighteen hundred gulden more than my cousin Henri told me that it could be worth.'

"The Baron turned towards your father and asked: 'Is this man trying to make a fool of me?'

"Then I began to count out the money, and he became very friendly. He invited us to dinner, but I wanted to be off with my hawthorn pot, so within half an hour of arriving at the house we were on our way back to Haarlem. Henri was extremely pleased that I had been able to buy the vase, but your grandfather and Barnett thought that I had unnecessarily thrown away at least two thousand gulden.

" 'And how much do you think I am going to get for it?' I asked them.

" 'You'll do well if you make a hundred pounds profit,' said Uncle Jaap, and this made Barney even more glum. But Henri said: 'You are right, Joel. You have bought a unique thing.'

"But then another difficulty arose. I knew that I had no customer in the North who would buy this piece, and I also knew that even in London there were only a very few people who would pay such a high price for a single piece of Chinese porcelain, so I asked your father if he would come to London with us to introduce me to a likely buyer. I particularly remember his telling me that his friend Grego, the artist, was very friendly with a man who was willing to buy the very finest at any cost. The next night we travelled to London. At my suggestion, Henri had sent a telegram to Grego, who had replied that he would wait for us in his studio in one of the Bloomsbury squares.

"The end of it was that Grego took us to James Orrock, at that time the greatest collector of fine Chinese porcelain in the world. Orrock already knew your father, and he received us very kindly. When he saw the vase, he exclaimed: 'My God!' After looking at it for a few minutes without uttering a word, he picked it up, took it to the window, and absolutely gloated over it. Then, after another examination from every side and under various lights, he suddenly asked: 'How much?'

" 'Twelve hundred pounds, Mr. Orrock,' I replied.

" 'I'll have it, but you'll have to wait four months for the money, for I have spent too much lately on my collection.'

"I paid your father one hundred and twenty pounds, and I made Grego a present of one hundred pounds, so that I left just five hundred and forty pounds for Barney and myself. But, my boy, that entry into the London market was the first rung on the ladder. I realized the possibilities at once, but Barnett would not listen to one word about opening a gallery there. So for many years we had to sell our finest goods through others."

This vase is now in the Victoria and Albert Museum (see illustration), and bears James Orrock's initials, cut into the base with a diamond. It is considered to be the finest in the museum, and is certainly the finest I have seen during my long career.

V

LONGING FOR LONDON

THE SALE of the hawthorn ginger jar for £1,200 had shown the two partners the great possibilities for their business in London; but Barnett would not agree to Joel Duveen's plan for moving to the capital. This enforced stay in Hull enabled the partners to make many more good private customers in the north-west of England. Nevertheless, Joel Duveen was constantly irritated by the knowledge that in London rich business men from all over the country were spending fortunes on beautiful things for their houses—mostly fine old French furniture and expensive tapestries. The partners lacked the capital for this very costly type of stock, and Barnett would not speculate in French furniture. Joel Duveen hated to "stagnate," as he called it, and faced by his partner's resolute opposition, he turned again to the whole-sale methods which he had learnt in the produce-business. Remembering the beautiful things in the rich farmers' houses in his native country, he asked his cousin Henri Hangjas to buy up as many Dutch old oak cabinets as he could find. At that time, about 1870, such things were still to be bought in Holland for a few pounds apiece; but whereas other importers of antiques bought them piecemeal, Joel Duveen bought them by the dozen. He always arranged for cleaning and repairing to be done by the sellers, since most of this very old furniture had been painted or varnished by the ignorant owners. He gave three months' bills in payment so that most of the purchases had been sold before the bills fell due. He told me many years later that he was in his element again, and practically without competition, as no other dealer had the pluck to buy vanloads at a time. But the most beautiful of all these cabinets could not be bought wholesale. They were the ebony-and-*palissandre* wood cabinets of the Dutch Palladian period, which were only to be found in the palace-like houses which the Dutch East-India merchants had built during the seventeenth century. These were not to be bought for a few pounds. The buying of them was entrusted to Jan Teunissen (Senior), of The Hague, and when Joel Duveen discussed this campaign with him, that very rich dealer offered him a year's credit if that part of the buying would be allowed to remain with him. This led to a vast business in all sorts of works of art during the next thirty years between Joel Duveen and Jan Teunissen, Senior, and his even more clever son, Jan, Junior.

The next wholesale business was done in the magnificent Dutch *staande* (standing) clocks—the majestic forerunner of the English grandfather clock. The best of these Dutch clocks always had a clever mechanical movement of ships or other scenes as part of the dial, as well as a carillon of from twelve to twenty-four tunes. They were already highly priced, and some of the finest fetched as much as two hundred pounds.

The dealing in old china and pottery went on, usually with Henri doing the buying, and *Oom* Jaap the financing.

Towards the end of 1871 Betsy Duveen (Joel's youngest sister and my mother), who was then twenty-one and who had been very unhappy after her father had remarried, came to live in Hull with her brother. Under his guidance, she made quick progress in judging antiques. She first undertook the complicated task of matching the thousands of old Chinese porcelain cups and saucers that were constantly arriving from Holland. Then she took charge of the girls who did the unpacking and packing of the most fragile articles. And, incidentally, she taught me this art when I came into the business just before my sixteenth birthday. In November 1872 my mother left Hull to get married to my father.

The Duveen-Barnett partnership continued rather longer than anyone expected. His marriage and the birth of a child every year lessened Joel's desire to take a leap into the difficult cosmopolitan business of London. But towards the end of 1876 a favourable chance arose for a friendly dissolution of the partnership. Barnett's father wished to retire, and an arrangement was made by which his son would take over the flourishing jeweller's business. As Joel needed every penny for buying high-class pieces for London, he was anxious to take money out of the dissolved partnership instead of stock that would be mediocre in the London market.

Barnett treated him very fairly; but because old stock could not be taken over at cost, this difficulty entailed a considerable loss to Joel. My uncle told me: "When I parted company with Barnett I had only eight thousand pounds in cash, but at last I felt a free man." As he said this he threw himself back in his chair, threw back his shoulders, and took a deep breath.

He was obviously enjoying that old memory, and I did not interrupt his pleasure; but seeing that he was in a reminiscent

47

mood, I could not let the opportunity slip and I asked a question that had been in my mind for many years about the projected partnership with my father.

"I knew only too well," he began, "that I could not do the buying and selling by myself. Buying meant constant travelling on the Continent, and private selling required my personal attention. I could not be in London and on the Continent at the same time. But early in 1877 your mother wrote me that your father had decided to open a business in London. So I telegraphed him, and we met the next day in London. I explained my plan, and offered him a one-third share in the partnership. He was to do the buying on the Continent, and I was to do the selling in London. The whole thing was settled in less than an hour; but then we added another scheme to the original one, for your father happened to mention that my young brother Henry, then twenty-one years old, was very unhappy in Amsterdam. His stepmother was making life unbearable for him, and to escape this he was consorting with a very wild set.

"I asked him whether there was anything wrong, but your father assured me that my brother was a good boy, and that it was all the stepmother's fault.

"At first I thought I would have him with me in London, but after talking it over we decided to send him to New York or Boston to open up wholesale connections between us and American dealers.

"We went into money matters. I told him about my capital, and he told me that he had done fairly well. He had nearly as much as I had, but it was almost all in stock. Although this was a more international one than Barnett and I had accumulated, your father did not think that the bulk of it was good enough for a first-class London business. After thinking it over for a moment, he decided to send his stock to be auctioned in London."

After they had come to an understanding on all points, my uncle and my father went to a leading firm of estate agents. They had decided that Oxford Street from Marble Arch to Oxford Circus would be the most suitable locality for their new enterprise, but they found that this was impossible at that moment. The agents suggested three places in Bond Street, but all were far too small for their purpose. As the agents were quite sure that it would take some time to find anything with plenty of space in the part of Oxford Street which they preferred, the two prospective partners decided to have a good preliminary look round the Paris dealers who would be their chief source of supply for the things in which they would have to deal. That night they left for Paris, and on my father's advice they first called on the important and very reliable Lowengard firm, where he was known and trusted. The head of the firm, a venerable old gentleman, after hearing the object of this visit, took them round his collection himself. During this inspection my father told him that they were going to open a large business in London and that they had come to Paris to establish relations with the Paris market. When M. Lowengard said that he would be only too glad to do business with them, Joel Duveen immediately explained that an opening on the best market in the world for fine French furniture and tapestries would be a great advantage to both parties. He admitted that he himself was not an expert on French art, but the fact that what they would acquire came from an admitted expert like M. Lowengard would enable them to sell everything with the utmost confidence. This settled the matter, and it was agreed that as soon as the two young men opened their galleries in London M. Lowengard would let

49

them have anything they wanted on "sale or return." This would be tried for three months after delivery in London, provided that at least ten per cent was sold at the end of that time. Henri hesitated, but Joel agreed immediately, on condition that they could choose the articles themselves.

The auction in London took place early in May 1877, but it was a complete fiasco. There was very little private bidding, and the dealers did not want to buy another dealer's stock. The result was that my father bought in all the best things, while the rest fetched ridiculously low prices. He not only lost a great deal, but he was unable to put up the capital which he had promised to invest in the projected partnership.

The unsold articles were repacked and left in a London warehouse.

Two months later, when my mother went over to England, these cases had disappeared. The auctioneers disclaimed all responsibility, and they were never traced.

Nearly a quarter of a century later, during the auction at Christie's of the Henry Huth collection, my late father's good friend Henry Grego told me that the hawthorn vase in that collection had belonged to my father. It had been bought from a barber in Soho for 12s. 6d. and had then been sold to Mr. Huth. This barber was a native of Haarlem, and my father had used him a good deal for various small matters. The fact that this man had sold the hawthorn vase tends to show that he must at least have had a hand in the disappearance of those cases.

At the Huth sale that hawthorn vase was sold for the ridiculously high price of £5,900. It was a fight between my uncle Joel and Robert Partridge. The latter was the Pyrrhic victor, but after some years he managed to sell it to the first Lord Astor, I believe at a loss.

VI

BETSY DUVEEN

MY MOTHER, Betsy Duveen, was the third child of Joseph H. Duveen, of Meppel, and his first wife, Eva van Minden. She was born on November 4, 1850. Her eldest brother, Joel J. Duveen, was nearly eight years older, and her younger brother, Henry J. Duveen, was her junior by five years. When her father remarried in 1870, life became very difficult for her, and after a few years she left home to live with relatives.

My father, Henri J. Hangjas, a distant cousin of hers, fell in love with her when, at sixteen, she came to stay with his parents at Haarlem; and six years later, on December 6, 1872, they were married. On marrying, my father joined his wife's name to his own and opened an antique-business in his native town, Haarlem. In 1876 he moved to The Hague. Then, early in 1877, he agreed to join Joel J. Duveen, his brother-in-law, in an international art-business with galleries in London and either Boston or New York. Joel Duveen was to run the business in London, and his young brother, Henry J. Duveen, was to open in America. My father was to have charge of the buying on the continent of Europe.

This great plan was frustrated by the untimely death of my father at the age of twenty-nine. My mother was left at the age of twenty-six with four little children, and expecting a fifth. I, the eldest, was three years and ten months old. The business, which had greatly prospered until a few months before my father's death, was in a state of chaos. As I have already mentioned, several large cases of valuable old Chinese porcelain that had been left in a London warehouse had disappeared when my mother went there to claim them. Moreover, many things which had been left on approval with dealers in Belgium and France on my father's last journey to Spain could not be traced. As was usual in those days, my father had booked all transactions in a note-book. Nearly all this writing had become illegible during a night journey from Leyden to The Hague in an open carriage. My parents had been to the wedding of some friends; a thunderstorm had overtaken them and both had been drenched. My father had contracted a chill which became complicated by typhoid fever, of which he died. The doctors declared he must have caught it on his Spanish journey. A family council decided that the business should be liquidated and that my mother and her children should be properly provided for by the family; but when my mother heard their decision she refused to let the well-established business be sacrificed. She told the family that she had to think of her little children's future, and she was going to see to it that they would not have to live on the family's charity.

My very kind-hearted grandfather considered this a mistake, and it led to a few months' coolness between my mother and him. Later I heard that the idea of liquidation had come from a man who had recently married into the family. He was anxious to open an antique-business in The Hague, and my father's house was not only in the best position, but it was also

The Duveen Family, a Wedding Photograph

Men (left to right): 1. Louis Duveen. 2. Captain Montague Abrahams (bridegroom). 3. Charles J. Duveen. 4. Captain Edward J. Duveen. 5. Henry J. Duveen. 6. Captain Ernest J. Duveen. 7. ———. 8. Henry J. Duveen, Jr. (son of Sir Joseph). 9. Sir Joseph Joel Duveen. 10. Lord Duveen. 11. Benjamin J. Duveen. 12. ———. 13. James H. Duveen. 14. Geoffrey Duveen (only son of Henry J. Duveen). 15. John J. Duveen.

Ladies (left to right): 1. ———. 2. Mrs. Louis Duveen. 3. Annette Duveen (bride). 4. Esther (Mrs. James H. Duveen). 5. ———. 6. ———. 7. Lady Rosetta Duveen (wife of Sir Joseph). 8. Mrs. Henry J. Duveen. 9. Elsie (wife of Lord Duveen). 10. Eva Duveen (Evaline Lady Abrahams). 11. Florence Duveen.

Sir Joseph Joel Duveen
The Founder of Duveen Brothers

let at a very moderate rent. It had been let to my father on a yearly contract, and three months before the expiration of the year my mother received notice. The house had been let to the man who had proposed the liquidation of the business.

My uncle Joel, who had in the meantime been appointed trustee of the children, came over to see what could be done about this, but the new contract for the house had already been signed, at a somewhat higher rental. And, as if this was not already bad enough, two dealers insisted on the immediate return of valuable porcelain and a collection of silver, which were missing. My mother knew that some of these things had been left on approval with Brussels dealers, and that the whole of the silver had been deposited with a Lille dealer; but he denied all knowledge of it, and this silver was never returned to my mother, in spite of a lengthy correspondence between him and her notary.

My mother went to Brussels a few months after my father's death. She met with no difficulties in collecting her property, but the visit nearly cost her her life. She was in one of the ramshackle old fiacres, going up the steep hill of the Sainte Gudule. The old horse's progress was less than half walking-pace, and fearing that she would miss her train for The Hague, my mother had asked the driver several times to stop because his horse was going too slowly. The sleepy or half-drunk coachman took no notice, so at last my mother took hold of her small valise and stepped out. The long train of her dress caught on something. She was swept off her feet and dragged along for a short distance before the man stopped his vehicle. The inevitable crowd gathered, and seeing my mother's bleeding hands, pulled the man off his box and beat him unmercifully until a policeman turned up and saved him from them.

53

My mother refused to bring a charge, as she realized that this would mean at least a day's delay. She managed to get to Mme Mareyne's shop, and after having her hands bandaged, she finished her business and caught the train back to Holland.

Her losses left my mother with little to pay the money owed to various dealers, but the Persian rugs that my father had brought with him from that fatal Spanish journey saved the situation, for my mother managed to sell them to the one man at The Hague who understood their value, the Marquis d'Arcicolar, Spanish minister to the Netherlands government. But neither the silver at Lille nor the fine Chinese porcelains which had been left in London were ever traced, and the auctioneers could not be made responsible. Many years later, my mother told me that all that was saved was about 40,000 gulden—about £3,000 in those days—nearly all in stock. The thought of her orphaned children kept her going, and her innate taste for the finest soon made her a prominent figure among the many experienced Dutch antique-dealers.

She, like her brother Joel, had learnt a good deal from the Ridder van Esso, and this experience, added to that year with her brother at Hull, now proved of great value to the business. Soon this beautiful young woman became a figure in the international market. Her greatest problem was the finding of a suitable house on the Hofspui, the fine avenue where her husband had established his business. She had almost given up hope when her notary informed her that a house only a few doors away from the old one, and even better than it, would come into the market. The difficulty was money, and as at that moment her brother Joel was going through a most difficult time and there was a good deal of bad feeling between her and her well-to-do father-in-law, she went to see a wealthy old art-dealer in Gouda. He had done much business with her husband, and during the last few months she also had bought many expensive things from this old gentleman. He admired her courage and energy, and put the money at her disposal at a very low rate of interest. She had won through, and on May 1, 1878, moved to her beautiful new house. From then on, affairs improved by leaps and bounds.

A year after my father's death, my grandparents took me to The Hague to visit my father's grave. We stayed with my mother in her large house with a garden at the back. My grandmother and I remained for some time at The Hague, and one day I was called from the garden because an uncle had come to visit us. Some years afterwards I heard that this uncle, Joseph Duveen, a member of the Zwolle family, had come that day to propose marriage to my mother; and then I remembered the conversation between my mother and my grandmother after the uncle had left. My grandmother had said: "But he is such a kind-looking young man." And my mother had replied: "I will never give my children a stepfather."

One day my mother spoke at breakfast about having to go to a country sale near Leyden. As my grandfather and uncles had already taken me several times to some of these country sales, I begged my mother to let me come with her, and when my grandmother told her that I had often been to auctions, I was taken. We first passed through Delft, and then, after a long drive by the side of the Rhine, we drove through wrought-iron gates and past one of the large Dutch sun-dials to a beautiful country-house. There were lots of articles standing on long tables in a tent in front of the house, and nearly everything was damaged.

I saw my mother handle many things, but every time she

put them down again almost as soon as she had taken them up. On one small table stood a pleasant-looking dark-green leather box. My mother opened the lid, and I saw two very pretty pink vases; but the moment she lifted the lid, old Mr. Mozes Hamburger, who had many a time given me some beautiful saucers for my little toy glass cabinet, said to her: "German imitations." My mother did not even handle them after this, and we moved on.

The next box was full of beautiful bits of lace, and I saw that my mother was quite excited about it. She and Mr. Hamburger stood talking animatedly about the lace. I heard my mother ask him whether he was going to bid for this lot, and he answered that if she wanted it he would not bid. I was very fond of old lace and began to beg my mother for some of the pieces. Mr. Hamburger said that he would give them to me if my mother did not.

It seemed a long time before the lace was up for sale, but when it was brought by a man from the long table, my mother bought it. She took the box from the man at once and began to show it to me, so that I could pick out a few pieces for myself. Mr. Hamburger was standing near us, and then, while my mother was handing me a pretty piece of lace, she suddenly called out: "Mine!" very loudly.

Mr. Hamburger growled: "Well, I'll be damned." He said some rude words to my mother, but she reminded him that he had said the vases were imitation. She had bought the vases by "Dutch auction." Dutch auction is a very complicated method for stopping the dealers from joining in a "knock-out." As I grew up I had often to go through this complicated and nerve-racking procedure. It begins with the customary selling by bidding upwards, which is a way of establishing the approximate value. The highest bidder is then the provisional

owner. But then follows the Dutch auction process. The auctioneer, who has now ascertained the opinion of the general
public, begins by calling out a figure usually about double the
provisionally highest bid. In the case of the vases the provisional bidding had ended at a little over 200 gulden, or about
£17. Then the auctioneer had started the Dutch auction at
500 gulden, and after he had called out the first three figures—in this case, 500, 475, and 450—my mother had
"mined" at the first possible amount, 425 gulden, about £35.
If someone had called out the decisive word before the fourth
figure had been called by the auctioneer, the sale would have
been void; and in such cases the auctioneer recommences his
chant at about double the previous starting figure. This is to
prevent anything being sold too much below its value; it is a
very useful selling method when rare works of art are sold in
the presence of a knock-out.

The provisional bidder is usually paid a premium of about
two per cent on what he has bid. This is to encourage provisional bidding. If, on the other hand, no one "mines" during
the final Dutch-auction bidding, he remains the owner. This
happens sometimes and is usually greeted with an ironic "He
hangs!"

On the way back my mother took the vases out of their
silk bed and told us that they were Sèvres worth at least
£2,000, and that she had been afraid of Mr. Hamburger all
the time. She had seen at a glance that they were old, and
knew quite well that he had tried to fool her. She used the lace
to make him think that she had believed him when he said
that the vases were imitations.

"What a bad man to do this to a widow," observed my
kind-hearted grandmother. The good soul did not know that
art-dealing is a keen battle of wits; but very few people ever

got the best of my clever, courageous mother. That night the two vases stood on the piano, for many years the pedestal for beautiful things to be admired and judged by my little sister and myself. The next day Uncle Joel came along and bought the two "*rose du Barry*" Sèvres vases from my mother for £2,000.

My mother, however, was to find out that things can be much more difficult for a woman than for a man. One day she was asked to come and see a collection which a young nobleman had just inherited from an old aunt. He wanted to sell it. The house was one of the magnificent old villas in the fine avenue that leads from The Hague to Scheveningen. A liveried manservant opened the door, but he seemed uncertain about announcing my mother. She protested that she had come all this way by appointment, and then the man mumbled something about his gentleman being slightly indisposed. He went upstairs and returned to show my mother up to the salon on the first floor. The gentleman was reclining on a sofa and after some trouble managed to get to his feet.

"I saw at once that he was drunk," my mother told me many years after. "He leered at me with a bestial expression on his face, and before I had recovered from my surprise, he had turned the key of the door. Then he came towards me, but by that time I had made up my mind what to do. I ran to the window, hoping that this would stop him, but as he came slowly after me, looking more like a huge ape than a human being, I caught hold of a Nankin vase and crashed it through the window. As he still came nearer, I pulled out a large pointed piece of the broken glass; then he paused. The crash had attracted the attention of the passers-by, but I hated the idea of a scandal, so I said to him: 'Open that door or I'll call for help!' That sobered him, and as he opened the door, the manservant came in and assisted him into the other part of the double room. I realized then that there were certain things not safe for a woman to do."

Buying privately has always been the most important part of antique-dealing; so my mother made an arrangement with an old friend of my father to look after this part of the business. But after some time the arrangement proved almost ruinous. Her partner, although he had good taste, could not distinguish between a good copy and an original, nor had he the least idea of valuation. This association lasted for a few years, but finally his irresponsible buying caused great financial difficulties. The contract was to extend for ten years, and final ruin was staring my mother in the face. She wrote to her brother Joel, who had been very much against this partnership at the time of its inception. He had insisted that a clause be inserted into the contract stating that my mother's remarriage would bring with it the right to abrogate the contract. My uncle was a man of deeds, so he came to The Hague with his wife, who also had a great influence over my mother. He argued that the only way out was to marry her cousin Joseph. My mother replied that although she liked him she did not love him, and that she would never give her children a stepfather.

Here my Aunt Rosetta intervened. She said that Joseph was the kindest young man she had ever met; that he adored my mother; and that although many of their friends would like to have him as a son-in-law, he had always refused to get married.

This made a great impression. Uncle Joel added that he had learnt the business very quickly, and that she would neglect the happiness of her children if she did not marry him, for she would be penniless in a few months. In his usual masterful manner he concluded: "I am going to telegraph him to come over by tonight's boat!"

He came, and my mother, seeing how her children all favoured the new uncle, gave in. She never regretted doing so, for our stepfather proved an affectionate father and an adoring husband. They were married on February 28, 1883, and lived happily together until our stepfather died in 1910, after having made our mother and us happy for twenty-seven years.

VII

HENRY J. DUVEEN'S ENTRY

I MUST now turn back to narrate Henry J. Duveen's entry into the art-business. This youngest member of the Duveen (Meppel) family lost his mother when he was eleven years old. After the debacle of the Meppel ironworks and his father's move to Amsterdam to open a small cotton-wool factory, the boy was immediately sent to the excellent Amsterdam Burgher High School, where he received a first-class education.

The second marriage of my grandfather, Joseph H. Duveen, caused a great deal of unhappiness to his younger children, with the result that his eldest daughter made an extremely unhappy marriage with a drunkard whose cruelty and neglect drove her out of her mind. My mother, the next in age, was also forced to leave home and live with relatives; but young Henry had to put up with his stepmother's cruelty. This resulted in much wild life when he was still in his teens, but, although he constantly mixed with the young wastrels of the Cape diamond-boom of the early seventies of last century, he never took to the gambling and drinking which demoralized these profiteers. When he fell in love with my father's sister,

Jeanette—then sixteen years old—and planned to elope with her, her father appealed to my mother to stop this nonsense. She wrote to her brother Joel, who rushed across from London with the intention of shipping the young lover off to America as quickly as possible.

As usual, Uncle Joel dealt energetically with the situation. He decided to carry out the Boston-New York plan without waiting for the co-operation of his brother-in-law, my father. Fortunately for the business plan, young Henry Duveen had a fairly good understanding of Oriental porcelain, the better class of delft pottery, and the various styles.

On their way to London, they called at my parents' house at The Hague for a further discussion of the American plan; however, my father had not yet returned from his ill-fated Spanish journey. My mother noticed how unhappy her young brother was at being dragged away, as he called it. He confessed that he was madly in love with Jeanette, and he wanted my mother's help in persuading their elder brother; but she was able to make him see reason by pointing out the madness of marrying a sixteen-year-old girl against the wishes of her parents and before he was even able to earn his own living. Then he tried to gain time by begging to be allowed to remain for a few weeks with my father and mother so that he could learn more about works of art in general. But his brother Joel was adamant. He insisted on his plan, and that same afternoon they left for Rotterdam to catch the Harwich steamer.

During the long journey down the Meuse, Joel outlined the plans, which Henry had to write down in a note-book. A stay of three days in Hull until his boat sailed was considered sufficient by his elder brother to teach his junior the differences in quality and value of his stock. He also allowed him to listen to the conversations with customers, and Uncle Joel admitted to me many years after these hurried lessons that Henry had been a very apt learner.

I have had the advantage of knowing both brothers in their heyday, and I was able to observe that both were men of great taste and extraordinarily quick thinkers. Joel was undoubtedly greater at convincing collectors that they were standing in front of something they could not afford to miss, but Henry was eminently able to obtain the same result in a less sweeping manner. Both convinced the customer that he was not only acquiring something very rare and beautiful, but that the object in question would always be worth at least what he was being asked for it. Their judgement was so good that they were always able to repurchase at the prices for which the things had been sold. In many cases they paid considerably more than the owners had paid.

To illustrate this statement, I must mention a conversation I had with Uncle Joel at a time when the younger brother was already at the top of his form as a salesman.

"Henry," my elder uncle said, "has done marvellously well, and he will do even better still; but he can't sweep the clients off their feet. He makes friends of them, and that is easier in America than here. I can make the buyer see in a few minutes that the thing I show him is not only just what he wants, but that it is a safe investment. I can prove to him that that particular article is the finest of its kind he has ever seen, and, my boy, that is why I am always willing to pay much too dearly—as the others think—for anything that is just a little finer than the finest. Henry makes friends of a few millionaires; I do business with almost every collector who comes in. He hasn't my temperament. He gets on friendly terms with them, but then he keeps them, for they trust him implicitly, and I will say that he deserves their trust. That is why he has been able to make great collectors out of those rich Americans."

"And what about Joe?" I asked.

"Joe will be the finest salesman of us all. He absolutely masters the client; but the difference between us is that when I have done a deal with someone, he feels that he has had the best of me. When Joe does a big deal the client goes away thinking that Joe has had the best of him."

I asked: "But does this not result in the client's wanting to return what he has bought?"

"Of course that happens at times, but Joe restores their confidence by agreeing at once, and this bluff usually succeeds in making the buyer anxious to keep the things. But his cleverest move is that when he notices that a client's enthusiasm for a particular thing is fading, he begs him to sell the thing back to us at a profit."

One of my own reminiscences of Joe's almost exclusive interest in his business is of a day when he was laid up with overwork—and rich eating. I said to him: "Joe, why don't you take up some pastime or some sport?" and he answered: "Yes, I know you are very fond of your sports, but my sport is my business." Not many years later, I had good reason to know that his business was not a sport but a relentless war on all competitors, with no holds barred.

Uncle Henry left for Boston in a steamer which, he told me, took nearly three weeks; and when he went to visit his cousins, the Koopmans brothers (sons of a Duveen mother), who had established a good wholesale business in old Dutch works of art, his efforts to bring about a business connection failed because they feared that this would soon change into competition—a not unlikely eventuality. Anyhow, his efforts in Boston came to nothing. Then he moved to New York, where a week after his arrival he received the news of my father's death. He was very upset at these tidings, and he wrote a heartbroken letter to my mother in which he said—among other things—that he had made up his mind to return to Europe, as he did not want to be so far away from all those he loved.

About the same time, Uncle Henry wrote a letter to his elder brother which hung for many years in the Fifth Avenue Duveen Galleries [1] as a tribute to the great founder of the New York business.

The letter began by mentioning Henry's disappointments in Boston and continued with a hopeful opinion of the New York market. Henry noted that Gobelins were in good demand, but he also wrote that he intended to return to England to talk matters over.

Joel Duveen, realizing that his young brother was merely homesick, cabled, ordering him to stay in New York and to hire some shop or warehouse to show the goods that were being shipped by the next White Star steamer.

In a few weeks Henry was able to start business in a downtown place, and he did well from the beginning. His brother had sent him a well-chosen selection from decorative, inexpensive pieces of delft to fine-quality Chinese porcelain; fine old English and old Dutch silver; and good pieces of old Dutch furniture that the New Amsterdam families bought eagerly. There were also several good seventeenth- and eighteenth-century portraits that were eagerly "adopted" by very distant "relatives." But the best of the stock consisted of fine French furniture of all periods and good decorative Flemish and French tapestries.

All these things had been chosen with Joel's good taste and

[1] See Author's Note.

judgement. Henry's enthusiasm, joined to a very friendly dis-
position, also proved a good asset in the combination. The
New York branch soon began to show good results, but Joel,
carried away by his energy, bought too far ahead of the New
York clientele. As was usual with him, he had overbought.
So, to hurry matters, he booked passage on the new White Star
liner, *Britannic*. As the London season was practically over,
he had sent some of his finest things ahead. Then, as luck
would have it, he was offered a very valuable set of Gobelins
tapestries by a titled English lady, a day before he was going
to sail. He was already considerably overdrawn at the bank.
Nevertheless, he bought the tapestries for £12,000, and,
what was worse, gave the cheque and took the tapestries with
him. Only then did he think of the bank! There was quite a
heated scene, but the banker was carried away by Joel's enthusiasm, and the extra credit was granted for two months.

My uncle told me the story of this transaction and of his
first trip to New York.

"I had to cash in on some of my finest things, and as Henry
had written me several times that Gobelins (tapestries of the
Manufacture Royale des Gobelins) were wanted, I felt sure
that this glorious set would fetch a big price in New York.
They were in the most perfect state of preservation, with the
colours as if they had only just left the looms. The background was *damassé* yellow, as in the Slangenburg "Don
Quichotte" set.[2] There were four large panels, measuring between about twelve feet to about twenty feet wide and about
twelve feet high. The two widest had two Boucher panels
each, and the smaller ones had each one central panel; all
these panels were framed in the lovely *alentours* of Jacques
(see illustration).

[2] See Chapter XX, "The 'Don Quichotte' Tapestries."

"As I had bought them at the last moment, I had to take these bulky tapestries with me on the *Britannic*. I took them by passenger train to Liverpool, but there the officials made trouble about taking such bulky packages as traveller's luggage, and in the end I had to rush to the White Star office to see one of the heads. I managed it, and had no more trouble until I had to pass the customs at New York; but Henry met me, and he knew how to get over troubles with the officials there.

"But what a shock I got when I saw our business premises! They were in a bad neighbourhood, and the place was not much better than a storehouse. Our beautiful stock was badly placed and badly lit, and the windows were not good enough for an old-clothes shop. In less than a week I had everything in a really good place with ample room to show the things and proper lighting. Of course the cost took even my breath away, but I knew only too well that trying to do things on the cheap meant ruin. Henry was very upset, but he gave in to me. The worst of it was that instead of being able to remit money to my London bank I had to use up practically the whole of the New York bank balance.

"Henry had told me that one of the richest men in America had asked him to find some very fine French furniture, and that this gentleman had visited some of the great palaces and museums in Europe, and so would be very hard to please. As soon as we had the place shipshape, word was sent to this gentleman, but he kept us waiting nearly a week before he turned up with a very showy French girl. I left the matter to Henry, but nothing was good enough for the client. Henry came out to me to tell me that the man had not even asked the price of anything. And then I realized the sort of mentality we had to deal with. I told Henry to go back to his customer and that I would send an assistant in to say that he was wanted by a lady. I would then come in to take over, and see what I could do. This was done, and I began to show the big man and his friend round our Chinese porcelain. There were several cases of these in the large show-room, but he did not like any of them. Then I took him to a small room where I showed him one of the finest pieces of French furniture I have ever had, a small table by Riesener, with ormolu mounts by Gou-thière. [A similar little table by Riesener was sold a few years later at the Hamilton Palace sale for six thousand pounds.] I had bought it cheaply from its former owner, Mrs. Green-wood, of York, and I asked fifteen hundred pounds for it.

" 'Show me something worth-while,' the big man grum-bled, and used one of my best Persian rugs as a spittoon. I answered him that I did not think that there was anything as fine in French furniture in the whole of New York. To this he replied that he did not care what was in New York. He wanted better than that.

"This time I was furious. I knew that he could not have seen anything finer than this table, and I had offered it to him much below its value. I realized that the only thing to do with this man was to show him something he could not buy. I smiled at him and said: 'I see you have been spoiled by the things you have seen in the French museums and palaces, but I think that I can show you something at least as fine as any-thing over there. Unfortunately, I am keeping it for an old customer, and you must give me your word that you do not tell any one you have seen it.'

" 'All right. Let me see it.'

"I took him upstairs where I had a strong top-light, and as I entered the room I drew the curtain of the largest panel aside. He said nothing, but I saw that this time I had made an impression. I took him right round the set, and told him that this was the work of the French Royal Tapestry Manufacture. Everything woven there was made for the king, and tapestries were only given to princes or ambassadors.

" 'Did you buy it from a prince?' he asked.

" 'No, I bought it from an English noblewoman whose great-grandfather had, about 1780, ordered it secretly through the British ambassador. A few years after this it was discovered that the head of the tapestry works, a Scotsman by the name of Neilson, had done a great deal of such clandestine business, and he was sent to prison.'

"For a moment he remained silent. Then he asked me how much I was asking for the tapestries, but I told him that I had bought it to offer to my brother's customer, and that we would have to give him the first refusal.

" 'I am not asking you to sell it to me, but I want to know what you are going to ask for it,' he growled.

" 'I want a hundred and fifty thousand dollars for the set, and I know that it is cheap at that.'

" 'I'll give you a hundred and seventy-five thousand dollars; money on the table.'

" 'I am very sorry, sir, but our other customer must have the first refusal.'

" 'Look here, young man,' he almost shouted, 'have you given a written option to this other fellow?'

" 'No,' I answered, 'but I think that my young brother has promised it to him.'

" 'Oh, you think, do you? Go and find out!'

"I had won, for I came back in a couple of minutes and told him that my brother did intend to keep it for the other customer, but as there was no actual option, I did not like to refuse it to someone who was so keen to have it.

" 'And what have I to pay?' he asked.

" 'A hundred and fifty thousand dollars, and there will be a condition on the receipt that we'll always take it back at ten per cent less.'

" 'Do you mean that you refuse my extra twenty-five thousand dollars?' he asked.

" 'Yes, sir. We like to make customers.'

" 'Right!' he said, and took out his cheque-book. And that, my boy, was our first big customer in America. For many years we did a great deal of business with him. The best of it is that within a few years he knew that I had bought a similar Boucher set for forty thousand pounds [$200,000]."

"And who was the customer?" I asked. But I had rushed in where angels fear to tread, and I just managed to escape the smack which I had earned. However, I have reason to believe that the buyer had been a great railway magnate, whose palace with all its treasures was destroyed at the time of the great San Francisco earthquake.

VIII

OXFORD STREET

WHEN JOEL DUVEEN left New York his courageous
move to a really good gallery had more than justified
his enterprise. Business was good from the start, and it increased by leaps and bounds through the joint efforts of the
two brothers. When the elder brother returned to England
he knew that the New York branch would ultimately become
the most successful art-business in that city. He explained to
me that the existing American dealers had always laboured
under great difficulties. They had to travel to Europe every
year during their slack period—May to October—to replen-
ish their stocks, but this meant that if the next season should
be a bad one they were unable to sell anything like the amount
they had been obliged to spend. As rents and other expenses
were extremely high, from time to time even big firms were
ruined in a few months. This was from the very beginning
the great advantage the two brothers had for many years over
the New York firms. Henry had only to cable for what he
wanted, and in a few days Joel was able to ship. He had the
whole European market within easy reach, and week-end
raids on the French, Dutch, and Belgian markets, added to

what he obtained from London auctions, were usually equal to the New York demand.

Towards the end of 1879 Joel felt that he was in a position to open his long-hoped-for London gallery, but there remained the difficulty of finding a place large enough, and in Oxford Street, the location that was his ideal. Then by accident he heard that Messrs. Phillips, leading English porcelain and pottery agents, were thinking of letting part of their too large premises in Oxford Street, two doors west of the Pantheon. As usual, he wasted no time, and within a few hours of hearing the news he had concluded the matter. He was to have the western half of the premises with part of the upper floors, and was allowed to remodel and redecorate his part. As soon as he had settled the plans he went to Paris to bring together the finest qualities of stock that he had planned for his purpose. He first visited Messrs. Lowengard, from whom he had already bought much fine French furniture and tapestries for the New York business; this time he asked for the arrangement old M. Lowengard had proposed during that first interview in 1877. This was arranged on the same terms: sale or return after three months; at least one tenth to be kept and paid for at the end of those three months. At that time he was already familiar with the qualities and values, and he selected forty thousand pounds' worth of French works of art. After this auspicious beginning, Jules Lowengard took him on a round of the Paris market, at that time the world's storehouse of works of art. Joel, with an eye on the rich English merchants and industrialists, selected only fine, decorative objects, rather than collectors' pieces. He was particularly attracted by the very beautiful coloured Chinese "mandarin" vases that had been mounted as *lampadaires* by the great bronze artists of the Louis XV and Louis XVI periods, and he secured seven pairs of these particularly effective pieces, each standing between seven and eight feet high. Several of his costly purchases had to be paid for in cash, and others with bills of exchange payable three months after date. In a few instances smaller dealers had insisted on bills payable two months after date, which ultimately led to severe worries. From Paris he went to Belgium and Holland, where he bought the finest old Chinese porcelain he could find.

When he opened in Oxford Street, he had a collection that would rouse the envy of all lovers of antiques. In Bond Street there were more important stocks of French furniture than his; but his Oriental porcelain surpassed anything ever seen before in London, and he had cornered the Oriental porcelain market. But his greatest strength was the tapestries. He had brought over the finest and rarest kinds of the Gothic, Renaissance, and eighteenth-century periods and felt certain that the great private buyers would have to come to him; but this overconfidence nearly ruined him. He had scored easily in the wholesale business and had had no difficulty in finding dealers to buy his purchases, but London private collectors of expensive pieces were, as he found to his cost, not easy to deal with. The worst handicap was that the big London dealers were very annoyed at his setting up in opposition, and he soon noticed that the few dealers to whom he had shown his stock were using this opportunity to spoil him with the big buyers. These dealers were well established and had their clients' confidence. Joel Duveen was a new-comer without any reputation in a business where the private buyer has to place the greatest trust in the dealer.

He soon found out that there was a campaign against him, waged particularly by those men to whom he had shown his finest things. They depreciated them by raising doubts about their genuineness, by ridiculing Duveen's "crazy" prices, and, worst of all, by faint praise. This stabbing in the back nearly ruined him; but it served as a great lesson, for never again did he allow any dealer to see his finest things. With the collectors who knew as much or more than any dealer, such as George Salting, he did some good business in the finest Oriental porcelain, as he did to a lesser degree with James Orrock. But the thought of his fine French furniture and, particularly, his very expensive tapestries kept him awake at night. The weeks were passing, and sales were slow. The Dutch dealers to whom he had given bills had known him for years, and they would not present these bills if he should ask for delay; but the French bills had been discounted by their holders, and these would have to be met on the due dates. Two thousand four hundred pounds would become payable in the first batch, and three weeks before this fell due he was still short of a thousand pounds. It looked as if Barney had been right: he had tried too high. It was not his lack of judgement or want of trying; he felt he was being ruined by the London dealers who were afraid of his competition.

Overwork and worry began to tell on his nerves, but he fought on. He visited every possible buyer, but with very small results. Only a very big deal could save him. At last, driven by necessity, he went to see the few dealers who were big enough to buy his sort of stock. But it was no use. Most of them were sarcastically sorry for him, and one was so pleased that he had helped to ruin him that he gloated openly over these difficulties while Joel tried to tempt him into buying under his own cost prices.

While telling me this story my uncle paused here for a moment. Then he continued with a most touching incident:

"Two days before the bill became due I was still short by five hundred pounds, and then I remembered a rich Hull brewer who a few times had lent me the money for some deal on condition that he receive a portion of the profit. As he had become too greedy, I had not applied to him for some years; but I had already tried everything else, and I decided to try him. I telegraphed him whether I could see him that evening on important business, but late that afternoon I received a reply that he was on his way to New York. I did not know where to turn, and that night, when I lay awake with worry, Rosetta suddenly said: 'Joel, you are worrying. What is it?'

"Of course I denied that I was worrying; but she told me not to lie to her because she was quite sure that I was badly troubled. In the end I had to tell her, and then without saying another word she got out of bed. In a minute she came back and handed me two hundred and twenty pounds in notes and the pearl ear-rings that I had given her out of one of my good deals.

" 'Here you are, dear; I have saved this money out of the house-keeping, and you will be able to borrow at least three hundred pounds on the pearls.'

"I was deeply moved, but I would not accept. Then she called out: 'Duveen!' and, my boy, I knew of old that when she said this it was the last warning before a very bad storm. So I gave in; but I vowed that one day I would cover her with pearls.

"The next day," he continued, "just as I was crossing Oxford Circus I caught sight of Mr. Arthur Wilson, the great Hull shipowner I had done a good deal of business with in Hull. He had always been very pleased with the things I had sold him; but I knew that his house was full up and that he did not buy French things. I was desperate, and I clutched at the straw. He was very pleased to see me, and after the first few words, I said:

" 'Mr. Wilson, if you want to buy beautiful things, now is the time. I have brought over the finest porcelains, furniture, and tapestries, but I have to meet very big bills before I have had the time to sell much. Come and look at them, and I will sell you the finest goods I've ever had at very low prices.'

"He laughed, and said: 'Duveen, I'm in the same boat. Things are bad with me, too. I've bought a big house in Mayfair for thirty thousand pounds, and my wife wouldn't go into it. I have had to buy another one for much more money, and now the agents can't sell the first one. I tell you what,' he added, laughing even louder. 'You sell that house for me and I will spend the money with you.'

"I knew that he meant it by way of a joke and that he did not think it possible that I should be able to sell the house; but I didn't hesitate a second.

" 'Do you mean that, Mr. Wilson?' I asked.

"For a moment I saw a dangerous flicker in his eyes; but then he burst out laughing so loudly that passers-by stared at us. When he stopped laughing he said: 'Well, now that you ask me, I was joking; but if you can sell that house it will suit me to buy the furniture for the new one, and it would only be fair to buy it from you.'

" 'Right,' I said, 'I'll sell that house for you within a week.'

" 'How?' he asked.

" 'That I don't know yet, but I'll do it.'

"We shook hands on that, and after he had given me his card with a few pencilled words for his agents, I started straight away.

"That day I had all the big agents working at the sale of

that house at double commission, half to be paid out of my own pocket. Within a week the house was sold, and Mr. Wilson kept his word. When I brought him the news he said that he had not come to see me before because he did not want to be tempted, but that he would now come with me at once. When he saw my stock he could not resist its beauties, and he bought far more than he had promised. He was a business man himself and understood the position. He took out his cheque-book and wrote a cheque for half the amount then and there. His house agents were a very fine old firm, and they refused to accept the extra commission.

"I was saved, and I never looked back after that. The decoration and furnishing of Mr. Wilson's house was the finest advertisement I could have had, and his rich friends almost fell over each other to get beautiful objects, too."

IX

ESTHER

THE FIRST MEETING with my then sixteen-year-old
cousin Esther, eldest daughter of Joel Duveen, was to
affect the whole of my future life. Before this meeting I had
heard her described by my uncle Joseph Hangjas while I
was still living in Haarlem with my grandparents. My young
uncle had been to Paris and London on important business,
and in London he had stayed with my uncle Joel. There he
had met Esther, then about twelve years old. She had made a
deep impression on him by her beauty, gentleness, and intelli-
gence. She had spoken to him in English, French, and German. "I can only describe her as a heavenly being," was his
phrase, which remained uppermost in my mind. When I returned to The Hague a year later, my mother was on the
point of marrying her second husband, Joseph Duveen, her
first cousin. He had stayed with his cousin Joel for over a year,
and both he and my mother always spoke of Esther as "the
angel." I was then nearly ten years old, and in my imagination
I always saw her as one of those glorious figures depicted on
sacred pictures. I had chosen an angel with long, dark tresses
in a large Italian picture as the model of my cousin. In the

summer of 1887 my two uncles and their wives brought
Esther with them. When I saw her I could not utter a single
word. She was totally different from, and much more beautiful than, the angel of my picture; she was quite fair with deep-
blue eyes. This was all I realized at that first glance; but her
expression and the smile which accompanied her gentle voice
transformed the usual terms of greeting into something celes-
tial. The only thing I remember of those first moments is that
my uncle Henry said: "Well, my boy, can't you say something to your pretty cousin? You are not so shy at other times."
Even then I could not speak, but I remember how our German governess had kissed my mother's hand when she left
us to return home; and to hide my inability to say something,
I kissed Esther's hand.

"Do you kiss the hand of every girl you meet?" teased my
uncle.

I made matters worse by saying that I had never done it
before. This time all my elders laughed, and after this *faux pas*
I had not the courage to lift my eyes again to look at her. I did
not know then what had come over me, but I realized later
that this first meeting of our eyes had been instantaneous love
on my side; and many years later I knew that it had had the
same effect on Esther.

By the time we sat down to dinner I had somewhat overcome my feeling of gaucherie. When I was placed beside my
cousin, I was able to attend to my table duties.

Gradually I regained sufficient self-confidence to keep up a
conversation with her, and I was much more at my ease until
Aunt Dora, Uncle Henry's young wife, sat down at the piano
and asked Esther to sing something. Esther sang a song out
of the then modern operetta *Dorothy*. The sweet but rich
tones of her mezzo-soprano voice made me tremble, and when

she finished I was again unable to utter a word. This song has ever since recurred to my mind, even though the memory of its loveliness brings pain.

Then my uncle, for whom I had sung frequently during his many visits, insisted on my singing also. My voice had changed from treble to high tenor, and I handed Aunt Dora Verdi's *Il Trovatore*. I sang the beautiful but sad *"Miserere."* I had already a powerful voice, and as I had heard this opera sung ever since my earliest youth I was able to surprise my uncles and aunts. Aunt Dora, a great performer on the piano, suggested that Esther and I should sing the duet for tenor and contralto *"Ai nostri monti"* from the fourth act.

In April 1888 I went to the Belgian École Moyenne de l'État at Hal. Shortly after, I was joined by two of my London cousins, Ben and Henry, who were my juniors by two and four years. They were very much out of their element, as neither of them knew a word of French or Flemish, the two languages spoken by the majority of the pupils; but I was supremely happy to be able to look after my two young cousins, the brothers of the angel who was never long out of my thoughts. Unfortunately, they only remained for about six months, as their father decided they should go to a school within easy reach of Paris, where he paid almost weekly visits for his purchase of French works of art. A few months after their departure I left school to enter my parents' business at The Hague. I left with the first Prize of Excellence.

On the first day after my return from school I was sent to Haarlem to deputize for the firm at an auction, because my parents could not go themselves. I did well, for I discovered that three small old Nankin bottle-shaped vases were of the very rare Ch'êng-Hua reign (1465–88) instead of the similar but very inferior pieces of Wan Li (1573–1620). I bought these vases for 90 gulden (£7 10s.) under the very trying ordeal of the Dutch auction and in the presence of my grandfather and his three sons, who had mistaken these vases for the very common Wan Li pieces of this type.

As I stepped out of the tram in front of our door that afternoon, I saw my uncles and my stepfather talking in our porch. They grinned at the large carpet-bag which my grandfather had lent me, but when I opened it and produced the Ch'êng-Hua vases they were obviously impressed.

"Where did you get those?" asked Uncle Henry. When I answered that I had bought them at an auction in Haarlem, he asked: "How much did you pay for them?"

When I told them that I had "mined" them at 90 gulden, he said: "I'll give you two hundred pounds."

"What!" interrupted my other uncle: "They are worth much more. I'll give two hundred and fifty pounds!"

"Three hundred pounds!" countered Uncle Henry; and this finished the comic auction on our doorstep. My stepfather told me afterwards that the vases were much too dear at that price, but that the uncles had been so pleased that they wanted to encourage me.

This success was followed shortly after by the discovery of some very valuable Beauvais and Lille tapestries behind the wall-paper in an old family house, also at Haarlem. My parents were in London and, as the house was to be sold within an hour after my discovery, I had the effrontery to "mine" this house at 17,000 gulden (about £1,400). After the tapestries had been removed, the house was sold at a loss of £420; but by then the tapestries had been sold for £4,000.

At the suggestion of my uncle Joel, I was next sent to England to sell old Dutch furniture to the dealers. I was then in my seventeenth year. Before starting on my business journey

I stayed two days with my uncle at his country-house, "The Hawthorns," opposite what now is Golders Green Station, London.

That evening my uncle praised me again for what I had already done, and as this was in the presence of Esther my secret hopes were raised sky-high. After dinner we went into the drawing-room, where at her father's wish Esther sat down at the piano and began to sing. Her cousin Ben Scott, of Hull, who was also staying at "The Hawthorns," stood at her side to turn the pages for her. He looked so debonair and behaved with such an air of a man of the world that I felt the first pangs of jealousy; but I found some consolation in the thought that he was an old man of twenty-seven! I soon noticed that he was not able to turn the page at the right moment, and Esther asked me to do it. I was now almost trembling with joy, and in this state of mind I nearly committed the same fault that had caused the hated Ben's downfall; but I pulled myself together just in time. When Esther suggested that we should sing another duet I eagerly agreed, and as my voice had now settled into a high baritone, we sang the duet for soprano and baritone *"De tant d'amour ne soyez pas ingrate"* from Donizetti's *La Favorite*. As this soprano part was a little too high for her mezzo-soprano voice, Esther transposed the not too difficult accompaniment into a slightly lower key. I let myself go, and after a slight whisper of "Don't shout" from Esther I toned down to the proper cantabile. This less dramatic singing blended our voices properly when Esther joined in. After we had repeated the duet twice Aunt Rosetta intervened with: "Esther, you must not strain yourself," and this was the end of that unforgettable musical evening.

The next day I left for Liverpool by the night train and began my first round of the North Country dealers. Much of this commercial travelling was unpleasant, but I secured some good orders with the various large photographs that I had taken along. This business rapidly increased as time went on; but my proud happiness was shattered by some hints I received about too much intermarriage. One day, while I was staying with him at his London house, Uncle Henry spoke quite frankly about the danger of marriages between first cousins. He began by telling me that my feelings for Esther had been noticed, and that her parents strongly disapproved. This was a terrible shock; but when I began to argue that this opposition to marriages between cousins was a mere superstition, he enumerated several terrible cases in the Duveen family. I had never heard of these; I was only seventeen at that time and inclined to disbelieve him. When even my dear mother spoke to me about what she called my "dangerous infatuation" I retorted that even she had married her first cousin. But the moment I had uttered these words I was sorry, for our stepfather had been a dutiful father to his stepchildren. I told her that I was very sorry for having said this, and she closed the discussion by reminding me that she had for this very reason refused for more than six years to marry her cousin; but that, fortunately, the children of her second marriage were strong and perfectly normal.

As time went on my business constantly increased, and by the middle of 1890 I had become well known to the Dutch and English dealers as a coming young man. I was happy in my interesting and exciting work, divided between business and studies in art libraries and museums. Nor had I given up my dream of happiness, in spite of the family opposition. I felt sure that my energy and capacity would change the opposition into consent, for I had increased our business in every direction. Then, in the midst of success and confidence in my happy future, I suffered the first great sorrow in my life. Aunt Rosetta wrote to my mother that Esther was engaged to a M. Lowengard, and she begged my mother to send my sister Evaline to her to take charge of the household in place of Esther. The wedding was to take place early in the coming year; and, as there were thirteen children, this was a very exacting household to manage. Aunt Rosetta explained that after giving birth to fifteen children she was too delicate to look after such a household, and that if Evaline could take over until Annette, then fourteen years old, would be able to take Esther's place it would be an ideal solution of all the difficulties. My mother consented, but I was dazed by the grievous news that Esther was going to marry someone else. It seemed impossible!

My uncle and aunt came over to fetch Evaline, but I could not face them, so I went off to an important auction in Friesland. When I returned to The Hague my sister had left with them. I was thoroughly shaken by the blow, and when a Paris friend told me that M. Jules Lowengard was a great gentleman and the leader of the Paris art-dealers, as well as an intimate friend of the various Rothschild families in Paris and Vienna, I tried to console myself with the reflection that Esther could fill any position, and that she had every prospect of being happy and honoured.

A few weeks after this, Uncle Joel and Aunt Rosetta left for New York on a visit that would last for some months because my uncle had undertaken the decoration of some great houses of American clients. This decorating always included enormous sales of precious things to fill these houses.

Almost immediately after my uncle's departure a letter arrived from Evaline saying that she was afraid Esther was very unhappy. They shared the same bedroom, and she had several

James Henry Duveen

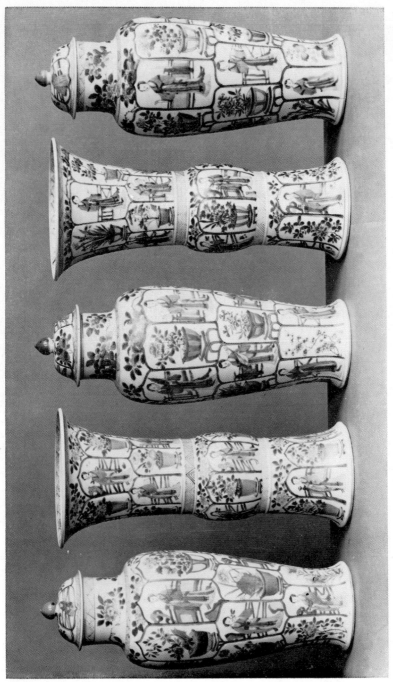

Nankin Vases, "Lange lyzen" Type

nights noticed that Esther was sobbing. At first Esther had explained that she was worrying about her parents' voyage, but she did not worry about that any longer. The crying, however, had increased; and finally Esther had confessed that she was unhappy about her engagement. My parents did not tell me about this, but another letter arrived in which Evaline wrote that Esther had asked her to write to my mother to beg Uncle Joel to stop this engagement. Evaline had also seen the fiancé and wrote that M. Lowengard, although very pleasant, was at least twenty years older than Esther.

I knew nothing about all this until a cablegram arrived from New York for my mother. In the temporary absence of my parents I opened it. It was from Uncle Joel. He thanked my mother for her letter and ended with the startling information that he had cabled his son Joe to break off the engagement.

But Joe, then twenty-one years old, had made up his mind that the engagement should not be broken off. He was already far-seeing and ambitious. The connection between Duveen Brothers [1] and one of the greatest art-dealing firms in Europe would mean an enormous increase in his firm's power in the world markets; although he dearly loved his sister, he made up his mind that this great prospect should not be upset by what he called a young girl's whim. He did his best to persuade her. He pointed out that she could not break her word and thus hurt and offend this great and kindly gentleman. It was far better to marry an older man whose conduct was known to be steady and honourable than marry a younger man who had not yet made his way and might make her very unhappy by unfaithfulness. Joe cited many cases in their own circle, and his sister began to waver. Jules Lowengard arrived from Paris the next day to plead his own cause. Thus urged by her

[1] See Author's Note.

adored brother and swayed by the eloquence of her fiancé, she gave in.

The wedding took place at the Savoy Hotel on March 9, 1891. My parents had gone to London for the wedding, and when Uncle Joel heard that I had not come with them he sent me a telegram that he expected me without fail; but I was too miserable and did not go. Instead, I went to stay with my Aunt Catherine in Haarlem, who did her best to console me; but even her kindness brought me no relief. On that ninth of March I vowed that I would never marry; and I kept that vow until twenty years later I married my beloved Esther.

X

INTERIOR DECORATION

THE LARGE PURCHASES by Mr. Arthur Wilson and the decoration of his house not only saved the critical situation that followed Joel Duveen's opening of his gallery in Oxford Street, but this decoration also brought out his exquisite taste. He had engaged an architect who made a specialty of decorating in old styles, but Joel soon noticed that this specialist's planning lacked harmony of colours and, even worse, he seemed to be unable to obtain the best effects from the lovely things Mr. Wilson had bought. The architect would brook no interference, and resigned. Already at that period Joel Duveen had seen many interiors of the great British houses and of the historical French châteaux; so, guided by his natural eye for effect and colour, he carried on without being hampered by a professional decorator. In a few days he had assembled some of the best French cabinet-makers and upholsterers who abounded in Soho at that time, and he soon found that what he saw in his own mind these experienced craftsmen could understand and create. The result was a quickly growing reputation for interior decoration in the French styles. He also greatly admired the Dutch and Flemish Renaissance styles. With the help of Teunissen, of The Hague, and Moens, of Brussels, he was able to buy many old wall-panellings of the sixteenth and seventeenth centuries, which he used for the decoration of the large dining-rooms of the great houses of London and the country in that long, prosperous period that ended with the First World War.

This decorating entailed a great deal of supervision, work that in itself was not remunerative; but, as the clients were only too glad to profit from Duveen's innate taste, they usually bought all the furniture, tapestries, pictures, and porcelains from him. Within a few years Joel Duveen was the most sought-after decorator in London, and his reputation soon brought him the very rich clientele among the great merchants and industrialists which he had foreseen and hoped for during those long years in Hull.

In New York, business also grew by leaps and bounds, but then there came another reverse. One night in 1883 the premises of Messrs. Phillips caught fire and were badly damaged. Though the fire did not spread to the Duveen gallery, ultimately the whole front of the building was taken down and rebuilt. New arrangements were made, and Duveen obtained the greater part of the ground floor and the whole of the three upper floors. The rent was increased from £350 to £750. Duveen used the opportunity to plan changes in the gallery; one of these was to build a large semi-circular show-window on the first floor. This space was to be filled with important and attractive works of art brilliantly illuminated at night to attract the attention of the theatre-goers. There was, however, strong opposition to this from the owner's architect, Mr. Cockshott. Joel Duveen explained that he wanted the semi-circular window to be free from all divisions so as to ensure an unbroken view of his works of art. When Mr. Cockshott observed that an eccentric gap in his façade would be the talk of the town, Duveen replied that this was exactly what he wanted. In the end the difference was settled by the architect promising that the divisions would be so designed as not to interfere with the effect of the show-window.

The rest of the incident I heard from the architect himself when nearly a quarter of a century later my uncle, Mr. Cockshott, and I were travelling by steamer from Monaco to Genoa. They were going to look at the old palaces for the model of a frieze for the enormous block of flats at the corner of Park Lane and Piccadilly which took the place of the antiquated Gloucester House. After lunch my uncle had gone to his private cabin for a rest, and Mr. Cockshott and I paced the deck while I listened to his praises of Joel Duveen. Their first meetings had been antagonistic; in fact, the architect admitted that he had hated the sight of Duveen at that time, and as he noticed my surprised stare, he explained. He began with their difference over the semi-circular show-window: "Duveen had been away for a few days, and the window framing had been set out in wood so that he could see the model on his return. I was just inspecting the work when I heard a roar behind me. I saw Duveen, and before I could interfere he made a rush at the woodwork and kicked it to pieces. 'You call that almost invisible?' he bellowed at me as he completed the destruction. Then he rushed off and went to see Mr. Phillips. The end of it was that he had his way, and I had to leave this yawning semi-oval to spoil the effect of my front. But when the building was finished and he made his first evening display it was indeed the talk of the town. He had placed a beautiful Louis XV lacquer-and-ormolu commode in the centre with a large gilt clock on it, with two candelabra to match, and as background a fourfold screen deco-

89

rated with scenes by Watteau. On the second night, I went to see the show myself, and there were crowds of people on the opposite pavement to look at the strongly illuminated sight. Hardly any carriage passed by without stopping, and I realized that this man whom I had looked upon as a brutal ignoramus had exquisite taste and that I had been wrong. Not only that, but I soon found out that in spite of his hasty and sometimes violent temper he was very good-natured, and we soon became firm friends. We have now worked together for many years, and the more I have seen of him the more I admire him."

I know from my uncle's own stories that the eccentric window brought him a host of new clients, and that his manner of doing business and his perfect taste made most of them not only permanent clients but lifelong friends as well. The sensation brought even the Prince and Princess of Wales to the new gallery, and, as I have already described in one of my previous books, during one of the Princess's visits she particularly noticed a Louis XV sofa covered with the finest Gobelins tapestry.

"She admired it more than anything she had seen and then, tempted by its look, sat down on it.

" 'What a lovely thing, and how comfortable,' she sighed in pleasure. 'I wonder how much it costs?'

" 'I sold it this morning for fifteen thousand pounds, Your Royal Highness,' answered Joel Duveen.

" 'Goodness! I daren't sit on so much wealth!' exclaimed the Princess, and hastily got up." [1]

In spite of his now enormous business, he was almost con-

[1] *Art Treasures and Intrigue* (Garden City: Doubleday, Doran & Company; 1935), p. 279.

stantly short of money because he could not resist buying any-thing beautiful and rare. As I grew up I heard hundreds of examples of this frenzy, and one which he told me to defend this weakness dates from this early London period. In the early spring of 1888 two old Chinese-porcelain vases were going to be sold at Christie's auction rooms. They were of the rare and priceless *famille noire* type, decorated with sprays of red hawthorn on a black ground, and formed part of the Lord Exeter collection from Burleigh House. On the day of the sale Joël Duveen was rather more worried than usual by money matters, and just as he was leaving to attend the auction he received a strong note from his banker about the state of his account. In the auction room he met the late Mr. J. C. J. Drucker, a wealthy Dutch collector who had made a fortune in the City of London. This gentleman asked him whether he thought that the vases were genuine. "Of course they are," answered Duveen, "but why do you ask me?"

"Because Wertheimer and several of the others think that they are Samson copies," replied the collector.

"Well, you buy them. They are the finest quality I have ever seen, and I would have bought them at any price if I could have raised the money."

"And what do you think I shall have to pay?"

Duveen answered with another question: "Are you sure that the Bond Street men really think that they are copies?"

"Yes, quite sure. They wouldn't dare to trick me," re-joined Mr. Drucker.

"Very well," said Duveen, "then I won't bid and will pre-tend not to be interested, and you may get them for very lit-tle. But I make one condition; if you ever should wish to sell the vases you will give me the first option."

"I am afraid that if I do get them I will never part with them; but if I should, I would certainly give you the first chance."

They parted, and when the bidding for the vases began Joel Duveen was talking to M. Coureau, the commission agent who attended all the London auctions. At first no one answered the auctioneer's invitation for a bid, and it was only when someone offered five pounds that the bidding began. Mr. Drucker was bidding against another private collector, and became the owner at 400 guineas. The moment the vases had been adjudicated to him he walked across to Duveen and asked him if he was really sure that they were genuine.

"What will you take for them, Mr. Drucker?" was the reply; this was enough for the lucky buyer.

In 1895 I was present when my uncle offered £10,000 for the vases that Mr. Drucker had bought ten years earlier for 400 guineas; and a few years later this offer was increased to £20,000.

In later years I became very friendly with Mr. Drucker, who spent his last years in Switzerland. He told me that he had intended to leave the vases to the Victoria and Albert Museum, but because of what he regarded as the unjust conquest of the Boer republics he had presented his whole collection to the Rijks Museum at Amsterdam. There they are the *clou* of the very rich Chinese porcelain collection.

XI

THE BREAK

FOR SOME YEARS the two brothers progressed rapidly. Joel, in his Napoleonic manner, was outvying everyone in enterprise and lightning action; Henry, in his more gentle and cautious manner, was building up a great clientele in America. At an early stage there, Henry had discovered that the good stock of inexpensive items was eagerly snapped up by the ladies; and the husbands whom they brought along almost invariably became buyers of the more expensive items. To Joel this seem an unnecessarily slow process and not worth the trouble of buying lots of trivial articles to be shipped to New York in large quantities.

I was still a schoolboy at The Hague when my uncle Joel, while driving round the town with me, said: "Henry wastes too much time on rubbish." When, some months later, I was accompanying Uncle Henry on the same round of art-dealers he spoke of his brother's mania of doing everything in a hurry, and, particularly, of always buying without thinking of what was at the bank. "Every few weeks I receive cables with our code word for 'remit all the money you can.'" These cables frequently forced Henry to visit people who owed him money, a most unpleasant way of dunning which had cost him quite a few good customers.

In spite of these difficulties, Joel's feverish energy led to enormous business; but the more he sold, the more pressing became his financial worries. Purchases from private sellers had to be paid in cash; purchases from dealers were usually paid for by acceptances, payable three months after date, and it was this last class of buying which led almost constantly to money worries. It may seem strange, but the three months' credit tempts the impetuous buyer to rely on sales before bills fall due. On the other hand, everyone who knew Joel Duveen believed in his unusual capabilities. Friends were always willing to help, and he insisted on paying them ten per cent interest. The time came, however, when these sources were fully exhausted. Then he had recourse to offering a share in the profit to rich speculating collectors. His many resources should have been sufficient to provide whatever might have been required; but nothing could keep pace with Joel Duveen's impetuosity when confronted by something unusually fine.

One day, shortly after I had entered my parents' business, my uncle astounded me with the statement that the more business he did, the more he was worried for money. He explained the apparent paradox by saying: "Customers hardly ever pay cash; the more one sells, the more one buys; but that has to be paid for long before the customer pays."

Early during my long life in the art-business, I realized that this financial difficulty was the real cause of worries in the art-dealer's world. My mother also had this family trait, and she was only rarely restrained by my cautious stepfather. And Joe, even when he had already become Lord Duveen, carried this weakness into the region of millions of pounds. His audacity led to triumph; mine partly to the ruin of my health and my business career.

The collaboration of the two brothers led to ever growing success, and when in 1884 Henry married Miss Dora Falcke, daughter of a well-to-do London stock-broker, the firm had already become a recognized power in the art-dealing world. By this time Henry was beginning to feel the results of his careful fostering of good connections with the American business men who were then surging towards financial world dominion. His young wife, although never mixing in the business, was very proud of her successful husband, and in her love and admiration she could not understand why his elder brother was apparently always giving him orders. She did not realize that this was caused by Joel's paternal feeling towards a brother younger by thirteen years. Joel never had time for long explanations. He knew that his brother understood him, and in spite of appearances the two brothers loved each other dearly. Both were quick-tempered, and in their impatient arguments their voices rose ever higher, with the result that those who did not understand them frequently concluded that they were quarrelling. Gradually Henry began to dislike being treated too high-handedly in the presence of employees and even of his wife. In the end, after many quarrels, there was a really serious clash that ended in the two brothers separating. Joel sent Charles, his sixteen-year-old second son, to watch over the assistants who had been engaged. The real manager was a very well-known New York art-dealer, the late W. Watson, a very extravagant, high-living member of the New York society of this period. For some years he had been a successful art-dealer, until his extravagance had ruined him. The business became fairly prosperous; but, as Watson told me when in 1896 I met him in Liverpool for the first time, the constant cabling for remittances soon caused trouble. Customers became annoyed, and finally Watson resigned.

The separation into two competing firms seriously aggravated the trouble between the two brothers, and after some time even the staffs of the two firms began to take part in this family quarrel. Henry was very popular and had made many friends, some of whom joined in the strife by belittling the elder brother's works of art. Several of these friends were high up in the New York custom-house; and, as at that time people connected with any of the public services could make serious trouble for any one they disliked, Joel's business stood in great danger. His employees began to notice that the custom-house officials were becoming increasingly difficult over the declarations of value, and that they were always looking for hidden drawers or compartments. Joel, receiving alarming reports from his New York branch, decided to look into the matter himself. He travelled to New York, accompanied by his wife and by Esther, their sixteen-year-old daughter, who was later to become my beloved wife. They travelled by the Dutch liner *Eider*. When they arrived at New York they were treated as smugglers and all three had to undress and be searched. They suffered all kinds of humiliations, but they had nothing to hide. At the same time the business premises had been occupied and were searched from top to bottom for goods that had not been passed through the customs. As this process involved all sorts of investigations through the stock and the books, Joel's legal advisers warned him that it would take weeks or even months before business could be resumed. He had to return home without having been able to clear up the matter.

Finally my mother intervened. Both brothers were travelling in Holland to buy works of art. She invited both to dinner for the following afternoon—at 5:30 in those days. Each accepted on condition that the other would not be there. Henry arrived quite half an hour before the arranged time, but Joel was late, as usual. After delaying about half an hour my mother had to order dinner to be served. We were already seated when an unusually loud clanking of the old-fashioned front door-bell caused Henry to exclaim: "Someone in a great hurry!" A moment after, we heard hasty footsteps along the old-fashioned marble-tiled corridor, and then the door was pulled open.

I shall never forget that scene. Uncle Joel called out: "What's this?" Uncle Henry jumped up and, looking furiously at my mother, said: "This is a mean trick, Betsy!"

For a few painful seconds the two brothers glared at each other, and then my mother said: "I am not going to have you two fools quarrelling any longer," and, addressing her eight-years-older brother, she said: "Here, Joel, sit down next to me. You are right, I did arrange this, and Henry knew no more about it than you did."

Joel took a step towards the seat that I had vacated, but then he turned and walked straight up to his brother. The next moment they were hugging each other.

It was one of the happiest meals I have ever witnessed, and even while eating, the two brothers were settling their plans for the future. They would travel to New York together, and as Joel did not consider either of their galleries good enough for his now much more important business he was going to find a bigger place farther uptown. The buying campaign in Holland was stopped, and after picking out all our finest porcelain the two very happy brothers left that night for Paris to collect and find stock Joel proposed for the new place. A long cable was sent to one of the leading New York estate agents

97

for a list of suitable premises in the neighbourhood of Union Square, and within a few days a satisfactory list was received.

During a quick campaign in Paris, Joel bought the most important French furniture and tapestries he could find. From the Lowengards he bought again a large quantity of the finest French tapestries, among them a set of three *"Comédies de Voltaire,"* glorious panels after special paintings by Boucher.

All these things had been bought for the opening of the New York galleries; and when Henry had at times expostulated about the enormous amount of credit that was being obtained on the usual bills of exchange, Joel assured him that most of these extraordinary works would be sold within a few weeks after they opened their new galleries. When the younger brother reminded his senior that they had not even found the gallery, he retorted: "You know me. We have offers of eleven likely big places, and I'll bet you anything you like that we will open in a fortnight after we arrive in New York."

London was ransacked for the best pieces of old English silver, and some of the finest things in Joel's Oxford Street gallery were picked out for the new business. A few days before their steamer was due to sail a telegram arrived from Mme Arens, the energetic widow of Antwerp's leading art-dealer, about what sounded like a find of the greatest importance. The telegram read: COME IMMEDIATELY, LARGE SUITE OF LOUIS QUINZE FURNITURE COVERED WITH BOUCHER GOBELINS.

A few hours after receipt of this message the two brothers were on the way to Antwerp. On their arrival Mme Arens told them that the suite was the property of an Austrian nobleman who had brought it in a railway van direct from his castle in Hungary. He wanted £20,000 for it, and it had to be in cash. The description proved that it was indeed a unique suite. No time was lost, and within a matter of minutes the two brothers stood in front of the finest suite of its kind they had ever seen. The richly carved and gilded furniture was of the most brilliant period of the Louis XV style. There were two large sofas, eight arm-chairs, six single chairs, two large stools, two low fire-screens, and two *"bergères"*—extremely comfortable low and wide easy chairs, with a luxurious down-cushion as seat. All these pieces were upholstered with Gobelins tapestries representing the famous *"scènes d'enfants"* by the Louis XV court painter, François Boucher. These scenes were woven in silk on a greyish-white ground, and they were surrounded by beautiful flowers on a delicate red background. The whole formed an ensemble of indescribable beauty and elegance.

Boucher had painted these scenes at the command of the Marquise de Pompadour, the luxury-loving favourite of Louis XV. This autocratic lady appreciated the beauty of the suite so highly that she commanded Jacques Neilson, the head of the *basse-lisse* [1] department of the Manufacture Royale des Gobelins, to make no more of these suites; and she also insisted on Boucher's pictures being sent to her. It is known, however, that Neilson made copies of Boucher's pictures, and that several suites were made with the same tapestry coverings. His great use of the Manufacture des Gobelins for many clandestine orders finally reached the ears of people who were unfriendly towards him, with the result that he was imprisoned for some time. He returned to the Manufacture later and died

---

[1] *Basse-lisse* is the method of weaving tapestry on a horizontal plane. *Haute-lisse* is woven on a vertical plane.

about a year before the Revolution. In 1902 my uncle Joel showed me the original suite Mme de Pompadour had ordered in 1751. He told me that the suite he had bought in Antwerp was just as beautiful but in a better state of preservation and that it consisted of several more pieces. In 1895 I had the good fortune to discover six backs and six seats of a similar set; but that is another story.

Joel Duveen was bewitched by the Austrian's suite, and in spite of his brother's remonstrances he concluded the deal for £18,000 on condition that the owner pay ten per cent commission to Mme Arens. As the vendor would not accept a cheque, Joel took him to Brussels, where with the help of his old business friend Handelaar a bank cashed the cheque on London. This deal was concluded four days before the brothers were due to embark at Liverpool.

On arrival in London the next morning Joel had to face his banker, Mr. (later Earl) Farquhar, who was then already head of Sir Samuel Scott's Bank, established about a century earlier. The banker admired Duveen's cleverness and energy. Time after time he had made his big deals possible, but he had warned his too-enterprising client on the last critical occasion that he must not draw over the fixed new limit.

My uncle told me that when he had informed the banker about the cheque for £18,000 Mr. Farquhar had sent for his cashier. When the latter appeared, he asked him whether he knew the state of Duveen's account.

"Overdrawn to within a thousand pounds of the agreed limit," was the reply.

Turning to Duveen, Farquhar asked: "And didn't you know that when you wrote that cheque?"

"I did not dare to risk losing this marvellous deal, Mr. Farquhar," Duveen replied.

"William," shouted the banker, "bring all the money from the safe and hand it over to Duveen. He thinks he has the right to all of it!"

And then he let fly at the culprit. "There is no curing you! You use our money as if it were your own. I am going to close your account!" But after he had raged for a few minutes the two parted on good terms, Duveen promising to draw no more than a few hundred pounds for his voyage, and to repay the extra overdraft within one month after his reaching New York.

Two days after landing at New York Joel decided to take the premises in Union Square that were to remain Duveen Brothers' [2] headquarters in New York for about twenty years. Much had to be done in the way of adaptations and decoration. Joel planned everything in a few hours, and he took personal charge of the decorations. All the walls were to be covered with silk or velvet in the colours best suited to the objects to be shown in the various rooms. Unfortunately, he could not find the right qualities and shades in New York so he cabled to Carlhian & Beaumetz, of Paris, explaining for which type of art objects the various lots were wanted. Within a few days a cable was received that the materials had been dispatched by the fastest steamer available. Meantime, alterations were being executed in a truly American manner. The men worked day and night in shifts, encouraged to hurry by Joel's generous distributions of largesse. The work was finished before the materials from Paris could arrive, and the time fixed for repaying the extra overdraft at Sir Samuel Scott's Bank was rapidly approaching. Forced by this very serious necessity, Joel took a bold decision. He had to sell something for a very big amount, and he decided that the Neilson suite

[2] See Author's Note.

of furniture was his best chance for providing a large enough sum to cover the overdraft and the large expenses that would still have to be incurred within the very near future. He had originally planned to give the Pompadour suite a "French grey" background; but, forced by circumstances, he used the *"Comédies de Molière"* tapestries, which had just arrived. He had been afraid that this background would interfere with the delicate beauty of the suite, but he found that they improved each other. He called for his brother, and after the two had thoroughly enjoyed the unique sight Henry pointed out that the big buyers were still away from New York and not likely to return until the second week in October. The same evening Joel heard from the hotel head-porter that the Californian who had bought the tapestries shortly after they had opened their first gallery in New York would be arriving at the hotel in a few days.

"I'll make him buy the Neilson suite!" said Joel to his brother, who told me many years later that he pretended to agree, but only because he would not discourage his brother. "We were in too big a hole, and I wanted to keep him up to his highest point of self-confidence."

The morning after the client's arrival Joel went to see him in his apartment. The big railway-builder said that he was really pleased to see the man who had sold him the tapestries everyone envied him. Joel then told him the history of the suite he had bought from an Austrian nobleman just before leaving for New York, and then, by a genial inspiration of the moment, he also told him about the banker's fury and the difficult position in which his anxiety to secure this unique suite had placed him. The client came with him then and there to see the suite and frankly admired it. Then he suddenly barked at Joel: "Young man, if you'll sell it cheaply I'll buy it now and pay before I leave the room!"

"Right," said Duveen, "I paid eighteen thousand pounds for it. I will take a hundred and fifty thousand dollars in cash [£30,000 at that time]; and if you wish to let me have it back in two years I will pay you ten per cent profit."

For a moment, there was no reply; then there was a shout: "Well, I'll be damned! Is this a mock auction?"

"No, sir, it's nothing of the kind. It just means that I am hard up, after all I have bought, to open this place in the proper manner. You will be getting the advantage for helping me out of a difficulty and you are getting something for a hundred and fifty thousand dollars that is worth a good deal more; and if you should ask me what it is worth I would have to tell you that I don't know what would be the real limit. It is unique, and I would not have any trouble selling it for much more if I could wait."

The big man walked up and down the room for a moment and then took another look at the furniture. Without another word he took out his cheque-book and wrote a cheque. When he had finished, Duveen asked him whether he had noticed the tapestry panels on the wall.

"No, and you are not going to make me take them, too. I'm off!"

Within two years Uncle Henry offered 225,000 dollars for the suite, but the offer was refused.

XII

GEORGE SALTING

SHORTLY AFTER my second arrival in London I went to see the Salting Collection of Oriental Porcelain at the South Kensington Museum. I had intended to spend an hour there, but stayed the whole of that day and again the whole of the next day. Even then I realized that, with the exception of the most outstanding pieces, I had only a superficial idea of this magnificent collection.

A few days after this exciting experience I bought from Messrs. Morgan & Son, of Hanway Street, London, eighteen odd covers for Chinese porcelain vases, and among them there was one for the well-known "long eliza" vases. It was of very fine quality and worth at least £25 to anyone who might have a coverless vase. My uncle was just going through them when a rather tall, spare, old gentleman walked into the office. "Good morning, Mr. Salting," my uncle said, but instead of replying Mr. Salting stared at my covers and asked: "Are these odd lids?"

"Yes," answered my uncle, "my nephew has just brought them in." Picking up the "long eliza" cover, Mr. Salting asked me whether I would sell it; and as I had brought them in with a view to selling them to my uncle, I looked at him, but he said: "All right, my boy. You can sell it to Mr. Salting if he wants it. Tell me what you paid for the lot." When I told him that I had paid £10, he said to Mr. Salting: "That lid is worth at least twenty-five pounds if you have the vase to match; so if you pay him ten pounds you do well and he will do well, too."

I was very pleased and said so. But this first meeting with the great connoisseur had many pleasant results, and the first of these was that he invited me to see his private collection in his sitting-room at the Thatched House Club, the next afternoon. When I entered his large sitting-room it resembled an overcrowded antique-shop, but even that first glance showed me that every piece was of the finest quality. During the few hours I spent in that room I realized that Mr. Salting was not merely a great collector of old Chinese porcelain but that his knowledge extended to practically every form of old art. When we had finished this memorable inspection Mr. Salting invited me to have tea with him, and soon after we had sat down he asked me whether we had sold a very fine *famille rose* dish to Joel Duveen. As we had sold a good many such dishes to my uncle during the last few years, I asked him to describe it. "The largest size, twenty-two inches in diameter, a very fine border and a scene of the Chinese emperor surrounded by a great many figures," he replied.

I immediately recognized the description of a dish my stepfather had bought shortly after I had entered the business, and for which 1,050 gulden (£87 10s.) had been paid. This was a record price for a Chinese-porcelain dish at that time. It had been sold to Duveen Brothers [1] for £100, a profit of £12 10s. We were under the impression that this dish had

[1] See Author's Note.

been sold to Mr. Salting, and I asked: "Didn't you buy it, Mr. Salting?"

I saw his face change and I feared that I had said something that annoyed him. After a few awkward moments he said: "No, it was not even offered to me, but I knew all about it. They sold it for five hundred pounds to Garland, of New York." After another short silence he added: "Duveen Brothers used to offer every outstanding piece of Chinese porcelain to me first, and I have been a good customer to them; but now all their finest things go to Garland, and you can tell your uncle that I am very annoyed with him."

As I was on my way back to Oxford Street I worried very much about this incident and particularly about Mr. Salting's parting words. I knew my uncle's fiery temper and feared that he would not even give me time to explain. During the long drive from Oxford Street to his private house, "The Hawthorns," I told my story, and to my great surprise my uncle took it very calmly. He began by telling me that Joe, his eldest son, had bought the dish from my stepfather and had beaten down the price too much. Joe had then sent the dish off to New York because he knew that Mr. Salting disliked him, and the dish had been sold to Mr. Garland. My uncle also explained that Mr. Garland already had spent nearly £100,000 with them, and was still buying, whereas Mr. Salting ran to Tom, Dick, and Harry, and was always a hard bargainer. He wound up with: "You can tell Mr. Salting that I have always treated him well and that I will pay him twenty-five per cent profit on everything I have sold him."

A few days later, I met Mr. Salting at a view day at Christie's. I had been afraid to carry my uncle's message; but when Mr. Salting asked me what my uncle had said to his message I merely told him that my uncle had answered that he had always treated him well and that he was willing to give him twenty-five per cent profit on everything he had sold to Mr. Salting.

I expected an unpleasant reply, but, to my great surprise and joy, Mr. Salting said: "That is easy enough, for the things have gone up more than that in value"; and he showed that he was not annoyed by walking round the saleroom with me and discussing the most important objects.

Soon thereafter, I had another eventful meeting with Mr. Salting. My cousin Charles had come to The Hague and asked me to visit the dealers with him. He bought a good many things in The Hague and also in Amsterdam, where we saw a fine pair of tall *famille verte* vases in the shop of one of the leading dealers. He asked £600 for them. Charley had doubts about the vases, but I laughed at his doubts and offered to buy them for joint-account with him. In the end we bought the vases for £450, and then the real comedy began. On our train journey to The Hague he took out one of the vases from the sheet in which it had been wrapped. I saw that he still doubted, but managed to reassure him.

A little later he took the other vase out of its sheet. I asked him whether he was still afraid, and when he replied that he did not trust them because they were too beautiful I roared with laughter. This pacified him and he showed no further nervousness. The next day we travelled to London with all his purchases packed in strong trunks. By the time my uncle arrived at Oxford Street all the things had been unpacked and were standing in a good light on the floor of his private office. He immediately walked to the big *famille verte* vases and after examining them for a moment he asked Charles: "Where did you get these?" When Charley told him his father shouted: "From those thieves?" He picked one up and took it outside into the yard. We followed him and Charley whispered to me: "I told you so," and to my great astonishment I saw clearly that my uncle mistrusted them, too. After a few seconds he turned to Charley and asked: "How much did you pay for them?" Charley, realizing that his father thought them imitations, answered: "I didn't like them, but Jack was certain that they were right, and we bought them in joint-account for four hundred and fifty pounds." My uncle turned to me with a suspicious stare. I knew that the vases were genuine, and when he called me a young fool, I answered that my mother had also said that they were the finest *famille verte* vases she had ever seen. "Then she is a fool, too," he exploded, "they are Samson imitations." This last insult almost goaded me into disclosing a valuable secret of their manufacture, but just in time I thought of a soft answer: "Uncle, I will sell them to Mr. Salting!" He stared at me again, and then agreed on condition that I did not involve him.

I put the vases into a four-wheeler and drove straight to Mr. Salting's club. He was still at his breakfast; but when I told him that I had brought two very fine *famille verte* vases he told me to bring them up. When I brought the first vase into the room he sat down in a low arm-chair and began to turn it in every direction. When I returned with the other one, he asked: "How much do you want for them?" Then I told him that I had bought them for £450 in joint-account with my cousin Charles, but that my uncle had said that they were Samson copies. At this Mr. Salting burst out laughing and after a moment remarked that my uncle had great taste, but he had still something to learn. Without changing his tone he asked: "What is the lowest you will take for them?" When I answered £600 he offered £500. As I looked disappointed, he added: "You know that you won't be able to sell them to any one if I don't buy them."

This not only hurt me but I also lost my temper and told him that this was unfair, for he knew that these vases were worth a great deal more than I asked. As I began to wrap them up again Mr. Salting asked me what I was going to do with them. "Sell them for eight hundred pounds," I replied, "and that will be only half their value!"

"I'll bet you a tenner that you won't!" he laughed.

"Done!" I shouted.

"Garland?" he now almost growled.

"No, sir, but I can *prove* that these vases are genuine."

He smiled again at this, but he changed his mind and wrote a cheque for £600, which he handed me with the explanation that, though no one could prove absolutely that the vases were genuine, he did not want them to go to Garland.

Again I was sorely tempted to give the proof, but I was able to restrain myself, for, after all, the vases were now sold to the greatest living connoisseur of Oriental porcelain, and his cheque would prove to my uncle that I was neither a fool nor a knave.

During the great period of Chinese ceramic art that coincided with the K'ang-hsi reign (1662–1722) the Chinese began to use a very beautiful enamel colour which is known by the name of manganese blue—rather more purple than the cobalt blue of that period. The latter was used for decoration *under* the glaze, and the former for the rich polychrome decoration *above* the glaze. This rich manganese blue had the disadvantage of affecting the glaze during baking, and this effect caused the glaze around the blue to shrink away for anything from an eighth to a quarter of an inch. The result was that as the years went by the atmosphere affected the exposed porcelain, and a slightly dirty surface was caused. Sometimes the deleterious effect during the baking has not been sufficiently serious to destroy the glaze, but then the glaze itself shows that it has suffered by a slightly iridescent appearance where the white touches the manganese blue enamel—something like the effect of oil floating on water.[2]

These effects can be seen only under a good light, and it is best to take the piece close to direct daylight and move it so as to let the light wander over the parts of the white where it adjoins the purplish-blue enamel. The test is infallible and has earned—or saved—me thousands of pounds.[3]

During the next few years I spent more time in London than in The Hague, and when in the summer of 1891 I was staying as usual at "The Hawthorns" with my uncle, the late Mr. Murray Marks of a firm of London art-dealers came to dine with him. After dinner my uncle asked Marks whether he could buy Mr. Salting's famous black vase for him. Marks laughed at the idea, but my uncle promised him £1,500 for it if he could secure it.

At that time such a sum for a single vase was enormous, and I could see that Marks was impressed. Shortly before leaving he remarked that he might be able to make an exchange. Mr. Salting was very keen on the very fine Verrocchio bronze that Marks had offered him for £1,200, but he did not want to buy it because he had already spent too much money that year.

[2] This slight defect ceased with the advent of the *famille rose* period (1720). I know of one exception in some *Chinese* imitations of *famille verte* which were made in the early nineties of last century; but these are easily detected because on these copies *all* the enamel colours have attacked the glaze.

[3] These remarks on Chinese ceramic technique are also included, in substance, in my *Art Treasures and Intrigue*, pp. 321-2.

The next afternoon, while I was having tea with my uncles in their private office, Marks was shown in. He had made the exchange, and a few days after, I saw that famous red-hawthorn-on-black-ground vase just before it was packed for shipment to New York. It was sold for a large sum to Mr. Garland, and a quarter of a century later, when Uncle Henry bought the Morgan collection of Chinese porcelain and the eighteenth-century French furniture back from the Pierpont Morgan estate for over £2,000,000,[4] this lovely vase was valued at £30,000.

[4] I do not know the exact amount but I do know that they were immediately insured at Lloyd's for £3,000,000.

XIII

CHARLES DUVEEN

CHARLES JOEL DUVEEN, the second son of Sir Joseph Joel Duveen, was born in Hull in 1871 and died shortly after the outbreak of World War II. He was in his sixteenth year when he was sent to New York during the break between Joel and Henry Duveen. When the two brothers made up their quarrel Charles was left with his uncle Henry to assist in the new gallery, but their temperaments clashed. After only a few months Charles returned to London, but this roused his elder brother's anger against the possible rival. There were violent quarrels between the two brothers, and the father finally decided to send Charles on an independent business trip to Mexico. Mr. Murrietta, the banker, had informed Joel Duveen that there were quantities of fine works of art to be bought from the old Spanish families that had been impoverished since the revolution against Spain. Charley, who was only seventeen at the time, left for Mexico with a letter of credit for £1,000 and letters of recommendation from Mr. Murrietta to several great families. When he arrived in Mexico City a German nobleman was recommended as companion-interpreter, and within a very short time Charles bought some fine Chinese "mandarin" vases at advantageous prices. After a short time in Mexico City they went inland to visit the old haciendas; and here, too, some fine Chinese vases were bought, as well as quantities of sixteenth-century armour and weapons. In the isolated monasteries many beautiful crucifixes in ivory, ebony, and tortoise-shell were bought also, at small cost. So far, they had travelled in the more populated regions, but on the advice of the companion they penetrated on horseback into the less civilized areas, and, as he had foretold, beautiful things were bought at ridiculously low prices.

One evening, while they were staying at a fairly large hotel, the companion was invited to join a poker-party. At first he declined the invitation, but after looking on for some time he accepted, and soon he won some big pots. Charley, who had played a good deal of poker in New York, wanted to join in, too, and after refusing several times to allow this, the companion finally consented. From the beginning Charley's bluffs were successful, and he had won a considerable amount when his luck turned. The end of it was that he and his friend lost all the money they had on them. Charley told me himself that he lost nearly £700 that night, and that the next morning his companion had disappeared. The hotel-owner told him that this gentleman had gone off with the others, who were a notorious gang of card-cheats.

Charley had not sufficient money left to pay the hotel bill, but the host advanced him money for the necessary cable. He telegraphed his father to send him £500 through the Murrietta Bank. The money came, and Charley continued on his way through the mountains, accompanied by a guide. During the second night of this journey the guide decamped with both horses and with the whole of Charley's baggage, including his money as well as the suit he had laid on the chair by his bed. Another cable was sent, and his father remitted the money with peremptory orders to come home by the first steamer.

When, finally, Charley's purchases arrived in London, his father was away in New York. Charles had gone to Hull with his mother to visit the Barnetts, and when he returned to London he found that all the fine vases had been sold by his brother Joe to other dealers for about a tenth of what they were worth. The result was a violent quarrel between the two young men that was never properly made up.

I remember very clearly the words of my stepfather when he took me to London for the first time. We were walking west along Oxford Street when I noticed some magnificent tall Chinese vases in the first-floor window of an antique-dealer's house. I pointed them out to my stepfather, and he told me that these were some of the vases Charley brought back from Mexico and that Joe sold for practically nothing before their father could see them. Messrs. Agnew had bought the rest; but when the father saw them he was furious at Joe's obvious trick. Although Charley had made no mistake over the vases, it was otherwise with the armour and weapons, which, although they were in the sixteenth-century style, were at least a hundred years later, as the Spanish colonists had continued to make them until well into the eighteenth century. Fortunately, Charles had bought these at very low prices, but the various ecclesiastical objects were practically unsalable, and I remember seeing them for some years as neglected rubbish in the immense cellar at 181 Oxford Street.

It soon became impossible to have the two eldest sons in the same place of business, and Uncle Henry refused to give Charles another trial in New York. His father thought of starting him in business in London, but this nearly caused another separation between Joel and Henry. Ultimately Charles bought a timber business in Madagascar, but the corrupt French officials put every difficulty in the young man's way. After losing several thousand pounds, he left and tried his luck in the Transvaal. The new venture was also a fiasco, and the next thing I knew about Charles was when I met him at an auction at "Four Crosses" near Welshpool. There were some beautiful things there, among them the most exquisite Chippendale drawing-room table I have seen. It was oblong and measured about three feet six inches by two feet six inches. The shape was serpentine, and the carving was of the highest quality. The slender cabriole legs were most graceful, and the cross that united and strengthened these legs was crowned in the centre by a lovely small flower-basket filled with roses, with everything carved in the finest San Domingo mahogany. A charming gallery of carved fretwork surrounded the top, but one side of this fretwork had been almost entirely destroyed by ivy. This gem had stood for many years in a neglected green-house where everything had been overgrown by this destructive weed.

I was just examining the table when Charley slapped me on the shoulder. He recounted his misadventures and ended by informing me that he had gone back to the art-business, to which I remarked: "Cobbler, stick to your last." There were many second-rate dealers present, mostly Londoners. One of these came up to us and asked whether we would join the knock-out. I refused, but my cousin took me apart to explain that he was no longer in the firm but was doing business on his own—mostly with the dealers. He did not want to quarrel with them, and asked me to join. I agreed, and a number of lots were bought under this arrangement; but I was chiefly interested in the small Chippendale table. I had already told my cousin that I was going to get that table, but he was not greatly interested. The bidding for it began at ten shillings by a member of the "K.O." I bid against him, as I wanted to make sure of having it in my own name. The other dealers were annoyed with me at this, but I persisted. In the end it was knocked down to me at £35. Shortly after four the auction was ended, and we then adjourned to the local inn. There the auction began again, with a leading London furniture-dealer acting as auctioneer. When the table was put up again I became the final owner at £75. Towards the end of this bidding Charley tried to stop me, as he thought the table too dear. At that time fine Chippendale furniture had not taken the leap upwards it was soon to take; and before Charley had left on his African travels eighteenth-century French furniture had been the chief interest in the London art-business.

We had previously arranged that he would come with me to Liverpool, and when we entered the station at Welshpool, Charles told me that he did not wish to have a share in the table and also reminded me that he had tried to stop me from bidding. I replied that I was very glad, and that I liked the table so much that I was thinking of not selling it at all.

The journey to Liverpool was most tedious. We had to change at Oswestry, Shrewsbury, Chester, and Birkenhead. At each of these changes I had to rush to the guard's van to watch over the handling of my fragile little table. Charles was with me every time, and I noticed his increasing interest. It was the same sort of comedy as the journey from Amsterdam to The Hague with the *famille verte* vases. In that case he had become more and more frightened; but this time the attraction of the little Chippendale gem became ever stronger. As we were crossing the Mersey by the ferry-boat I remained on deck by the table, surrounded by a ring of curious passengers. On arrival at Birkenhead Woodside Station I had telephoned, and on the Liverpool landing-stage two of my assistants were waiting to take charge of the table.

Charley stayed with me that night, and on the following morning he returned to London; but shortly after lunch I received a telegram informing me that he would arrive that evening with a friend to see the table. The friend was Sydney Letts, the great English furniture-specialist of that period.[1] I telegraphed back that the table was not for sale, but they came all the same. Letts, on seeing the table in my sitting-room, began by saying it was not English but Portuguese in the Chippendale style. It is well known that the Portuguese and even the Italians had made a great deal of beautiful furniture after Thomas Chippendale's published designs; but these pieces always suffer from heaviness, and my table surpassed everything I had seen in English Chippendale by its graceful lightness. When Letts observed that I did not know what I was talking about, I turned my back on him and walked out of the room. After a few minutes Charles came into my study and told me that I had been very rude, to which I replied that he had brought this man despite my telegraphing him not to come, and, what was worse, that Letts had insulted me. Charley replied that Letts had already admitted to him that he had been rude; but that he liked the table so much that he was anxious to buy it for five times as much as I had paid. I replied that I would not part with the table. Charles pointed out that, although he had brought Letts, he would not claim any share in the profit of the table, which he had bought in joint-account with me, or any commission for bringing the buyer. Letts had

[1] Poor Sydney Letts went down with the *Lusitania* in 1915.

promised to give him a quarter out of the profit when he should sell the table to an American customer he had in view.

I remembered that Charles had gone through a very bad time in the last few years, and I realized that this deal would be a good beginning to his re-entry into the art-business. On the other hand, Letts's insult rankled, so I said that I would discuss the table only if Letts apologized.

Charles went out and in a few seconds returned with Letts. When the latter began by saying that he regretted the argument I answered that all I wanted before discussing business was his recognition that the table was English Chippendale. I also stated that I would describe it as such on the eventual receipt. This was agreed, and then I told him that I would not accept less than £500 for the table, although I thought that it was worth double that amount. This was accepted, and that night the two travelled back to London by the sleeper, with the table in personal charge of the guard.

Nearly twenty years later, I spent nine months in America and met many collectors. Among these was the famous Mr. Canfield, a collector of great fame. He had made his fortune during the wild period of the first gold-rush in California. He had dug his gold outside the mine-fields by keeping palatial gambling-houses in the style of Monte Carlo. He was only a small man, and his manners were quiet and gentlemanly. He showed me his collection, and there I found my lovely little table. I told him where and how I had bought it. Mr. Canfield reciprocated by telling me that he had bought it for £3,000 and that, ever since, other collectors had tried to buy it from him. He had even been offered more than double what he had paid.

During that last visit I did not know that poor Mr. Canfield was suffering from a deadly disease; but not long after my return home I read that he had walked into a fast-moving bus in Fifth Avenue, and that there was some doubt whether this was an accident. Soon thereafter, the First World War broke out, and I do not know what became of the glorious little table.

XIV

THE DUVEEN FORTUNE

AFTER MY FIRST and very satisfactory business trip to the north of England I extended my rounds to the whole of England, as well as to Edinburgh and Glasgow. I discovered that London was a most exciting field for exploration. Most of the smaller antique-dealers were rather ignorant, and I noticed that by careful search in these little shops it was possible to make interesting finds at small cost. I hunted chiefly for small eighteenth-century figures from the princely porcelain works of Meissen (Dresden), Höchst, Fürstenburg, etc., and the very rare figures of Nymphenburg. I was then in my seventeenth year, but I owed my early knowledge of these little gems to the late Sir Horace Rumbold, the envoy extraordinary and minister plenipotentiary at The Hague, and in an even greater measure to the late Baron van Zuylen van Nyevelt, whose small collection of Nymphenburg figures created a sensation at Christie's in 1955 by fetching many thousands of pounds.

Small pictures of the seventeenth-century Dutch masters could also be picked up for a few pounds, and I was particularly keen on the still-life pictures of game and the lovely flower pieces that thirty years later had more than centupled in value.

This search for treasure around London was much more exciting than the travels around the provinces, and most pleasurable were the evenings when I showed the day's finds to my uncle. He always encouraged me with praise, but was sharp in his criticisms when I showed him a mistake. Usually the younger sons crowded round us during these oracular judgements. At that time there were nine sons, but Joe and John usually went out at night, and Charles, the second-eldest son, was in New York. Four of the younger boys were already old enough to be keenly interested, and they were extremely quick at learning.

The keenest and most studious of my cousins was Edward, my junior by two years. As the Easter holiday had begun, he asked me to let him come with me on my hunts around the small dealers. My uncle liked the idea, and from then onwards Edward was my constant companion on these raids. He knew already the various marks on European porcelains and potteries, and after I had pointed out a quick and easy way to distinguish the character marks on Chinese porcelains he became quite familiar with these, too. One day when I was groping round a very small and dark shop in Noel Street, Soho, I heard him ask the price of some article lying near the entrance. The woman said: "Half a crown," and I saw Eddie take a coin out of his pocket and pay it over. I stepped across and saw my young cousin take up something very dark and put it in his pocket, but I could see by his expression that he did not want me to ask any questions. After a further look round we walked out, and then he told me that he had bought an old pottery imitation of a Chinese kylin. I expected to see a cheap imitation, not worth carrying away; but after we had turned into Wardour Street, the little dog-like figure he took out of his pocket took my breath away, for it was an old delft pottery replica of the Chinese fabulous animal called a kylin; and as I turned it upside down I saw the interlaced "A.P.K." mark of Adriaan Pijnacker, one of the greatest delft potters, whose work is literally worth its weight in gold.[1] When I explained to Eddie the rarity of his find, the value of which I considered to be at least £100, he said—very Duveen-like—that he was going to leave school at once and go into business; but he reckoned without his father.

Uncle Joel was late to dinner that night, and although Eddie was impatient with excitement to show his find, he knew that his father could not be interrupted when he was busy with a client. When at last, towards half past seven, Uncle Joel did turn up and saw what young Eddie had picked up on his own judgement, he at first disbelieved our story. I assured him that Eddie had bought it without asking my advice. Eddie said that, though he did not know what it was, he saw that it was very beautiful and unlike any kylin he had ever seen before. "You stick to that, my boy, and you'll go far," said Uncle; and then we sat down to dinner, where, by Aunt Rosetta's law, no business could be talked.

That night, while my uncle and I had our usual half-hour after the family had gone to bed, he told me that there was no demand for coloured delft in England, and that I had better take the kylin with me to Holland and sell it there. He said that he had never even seen such a figure in old delft pottery, and that, owing to the fall in values through the Paris imitations of polychrome delft, he thought that 1,000 gulden

[1] In 1917 the author bought two polychrome delft pottery dishes (15 inches in diameter) by the same artist and sold them shortly thereafter in Holland for £5,000 to a Dutch collector, the late Mr. Anton Jurgens.

would be the utmost that I could expect to get for it. As it turned out, I sold it to Boas-Berg, the Amsterdam dealer, for 1,500 gulden (£125).

After leaving the subject of the kylin we returned to Eddie's flair for beautiful things, and I happened to remark that he ought to be very happy that all his boys were so clever. "Yes," he said, "they are all right. I am bringing them up very carefully, and they know already that money and position bring responsibilities. I have taught them to behave like gentlemen, and they won't waste the money I hope to leave them; but, as I have seen only too often, their children will probably be less careful because their parents may be too indulgent."

These wise words recurred to me when my uncle died eighteen years later, for he left his large fortune so well tied up that the next generation could not touch the capital. His eldest son, Lord Duveen, had no son to succeed him, and he knew that his daughter had no family to succeed her. One day he told his six-years-younger brother Edward that he was worried about what to do "with all this money." Edward, with whom I began to write this history shortly before his brother's death in 1939, told me that he had answered: "Well, see to it that there will be no poor Duveens. Leave the bulk of your money in a trust or trusts, the capital to accumulate and to be divided after the death of your daughter among the great-grandchildren of our father." After consultations with great lawyers this was arranged; and as, humanly speaking, this accumulation will continue for a considerable time, the slumbering treasure may well amount to 15,000,000 pounds at the time of its division. Moreover, the thirteen children of Joel Duveen have not been as prolific as their parents, and it looks at present as if those of the third generation who will ultimately divide Lord Duveen's fortune will be only about the same number as those reared by their great-grandparents, Joel and Rosetta Duveen.

Apart from this fortune, Lord Duveen made many bequests and settled 1,000,000 pounds on his wife and double that amount on his daughter.

XV

JOEL DUVEEN'S ILLNESS

SHORTLY AFTER his daughter's wedding Joel Duveen had to rush off to Newcastle to see one of his most important clients. He travelled by the Scottish Night Express, and spent practically the whole day with his client, returning the next night to London. A blizzard had been raging for days, and he must have caught a chill during this journey. On his return to London, he found that he had to travel to Brussels on a very urgent business matter. His wife noticed that he had a bad cold and insisted on travelling with him. His fourth son, Louis, then a youth of sixteen, accompanied them. My parents, who had been to London for the wedding, had arrived back at The Hague on the thirteenth of March, and after a few days my stepfather received a telegram that his eldest sister had died suddenly from a heart attack. He left immediately for Apeldoorn, at that time half a day's journey from The Hague.

The next day further bad news arrived; my Aunt Rosetta telegraphed from the Grand Hotel, Brussels, that Joel was very ill and that she and Louis were ill with influenza. The telegram ended with: PLEASE COME AT ONCE. We just had time to pack our bags and catch the next train to Brussels. From the station we telegraphed that we would arrive shortly after two o'clock by the Paris Express, then one of the fastest trains on the Continent, which took four and a half hours to do the journey. At the Belgian frontier there was the removal of all luggage to the custom house, and after the usual twenty minutes had been exceeded by five, my mother became agitated. She went to the station-master, begging him to get the train away as soon as possible. She explained the reason, and he was very courteous. He came out of his office with us, and after a liberal use of very loud vituperation at the various officials, the whole station staff seemed occupied in throwing the baggage back into the vans; the passengers were herded back into their compartments, and we left without further delay. I had received another lesson in overcoming what may appear to be immovable obstacles.

When we entered my uncle's large and overheated bedroom we saw an enormously stout woman sitting by the bed. She rose with obvious difficulty and told us in a loud voice that the gentleman was dying. My uncle, looking very ill indeed, opened his eyes at this. When he saw my mother, he said in a wheezy tone of voice: "My sister. I'm saved!" He sighed with relief, and then my mother took charge. She ordered me to place a screen to divert air currents, carefully covered her brother's chest, and then, to the horror of the woman, pulled down the upper parts of the windows. She reassured her brother with: "Don't worry, dear. I'll remain with you day and night until you are better."

It appeared that, on arrival in Brussels, my uncle had felt very ill, and Mr. Handelaar, the business friend who had met him at the station, had sent for a very clever young doctor. When this young man seemed puzzled at the cause of the illness, Mr. Handelaar had sent for a second doctor, unfortunately also a young man. The next morning, after passing a very bad night, my uncle heard that both his wife and his son were very ill with influenza. He sent a message to his wife, begging her to telegraph to my mother. A telegram was also sent to Sir Andrew Clarke, Queen Victoria's favourite doctor, to come over at once. By the time we arrived a reply had already been received from Sir Andrew saying that he was coming by night steamer and requesting that rooms be reserved for four people.

My mother visited Aunt Rosetta and arranged with her that the daughter of a Brussels business friend should nurse her and that we two, my mother and I, should look after Uncle and young Louis. The immediate effect was that Uncle became less agitated and for the first time after two sleepless nights was able to get some sleep between the agonizing spells of coughing.

The next morning Sir Andrew Clarke arrived. The old specialist made a thorough examination and reassured the nervous patient; but when he accompanied my mother to the other two patients he told her that her brother was suffering from a dangerous attack of double pneumonia and that only the most careful nursing could save him. He prescribed the necessary medicaments for the patients and then went to take a rest after his night's journey. At about five o'clock that afternoon Sir Andrew made another examination. He said that it was impossible to foresee what would happen; but he again impressed on my mother that only the most careful and constant nursing could save the patient.

He paid one more visit late that night, and after another examination said that he would come in very early the next morning because he must catch the first boat train. The patient had a more restful night. Sir Andrew, when he came in for his last visit, complimented my mother on her nursing, but added that the best thing he could say was that the patient was not worse.

On leaving, he told my mother to inform the hotel-manager to charge his bill to Mr. Duveen's account, and that he had come with his wife, his wife's maid, and his own valet. He explained that he was an old man, and that he never travelled without his wife to look after him. Some months later my uncle told me that Sir Andrew had charged 300 guineas for his services, apart from travelling expenses; and when I expressed my surprise at what was at that time an enormous fee, he explained that this very busy man had left his large consulting practice for two days, and that it was only owing to their friendship that he had faced the tiring journey.

A few anxious days followed. We saw no improvement, but the patient was easier in his mind and not so restless. The fourth day there was a considerable drop in the temperature, and on the fifth day after Sir Andrew's departure the Belgian doctor was able to tell us that the temperature had dropped to normal. The pains in the chest had also disappeared. My aunt and my cousin were also much better and were already on normal diet. At the beginning of the third week my uncle, who during his convalescence had proved a difficult patient chafing at the inactivity, was allowed to sit up and receive visitors. As all the Brussels dealers knew that Duveen of London was staying at the Grand Hotel after an illness, several of them called, mostly to try to do business with him.

The day before we left for London a letter arrived from a Spanish duke. He wrote in French, explaining that he knew no English. He was staying at the same hotel and had heard that the leading London dealer in old Chinese porcelain was staying there, too. He went on to say that he had brought over from his castle near Seville a very beautiful and precious vase that had been in his family for more than two centuries. He wished to dispose of it and requested the pleasure of being allowed to show it. I replied for my uncle that he would be glad to see the vase that afternoon.

When the Duke entered the large but ill-lit sitting-room he certainly looked the great gentleman, and he was followed by a manservant who carried something wrapped in a piece of black cloth. After the exchange of the usual courtesies in French, the piece of porcelain was unpacked and proved to be a tall cylindrical vase with *famille verte* decoration on imperial yellow ground. The owner stated that he had refused 20,000 pesetas (£800) offered by one of the leading Spanish art-dealers for the vase, and that he would not accept less than 40,000 pesetas for it. My uncle walked to the window and asked me to bring him the vase.

The moment I lifted it I got a shock, realizing that it was too light for an old Chinese porcelain vase of this size. But my uncle was even quicker, for at the same moment he ordered me in Dutch to put down the vase at once. He then said in English to the Duke: "You are a swindler. Take this thing away."

The Spanish nobleman, who "did not understand English," exclaimed in very good English: "I will instruct my lawyers to bring an action against you for defamation of character!"

"In your character of a Spanish nobleman, or of a notorious English swindler?" asked my uncle.

I saw the expression of fury on the man's face suddenly change to one of fear. He took a step forward, and I stepped between him and my uncle; but to my surprise he only picked up the vase and strode out of the room without another word.

My uncle broke out in one of his uproarious fits of laughter. "I thought I knew him as he came in," he said, "but his false black beard and his dyed hair took me in until the light fell on to that vase and I saw that it was a Paris copy." Only then did my uncle mention the name of a young nobleman who had already made himself notorious all over Europe.

This exciting incident seemed to have restored my uncle's spirits, and he suggested a short drive through the Bois de la Cambre. That afternoon we all drove out in a roomy landau in the warm April sunshine through the lovely woods near Brussels. When we returned to the hotel my uncle came out with one of his typical surprises: "We are going to London tomorrow." However, in spite of his regained spirits, he was never the same man again. His mental energy remained as vital as ever, but his robust bodily constitution had been permanently damaged. He had to leave England every autumn and travel with the warm weather. Early in October he would leave for Biarritz or the French Riviera. He would stay some time in Rome, Naples, and Palermo, and leave there for Cairo; and during January and February he had to seek warmth and sunshine at Aswan. As spring began he would return by the same stages, until around Easter he would again be in Monte Carlo on his way home to London. He gradually became stronger, but he was obliged to keep to the same program during the rest of his life.

XVI

OLD BOND STREET

By the end of the 1880's Joel Duveen realized that a change from Oxford Street to Old Bond Street was essential. But two great difficulties stood in the way of this plan: the scarcity of good locations, and the comparatively small size of the properties. One morning while walking through Old Bond Street he happened to look at a coach entrance leading into an open yard and was accosted by the owner, who knew him. The man informed him that his firm had bought large premises in a street which was more suitable to their business, and that their present place would be just the right situation for a large art gallery. When Duveen pointed out to him that the only frontage on Old Bond Street would be the coach entrance, the other replied that his firm had an option on the large frontage occupied by another firm. Duveen then inquired about the price for the combined properties, but found it so prohibitive that he refused to make an offer. On the way back to Oxford Street he began to doubt the existence of the option on the all-important frontage. He drove at once to his solicitor and asked him to make immediate and discreet inquiries about this. It transpired that there had been some conversation about an option, but that nothing had been arranged and that no price had been mentioned. Within a few hours the important premises, the frontage of which provided a fair-sized gallery, were acquired. When the warehouse-owners realized that they now only had storage property reasonable terms were arranged, and Duveen Brothers [1] could now build palatial galleries in the best part of London.

Joel set about rebuilding the premises without delay. He decided that a gallery was needed in the top storey with roof lighting. When work started on raising the roof for this, the owner of the tailor's shop next door complained that he would have to invoke the law of "ancient lights" because he considered that this increase of height would affect his property. As it was higher than Joel's raised roof and the only effect was to take a little light off the tiny window of a single lavatory, my uncle made the generous offer of £500 compensation. When the tailor demanded some thousands of pounds, believing that he could hold up this work that Joel needed so urgently, my uncle, who would always pay generously for what he wanted but would not tolerate extortion, refused to be imposed upon.

His lawyer, when consulted, found after inquiry that the tailor was financially embarrassed and was clearly counting on saving his business by holding my uncle to ransom. He therefore advised that the wall should be raised to the required height during a week-end, because the courts would not then be sitting and no injunction could be issued to stop the work. Once the wall had been built it could be removed only after litigation, which would fix a fair compensation if it were allowed to remain.

A fortnight later the builders, who had all their materials and men ready, put as large a gang as the site would hold on

[1] See Author's Note.

to the building of the wall, starting on Saturday afternoon. The intention had been to work through the nights, but this proved impossible, with the result that by 10 a.m. on Monday the wall was still incomplete. The neighbour at once obtained an injunction to stop further progress. This happened more quickly than my uncle, who was in the building, had believed possible; and when he was informed that a man wished to see him, he guessed from the description that this might be an officer of the court waiting to serve notice on him of the injunction. The builder's foreman offered to have a large box constructed in a very short time, inside which my uncle could be smuggled out of the building as if he were builders' materials. As this scheme did not appeal to Joel, another way of escape was contrived. He took the clothes of one of the builder's labourers and was liberally sprinkled with building dust, and walked out of the building unnoticed with a party of workmen. The wall was finished before the injunction could be served. As was foreseen, litigation was threatened, but nothing came of it; and my uncle gave the neighbour the £500 he had originally offered. Within a few weeks the tailor's business closed down.

With these galleries in Bond Street, which had become the world's centre of the old-art business, Joel Duveen felt that he had really arrived at the top. Until then Duveen Brothers had dealt very little in pictures, apart from the lovely and decorative pictures by eighteenth-century French masters like Boucher, Largillière, Watteau, and Fragonard; and their first great effort in this direction was an exhibition of works of eighteenth-century French masters, arranged with the co-operation of Messrs. Gimpel and Wildenstein, of Paris.

This achieved little success, and the firm had now to rely on its own efforts to create a clientele for old masters of the Dutch and Italian schools. During Joel Duveen's winter absence his eldest son, Joe, appointed a clever young employee of one of the leading London picture-dealers to advise him on pictures that came into the market. This, too, proved useless, for the young man, who had very capably followed the lead of his experienced employers, proved by his personal lack of judgement useless to his new employers. Joel, shortly after his return from abroad, heard that one of the two Dowdeswell Brothers (high-class picture-dealers in New Bond Street) wanted to leave his firm, and terms were arranged for Mr. Dowdeswell's employment as adviser to Duveen Brothers. This arrangement had good results, and the Duveen picture gallery soon became one of the most important. Henry Duveen proved as clever a salesman in pictures as in the firm's other specialities, and clients such as Mr. Altman soon brought him into a commanding position in the rapidly growing New York market. The purchase of the Rodolphe and Maurice Kann collections set the firm on a commanding pedestal, and from then onwards transactions of hundreds of thousand pounds at a time became almost common.

Another change was caused by the ever increasing power of the professional experts, who were mostly men in charge of museums on the continent of Europe and who had studied in certain schools in which they specialized. They were always able to trace the history of a picture, and they knew where almost every work by their favourite masters was to be found. Most of these learned men gave their opinions gladly and usually free of charge, only sometimes expecting a present of some work in which their particular museum specialized. Until the outbreak of the First World War this help from the professional experts remained fairly respectable; but during and after that war "presents" and other *douceurs* changed gradually into very high fees. Even the redoubtable Dr. Wilhelm von Bode, head of all the imperial museums, began to expect more than a present to one of his museums. Such arrangements with the experts did not remain a trade secret, but, for example, came out under cross-examination in the sensational lawsuit in America about the portrait *"La Belle Ferronnière"* by Leonardo da Vinci, which had been offered to the Kansas City museum. Unfortunately, there was another *"Belle Ferronnière"* by Leonardo da Vinci in the Paris Louvre museum. Joe, then Sir Joseph, was interviewed by one of the New York papers about the impending acquisition by the Kansas museum. He laughed at the idea and pointed out that the real *"Belle Ferronnière"* was in the Louvre museum; and then the tragi-comedy began. The owner of the Kansas picture took action for "libel of goods"; and during the ensuing proceedings great numbers of renowned experts declared that the Louvre picture was the real one and an equal number declared the opposite. The reports of the interminable proceedings prove the truth of an English judge's well-known dictum that there are three kinds of liars: liars, damned liars, and expert witnesses. The farce ended with the inability of the jury to agree. Joe, unwilling to spend further years on this litigation, instructed his legal representative to settle the matter, and, as Edward Duveen assured me, the case was settled "for very little." Joe was now too powerful in the picture market to worry about such matters, and he remained the undisputed master of the market that he had created, in which prices of £250,000 for a single picture were not uncommon.

My cousin Edward, director of Duveen Brothers, London, when asked what his two Paris colleagues were doing now that all the business was being conducted by Joe in New York, replied that Joe "kept them busy travelling all over

Europe to collect experts to testify." This was an exaggeration; but Joe, then Lord Duveen, was extremely careful to
buy only pictures that had for centuries been recognized as
masterpieces by the greatest masters. Money to him was no
object when he could buy the finest works, unblemished by
even a breath of criticism. He knew from experience that this
could be obtained only by gaining the blessing of the experts;
then he could laugh at the curses of the rest. His unfailing eye
for beauty and quality, assisted by the recognized experts, enabled him to command the greatest field of collecting with a
success that so far remains unequalled.

XVII

EMBARRASSING VASES

M OST OF US have unpleasant memories of embarrassing situations into which we have been precipitated by circumstances beyond our control. For art-dealers, who are constantly thrown into contact with extraordinary things and with even more extraordinary people, nerve-racking experiences are of almost daily occurrence. Trained in a hard school, I had gained a mastery over my feelings and an almost complete immunity against minor misfortunes. Presence of mind, a little tact, and an ability to laugh it off became my form of protection. Nevertheless, one early misfortune, nightmarish in its quality, is still vividly engraved in my memory.

The "ogre" of the story is an extremely beautiful set of five old blue-and-white Nankin vases, whose outward beauty makes an unfailing appeal to even the least trained eye. Only ten inches in height and of a very graceful shape, two of the four sides of the vases are decorated with *lange lyzen* figures, while the other two sides are decorated with flower-baskets and foliage in the same colour. The borders are flanked by a striking key pattern in deep blue, which forms a most attractive frame to the decoration, at the same time accentuating the graceful outline of the vases (see illustration).

I had encountered a few specimens of this particular vase before I experienced the adventure that made me fight shy of them.

The first one was at an auction sale in Holland. My step-father was with me, and just as I was taking the vase in my hands for close examination my good-natured relative exclaimed with a most unusual growl: "Put that down!" I was only sixteen at the time and I obeyed; but just because of my youth I managed to slip back unseen. I took the vase in my hands again and could find no reason for this mysterious taboo until I turned it upside down to look for a mark. I then beheld one of the most indecent pictures I have ever seen, and a sharp smack on my ear helped to impress the memory of vase and mark on my mind.

I must explain that the Chinese usually painted the name of a reign, a symbolic flower or figure, or sometimes a sacred animal, and on very rare occasions a miniature scene on the bottom of the pieces, by way of mark. I soon noticed that certain shapes and decorations invariably bore the same distinctive marks, so that I knew what to expect as soon as I saw a particular piece.

The second specimen I came across, however, was the lower fragment of one I found among the broken wreckage that had accumulated in our chests and cupboards during generations of art-dealing. Remembering my early lessons, I looked hastily round before taking it from its forgotten corner. Turning it round I found to my surprise that this particular one was free from any undesirable mark. Obviously, the Chinese sense of humour had not extended to this piece, and from that moment it was one of my many youthful ambitions to find an entire set un-besmirched by a disfiguring scene.

A few years passed and I had already realized a good many boyish hopes when one day I was asked to look over the collection of an old lady, last descendant of a family of Liverpool merchant-princes. I had been invited to tea, but no sooner had I entered the drawing-room than I received my first shock. Opposite the door a set of the dangerous vases was staring at me from the top of a low cabinet. I did not dare to let my eyes dwell on them lest my hostess, observing my interest, should begin to discuss them. Meanwhile, the talkative old lady poured out a never-ending stream of comment and information about her treasures, but her failure to mention the vases—the most obvious pieces in the room—only served to increase my embarrassment.

Fortunately, a gorgeous pet macaw brought diversion and relief. The great bird with its murderous-looking beak took a fancy to me and clambered on to my shoulder before I could stop it. I had a large cockatoo myself and was used to such little tricks, so I took things calmly while the bird used his beak only for "kissing" and whispering in my ear. "The sweet little darling!" exclaimed my hostess. "He seems to have taken quite a fancy to you! As a rule he bites any one who comes near me."

This flattering remark held a powerful antidote for my embarrassment. I just sat still, taking great care not to make any sudden movement or to emphasize any words for fear of startling my unwanted companion. When eventually we rose for a walk through the vast early-Victorian room, I hoped that the bird would hop off; but, to my disappointment, he insisted on staying where he was. His mistress tried to remove him, but that gave him a chance of proving his character by making vicious-looking lunges with his beak at the "beloved hand that fed him." By this time I felt quite sure that the bird would not bite me, so we continued to walk through the room, stopping to discuss the many pieces of the collection, until the dreaded moment approached when we would reach the Nankin vases.

Just before we reached the cabinet the old lady went back to the tea-table for a moment. This gave me an opportunity to ascertain by one swift movement whether the vases were value-less because they bore the unspeakable mark, or very valuable because of its absence.

The cabinet was about six feet high, so that a slight lift and tilt would give me the eagerly wanted information. Quick as lightning my arm shot out. I lifted the vase and saw that the entire base was covered by a thick piece of white paper. Then the satanic macaw let out a shriek that for a split second almost petrified me. My hostess gazed up, startled, and our eyes met. After that neither of us had any doubt as to the other's guilty knowledge.

Again the bird saved the situation. Maintaining his ear-splitting scream, he added to it such a beating of wings that this time I had to remove him by sudden force. He matched my quickness, however, by giving me a nip in the bone of my thumb, the mark of which is still with me. The sight of the blood was the last straw to my hostess's shocked nerves, and she gracefully slid down in her chair with all the ceremony of the eighteenth-century "vapours." Her maid now took charge, and as soon as the old lady had recovered I made my hasty adieux. The keen air of the frosty December evening was an intense relief to my oppressed feelings; but I had to walk around aimlessly for a couple of hours before I was in a fit state to return home, and it was a long time before my own nerves completely recovered from this very awkward episode.

Yet, strange though it may seem, I was forced again to encounter this devilish set on several other occasions. About eight months afterwards I was spending a few weeks at The Hague, and, being on holiday, I used to stroll every morning through some of the many antique-dealers' shops for a friendly chat. Soon after my arrival, I happened to enter the charming little place of our old friend Mr. Croiset, once a partner in our business. He was a man of excellent taste, but he had the weakness of permitting his taste at times to run away with his judgement. The moment I entered I realized that this little weakness had led him into trouble again.

"Look at these, Jack!" exclaimed the old man, who had the right of calling me by my nickname because he had many a time spanked me when I was "rising six." I did look, and, behold, there were the identical vases I had seen in Liverpool!

In order to tease my witty old friend I retorted with a sarcastic "Have you looked at them yourself, Mr. Croiset?" He stared at me for a moment, and stroked his red, pointed beard, a typical gesture when he was puzzled and needed time for reflection. I understood the invitation and decided to answer with facts. I lifted the vases one by one and saw that the paper was still pasted beneath them.

"What are you looking at?" asked Mr. Croiset, extremely surprised at this seemingly useless examination of the least important part of the vases.

"Do you know what is under this paper?" I countered.

He wasted no words but took a penknife out of his pocket and began to scrape. This time I was no more a boy from whom certain things had to be hidden so I watched eagerly for the removal of the last shreds that covered the miniature painting. Then my venerable friend made his discovery. Even then, I fled his too-ready hand and ran out of the place roaring with laughter.

Poor Mr. Croiset had to dispose of the set at a great loss, and a few weeks after my holiday I called on the late Lord Leverhulme at his Cheshire home, "Thornton Manor," to do my periodical "vetting" of his new treasures. The then Mr. W. H. Lever was an extremely serious man of a somewhat religious turn of mind. So my feelings can best be imagined when I beheld among the new-comers to his vast collection this accursed and embarrassing set of vases. For a moment I hesitated; but because of my duty to my client I took the plunge.

"Did you buy these at The Hague, Mr. Lever?" I said, pointing at my pet aversion.

"No, I bought them in London. I suppose you know them?"

"Yes, I have known them for some time," I replied. "In fact, they used to belong to a Liverpool family and later went to Holland!"

"Then why didn't you buy them when you had the chance?" asked the soap-king with an expression of having scored over me.

"Have you ever looked at the mark, Mr. Lever?" My question caused the same sort of puzzled expression to cloud his face as I had seen on that of the Dutch dealer.

"The mark? There is no mark!" he said.

I then took one of the vases in my hands, and when I turned it round there was no mark; just a plain white surface. I did not have to think of the possibility that it might be another set, for the plain white did not react to the play of light as it should: the offending mark had been carefully painted over by a clever restorer, and the varnish glaze had all the appearance of the kaolinic glaze of the K'ang-hsi reign until I made the necessary motions in the full light of day.

I was now in the same sort of predicament that the vases had caused me the first time I beheld them; moreover, it was my duty to tell this very serious, strait-laced man what I knew to be under the paint, and for a moment I did not know how to begin. During this momentary hesitation my client was visibly mystified by my manner, possibly anticipating one of the many tricks that were played on him by rival dealers in their internecine war for his custom. I realized the danger and took the plunge.

"Mr. Lever," I said, "you ask me my opinion and I must tell you the truth, even though unpleasant."

Pointing to the base of the vase I held in my hand, I continued: "This bottom has been painted over to hide a very unpleasant mark." Mr. Lever snatched the vase from me, and, after a moment's examination by the window, said somewhat crossly: "There is no paint; this is the old glaze right enough!" He was losing his temper, which made things even more unpleasant. However, now I had started and had to continue. I pointed out the difference between the effects of moving light on the old glaze and on the new varnish and tried without success to demonstrate it.

Only one thing now remained: I used a penknife and scratched the paint. This revealed proof positive, even to my somewhat self-opinionated client.

"Go on!" he exclaimed when I paused, having revealed part of the scene. But it was impossible. I knew I was going to offend my great and powerful client by my refusal, but I had no choice.

"I prefer not to, Mr. Lever," I stammered, while the blood rose to my head. For a moment he stared at me with his light-blue eyes that pierced one like gimlets. I was still very young, and he must have seen my mute appeal. Suddenly he turned on his heel and began to walk towards the door.

"Come in to lunch!" he said without looking back, and I followed him somewhat sheepishly, thinking what a pity it was that even in an artistic and pleasant business like ours such moments occurred. The luncheon was rather dismal; each of us felt the air of restraint caused by the equivocal subject neither of us wished to discuss.

Some months later I had to supervise one of the periodical migrations of the collection to one of Mr. Lever's other houses, and once again the vases passed through my hands. When the time came to deal with them I could not resist my curiosity. I looked for the one I had scratched; but there were no scratches now, as the mark had been re-covered by the same clever imitation of the old glaze; and this could have been done only after the whole of the scratched paint had first been totally removed!

Since then I have seen a few more of these vases, but the mark was always decently hidden by paint or paper. The only ones not thus protected are the pair in the Chinese-porcelain collection of the British Museum, but they are behind glass in a locked show-case.

XVIII

THE POMPADOUR CHAIRS

THE FEVER for treasure trove, which mastered me when I was a schoolboy and was heightened by early successes, remained with me throughout my life. Auctions and dealers' shops have provided me with my greatest finds. This is the story of the coup that provided me with a protracted thrill and brought me at the same time into closer contact with that forceful character, the late Robert Partridge.

It happened not long after I had made Partridge's acquaintance at the sale of the old home of the Davenport family, of porcelain fame, where I bought an old packing-case full of mediæval stained glass for a few shillings. This second meeting took place at a sale at an old family house in the Dingle, Liverpool, and I cannot remember seeing a more complete collection of mid-Victorian monstrosities. But even in these discouraging surroundings my passion for treasure trove was as ardent as ever. I searched through the servants' bedrooms, the attics, the cellars, and even the outbuildings but met with no success.

Disappointed, I went in search of my old friend Petty, the trusted commission buyer of all auction-goers in Liverpool. I found him in the housekeeper's room on a long sofa, the seat of which was covered in a very loud chintz cover. "Nothing but rubbish, Petty!" "I told you so," was the consoling rejoinder.

It was a very warm day, and the cool room tempted me to sit down for a moment. Few people were interested in this part of the house so we had the room to ourselves and indulged in a quiet chat about other matters. After a few minutes one of Petty's clients came in to give him an order and the two left together. No sooner had they gone than I rose and was about to leave when I turned my head for a last glance round. I realized that I had failed to look under the chintz cover of the sofa. The uncovered seat showed it to be entirely upholstered with Victorian rubbish. Nevertheless, I resolved to investigate properly.

I inserted my fingers through one of the openings left by the many tape fasteners at the back and felt for the upholstery beneath. To my amazement I encountered the same feeling of fine silk tapestry which I had experienced the day I had discovered the Beauvais tapestries behind the wall-paper in a house at Haarlem, and which had resulted in a deal that had brought me prestige in the firm before I was seventeen years of age. But now, more experienced, I did not take the same foolhardy risks I had been forced to run at the Haarlem auction.

The sale was not due to start until after a couple of days' view, and a hasty glance at the catalogue showed me that the sofa would not be reached until early on the second day of the sale. However, it had become imperative that I should know exactly what was under that needlework. Half a dozen times I started to undo one of the tape fastenings, and each time I was forced to desist by the sound of approaching footsteps. I came to the conclusion that the simplest thing to do was to close the door gently and turn the key in the lock.

Within a few moments I stood in front of six small panels of Gobelins tapestry that had been joined to make the covering of the sofa back. They were chair backs of the finest weft of the Manufacture Royale des Gobelins. Each piece represented a child engaged in some rural sport or occupation. There was a little sleeping shepherdess; a little girl with a bird-cage; another carrying fruit in her apron; and three others of boys, one a fisherman, another carrying a birds' nest, and the other carrying two small birds. I recognized them immediately as part of one of the sets woven after the paintings "*Les Enfants*" by the great François Boucher.

These chair-coverings had first been woven for Mme de Pompadour, Louis XV's art- and luxury-loving mistress. When she heard that the Manufacture intended to make some more sets after the same pictures she forbade it and insisted that Boucher's original pictures should be delivered to her. After her death in 1764 the paintings returned to the Manufacture; and I knew that more of these glorious sets had been made. Here, in a servants' room of this most prosaic house, I had found six fragments of the very gems La Pompadour had thought too beautiful to be sat upon by less exalted personages than herself. How, indeed, are the mighty fallen, I thought to myself. The six backs had been clumsily stitched on to a dark brown rep, and it was evident that they had been intended only as a temporary covering until the artistic hand that had perpetrated the "slipper work" tapestry on the seat had completed a similar horror for the back.

As I replaced the cover another idea struck me. The seats must be beneath the needlework! I therefore extracted some tacks at the back of the seat, but when I inserted my hand under the needlework cover I found only the hair stuffing. After smoothing the opening I had made I opened the door and began a new search for the missing seats. I probed any chair or sofa that looked promising, but without success. Every few minutes my search was interrupted by meeting with some dealer. I followed any potential rival unobtrusively until the danger was past, and this trailing had so often stopped my search that closing-time approached before I had finished. The most crowded apartment of all was the enormous drawing-room; its three high windows provided plenty of light, as well as seats for the crowd of curious women. Every chair and sofa of this room had been occupied ever since I started my search. It was as I was passing through once again in the wake of a provincial dealer that, most unexpectedly, I saw, decked out in very loud tweeds, the imposing figure of Bob Partridge—and I had been so sure that no London dealer would attend this unpromising sale!

"Hallo, young Duveen!" bellowed Bob as soon as he saw me. As everyone turned towards us I felt terribly self-conscious. "What are *you* doing among all this tripe?" he demanded, approaching me.

"I've promised a few clients to be here; they want to buy some of the silver and they wanted my advice," I answered, gaining confidence as I spoke. Bob dismissed it all as "a fine lot of Victorian melting-stuff." I asked him what had brought him there. He replied that he was on his way to Dublin that night, but wanted to view the sale on the way; and he made a grimace of disgust.

At that moment some ladies rose from one of the window-seats, and Bob, who was wiping his perspiring face, sank down in the vacated places and pulled me down next to him. "I'm on the look-out for something very important in French eighteenth century for a great "takkef" [antique-dealers' jargon for rich man]. Have you got anything really fine in that line?" I thought with a stab of anxiety of the French tapestries that I reckoned already mine, but I answered without pausing: "No, we don't keep French things in Liverpool. There is no sale for them."

"Doing anything tonight?" Bob asked next. "My boat does not go until eleven, and I don't know what to do with myself. Come and have dinner with me at the Bear's Paw." I proposed instead that he should come home and dine with me. He accepted my invitation, and since I could not resume my search, we remained on the window-seat. As Bob had placed his small bag between us, we were sitting slightly apart. He was talking away about a profitable trip he had just made to Antwerp when I noticed something that again set my blood tingling. The long window-cushion we were sitting on was covered with the same brown rep on which the other tapestries had been stitched.

Partridge continued excitedly with his story while with one of my fingers I managed to bore a small aperture between the rep and the lining that covered the under part of the seat. Slowly I wormed my finger beneath it and felt again the unmistakable weft of Gobelins tapestry. I felt triumphantly that I had found the six seat panels to match my other find. At the same moment I realized the danger of such a keen hunter as Partridge sitting on my discovery. My problem now was how to get him away without rousing his suspicions.

"What do you think of that?" Bob exclaimed. He had come to the end of his Antwerp story. As he noticed my blank look, he followed his question with a sharply spoken "You are not even listening."

"I was just thinking of an important telegram I have forgotten to send off," I explained. "Come," I continued, "I must look for a shop where I can telephone to our book-keeper."

He followed me out and we walked to the main road. While I telephoned my imaginary telegram Partridge stood outside holding my bicycle. When I rejoined him he took the old-fashioned horse tram while I cycled behind, busily work-ing out my plans for the next few days of suspense. Late that night I saw my guest off to his steamer, and early next morning I resumed the trail.

My plan now was to wait until there was a good crowd in the drawing-room before I sat down on the two seats that I had not yet investigated.

I was talking to a client when two London "runners" strolled in. They knew me and I was careful not to follow them; but I took up a strategic position in a lobby from which I could command the road to the two rooms that held my se-cret. This was a mistake, for these men, who had no real knowledge but plenty of cunning, must have noticed that I took an interest in their movements. From being the watcher I now became the watched. I realized that if I left the lobby I would prove beyond question that I had been watching them; I therefore decided instead to stay there until a client came past so that I could make it appear that I had been lying in wait for him.

The opportunity came within a few minutes when the con-sul of one of the Central American republics approached. This man had taught himself "all there was to know" from a few out-of-date books and had amassed a vast collection of paint-ings of all schools without ever having succeeded in buying the right thing. He was confident in his own knowledge and was proud of the way he scored over everyone when he bought another fake.

We had been in the drawing-room only a few minutes when I noticed the two men standing behind a gilt screen. I knew they were watching, and of this knowledge I made good use. While talking to my client I saw a nineteenth-century imitation of a Sèvres porcelain inkstand of the type that came to England after the first great International Exhibition. It was attractive enough, for the Sèvres blue of the imitator closely approached the original, and the flowers, too, had been cleverly painted. After glancing carefully round the room, except at the corner from which I knew I was being observed, I nudged my client mysteriously with my elbow. "What's the matter?" he whispered excitedly in French, the language we always spoke together.

"What do you think of that little inkstand on the little table behind me?" I murmured; and as he moved impetuously towards it I added the warning: "Be careful! Someone is watching us from behind that screen. Don't pay more attention to the inkstand than to the other things on the table."

My school-boy trick, much too clever, had the effect that I had anticipated. The Consul made his discovery. "Ah, *délicieux!*" he exclaimed softly, but with such excitement that half the crowd in the room must have become aware of his admiration. "Sèvres of the finest quality," he informed me as he concluded his inspection.

"I think it is only a Louis Philippe copy," I ventured to remark diffidently.

"*Mon jeune ami,* you have a lot to learn. You are too ready to see imitations in everything," was the patronizing retort.

When my client left, the two touts approached me. I could

see by their amused looks that they had swallowed the bait. "Now, my boy," began the bigger of the two, a former chucker-out of a notorious Soho public house, "we're not going to waste words. We want that Sèvres inkstand. Are you going to stand in, or is it going to be a fight?" "Standing in" meant forming a knock-out. I had overreached myself with my clever trick, and now I had made certain of their remaining at the sale.

"I'm very sorry, but I can't do that, as my client wants it," I replied.

"All right, clever boy. It will be a fight then. We're going to buy it, no matter what you bid."

Some of my anxiety was relieved when, shortly afterwards, the pair informed me that they were going, but that they would be back in time for the sale of the inkstand.

The rest of that day I kept to my self-imposed role of adviser to clients, and by the next morning, when the sale began at eleven o'clock, I had been able to collect some commissions for my friend Petty, who, as usual, bought a goodly proportion of the lots. I was a more than bored spectator, keeping my eyes open for London or Continental dealers. Only a few more touts looked in, but these soon left in disgust.

That evening I arranged with two young friends to bid for the two lots I wanted. They readily entered into the spirit of the thing, and I told them to continue bidding until I should stop them by an agreed signal. I had been unable to ascertain the presence of tapestry in the other two cushions, but as all three were catalogued in one lot under the heading of "three window-seats," I decided to take no further risks but to leave it to chance.

George Leete, of the now extinct firm of Branch & Leete,

was in the rostrum, and that morning he was inclined to "dwell"; consequently, it was about twelve thirty before we reached the contents of the housekeeper's room containing the sofa I wanted. During the whole of this time I had the feeling that some danger to my tapestries would arise. The room was overcrowded and the atmosphere oppressive. I could not even see whether the friend was present who was to bid for the sofa. My excitement became physically painful as the great moment approached. I was still trying to discover my friend when, looking towards the door, I beheld a spectacle much exceeding my worst fears—Bob Partridge himself, evidently looking for me! He shouted to me and began to force his way through an indignant cluster of curious women.

It flashed through my mind that he must have known all the time. His return to this sale I accepted as sufficient proof. All I could do now was to await developments; but I made up my mind to arrange a joint-account purchase if he should indeed begin to bid. Any doubt that I may have entertained was turned to certainty when he whispered to me: "I know your little game, my boy." Sullenly, I awaited Partridge's terms. Several long minutes passed and still he made no overtures. At last he sarcastically asked if I was annoyed. Just then the auctioneer announced the sofa.

I still could not see the friend who was to bid on my behalf. I tried to move to another part of the room, but Bob held me back, saying that he had to talk to me. Even as he ceased speaking I heard the auctioneer's tap, followed by the word "cash," which meant that the sofa had been knocked down to someone unknown to the auctioneer and that the money had immediately to be paid by the bidder. Partridge's loud voice had drowned the sound of the only bid that had been made. Who had made it I did not know, and I was no wiser when the money was passed through the crowd to the auctioneer's clerk.

I had lost the sofa; my stupid friend had let me down! Again I moved to go out, for I still had a chance of obtaining it, I thought, at a profit to the unknown buyer. Partridge loudly told me not to run away. I asked him what he was after. With devilment in his eyes he whispered: "You'll have to join me and the boys over that bit of Sèvres."

For a fraction of a second I did not grasp what he meant; then I remembered the episode of the imitation Sèvres inkstand and broke out in almost hysterical laughter of relief. Partridge demanded that I explain what the joke was while his eyes narrowed to mere slits. I realized that I had to continue with the comedy of the inkstand lest his suspicions be aroused. "I suppose your friends telegraphed you to return for that?" I inquired, not so much because I doubted the fact, but to gain a few seconds more time.

"Of course they did, my clever lad, and now you'll join or we'll fight you for it. So what is it going to be?" he concluded.

"The joke is, I have promised my client not to oppose him, so you'll have to fight him for it." And again I laughed, this time in order to make him think that this really was the joke. But from this time Bob would not leave me and effectively prevented me from looking for my missing friend.

When the contents of the drawing-room were reached I noticed my client, who had arrived to bid for his "find." One of the first items to be offered was the lot of three window-seats. Then I saw the other friend who was to do the bidding standing almost opposite to me. "How much for the three window-seats?" demanded the auctioneer impatiently. "Shall

I say ten shillings?" he asked, looking round the audience for some sign. My friend, who remembered my instructions, did not move. "Let me have a bid. Shall I say five shillings?" called the auctioneer. My friend nodded, and he had hardly done so when the hammer tapped out the "sold" signal.

A few minutes later I told Partridge that he would have to excuse me as I had to see my client. "All right, you clever devil. I see your little trick, but it won't work!" was his threatening rejoinder. When the inkstand was offered I was standing next to my client, who began the bidding at a pound. Partridge, obviously on the war-path, countered with a shouted "Ten pounds," adding, "I'll have no shenanagging."

Scenting a sensational fight, the auctioneer turned to the Consul with his most flattering smile. "Shall I say twenty pounds for you, Baron?" This was a piece of clever flattery, since my client loved to hear "de" before his name, although he had not the slightest pretension to any title. I did not want to see him walk into any such ridiculous trap; I also did not want Partridge to be stuck with this worthless copy at a big price, and I decided that the matter had gone beyond a joke. Whispering to my client, I gave him my word of honour that the article offered was a Louis Philippe copy and that the dealer was only bidding because he saw us together.

These words, coupled with the fact that he was only keen to pick up great bargains at very small sums, caused him to hesitate; and the auctioneer, guessing I was spoiling sport, called out again: "Come, Baron, this thing of beauty would fetch hundreds of pounds at Christie's!" The Consul was visibly affected by this new lure, but Partridge saved the situation by calling out sneeringly: "Come on, Mister Baron, if you have a few hundred pounds to spare. I'll buy it or stick you with it at much more than it is worth!"

This was Bob Partridge's early manner of bluffing a private buyer away, and he succeeded where I might have failed. My client was nonplussed and frightened, and the hammer finally fell at the ten pounds that Partridge had offered.

Partridge was now the puzzled party. He crossed to where I stood and took me aside. "Thanks for stopping your client," he said. "You are 'in,' I suppose?" I knew his meaning immediately. Partridge mistrusted his easy victory and wanted to ascertain from my attitude whether the article was of value or not. I declined with thanks. For a fraction of a second his face registered a whole scale of emotions, from disgusted disappointment to pretended elation. Big Bob was game even in those days of his difficult beginnings; but I had already seen too much of this sort of acting to mistake the situation. He returned jauntily to the two runners who had been the cause of his mistake, and I could see by the expression of those less accomplished actors that they were not elated with what Bob told them.

This was my chance. Slipping out of the room, I soon found the friend who had bought the window-seats, and he informed me that my other friend had bought the sofa for one pound. Greatly relieved, I asked him to arrange delivery with one of the touting carters who were always to be found at these sales.

My business at the sale was now over, and I waved a hand by way of good-bye to Partridge. He followed me out again, however, exclaiming: "Jack, it's my turn to stand *you* dinner now. I'm not leaving for London until tomorrow, so let's spend the evening together." I felt too happy to refuse; so after he had claimed and paid for his "Sèvres" inkstand we left the sale. Bob accompanied me to our Bond Street premises, and after I had signed some letters I took him out to tea. When we returned at six o'clock the furniture had not yet arrived; and after another half-hour I came to the conclusion that the carter had taken on some other jobs at the sale, and that I would most likely have to wait until the next morning for my purchases. I arranged that one of the men should stay until eight, in case the cart should turn up.

Partridge and I enjoyed a good dinner at the Bear's Paw, then one of the best restaurants in England. Towards the end of the meal the man who had been awaiting the carter brought me a note informing me that the things had been delivered and placed in the basement. Partridge and I spent another very pleasant hour chatting and exchanging the inevitable anecdotes. Then he became serious again.

"I have had a bad time lately, Jack," he said. "This journey to Ireland was a wild-goose chase, and this inkstand is rubbish, too! Oh, yes, I've tumbled all right. It's my own fault, but I'm a sport. I did it myself, and I bear no ill will to any one. The point is, have you anything really fine that I could take to London with me? If I can ever do you a good turn I will." I felt really sorry for Bob, and I was also on tenterhooks to see my treasure. "Come on, Bob; I may have something for you in eighteenth-century French, after all," I told him.

We took a hansom and in a few minutes entered the basement where the sofa and window-seats had been placed. To all Bob's excited inquiries as to what I was going to show him I told him he would have to see for himself, and in the end admitted that I had not yet seen the things properly myself. I told him to take the cover off the back of the sofa while I undid the window-seats.

In a few seconds I had ripped off the brown material that hid the secret while Bob, having undone the first few tape fastenings, was also roused and irretrievably ruined the chintz cover by tearing it to shreds. We took no notice of each other for a few seconds; we were both much too excited. The six missing tapestry seats were all complete. They were worn a little, but it would cost a mere £30 or £40 to put that right.

Bob broke the spell by demanding where I had found them.

"Under your nose, today!" I could not help boasting.

He gave me a short glance, then nodded his head very slowly. "Jack, my boy, you've been too clever for me; but I'm a sport and I'm glad for your sake. Now, you be a sport too, and let me buy them at a fair price. I don't care a tinker's cuss what they cost you, but don't be heavy-handed."

He used the right argument, for if he had tried to argue that I had played him a trick I would have been much more difficult to deal with. After a few moments' reflection I said: "Twelve hundred pounds and no bargaining!"

"Done!" exclaimed Bob, but added: "You'll have to take a cheque, as I have no cash on me. As a matter of fact, I will have to draw the cheque for twelve hundred and ten pounds because I have only a sovereign left until I reach London."

The financial standing of Partridge was at that time unknown. I stared at him for a fraction of a second, and his obvious anxiety did not increase my confidence. However, I felt that even if he were not a good risk from the orthodox point of view he was certainly clever and a sportsman. Concluding that he would not play me a dirty trick, I agreed. When he wrote the cheque he gave me a further shock by informing me that he was going to take the tapestries to London by the night-train.

That night I resolved to have the cheque presented in London for special collection. In the morning, however, I changed my plan and decided to give Partridge time in case he had drawn the cheque with the intention of covering it before it came through. The money was duly paid, and that day I invited to dinner the two friends who had bid for me. Just before it was served I slipped into the dining-room and placed a £100 bank-note in each napkin.

Some ten years later, when Bob had become one of the leading dealers in London, I was having dinner with him and his wife at their house in St. John's Wood Park. "Doris," he said when he introduced me to his charming and clever wife, "this is Jack Duveen, who put me on my feet!" By then I had done several important transactions with him, and the memory of the tapestries was already dim. Observing my surprise, he added: "Yes, my boy! You let me have those tapestries, and you took my cheque for over twelve hundred pounds when I hadn't a stiver at the bank. I made a thousand pounds profit on them a few hours after I arrived in London, and I was able to provide for your cheque. It was the first big money I made."

XIX

THE MONS FIGURE

I HAD BEEN in charge of the Liverpool business for a few years when I received from a friend in Antwerp the catalogue of a collection that was to be sold at Mons, in southern Belgium. On looking through this catalogue I was struck by the description of a Chinese *famille verte* figure standing about forty-three inches high. The description and the most unusual height left me in no doubt that it was the unique figure my mother had described to me. My own father and my uncle Joel together had bought it in Belgium about 1875, but a few days later they had, through shortage of money, resold it at a low profit to an old friend of the family, M. Joseph Volant, of Brussels.

I sent a long telegram to my stepfather at The Hague, begging him to go to that sale and to buy the figure at any price if it should really be of the finest quality. When this telegram arrived at The Hague my stepfather was attending an important sale at Zaandam and did not see the telegram until the evening of the next day. Moreover, he had spent a great deal at this auction and had bought for a much larger amount than he had intended. Accordingly, he telegraphed me in our private code for the state of the Liverpool banking account, the reply to be telegraphed to him Poste Restante, Mons. But when this telegram arrived at Liverpool I was on my way to a sale at Amlwch in the Isle of Anglesey, with the result that the telegram reached me the next morning. I replied that our bank balance stood at between £1,500 and £1,800.

This news reached my stepfather at Mons when the sale was over. Fearing that the financial position was difficult, he had let the figure go for 2,500 francs (about £100 at that time) to the Paris *revision*, the French equivalent of the English knock-out at auctions. A few days after this I had to go to London, and as usual I stayed with my uncle Joel. After dinner we went to the library for our usual chat. As soon as we sat down I asked whether he remembered a very fine *famille verte* figure over a metre high that he and my own father had bought together and sold again to M. Volant.

"Have you got it?" he exclaimed excitedly. I told him what had happened and finally showed him the catalogue. He glanced at the description and rang the bell.

"What are you going to do, Uncle?" I asked.

"Go and pack your bag. I'm ordering the hansom to take you to Charing Cross. You are going to Paris by the night-boat to find out where that figure is and bring it back, no matter at what price." He added as an afterthought: "I'll give you a blank cheque to take with you. Try to get it as cheaply as you can, but *get it!*"

He signed a cheque, and by the time I had packed my bag the hansom was at the door. As the horse moved off he called out: "I know you'll do it!" This gave me the will to persist in spite of the unending difficulties and rebuffs I met the next day.

At nine the next morning I started on the trail by questioning a Flemish dealer in engravings whom I had been able to oblige several times. He had been at this important auction at Mons, and he also knew that the *revision* had bought the Chinese figure. He was able to give me the names of these men, and the first name he mentioned was that of the elderly head of the Paris *revision*.

When I entered the man's small but well-stocked shop he was out, but his wife, a clever old business woman, told me that she knew nothing about such a figure; but when I told her that my stepfather had seen her husband at that sale in Mons she admitted that her husband had been there, but that he had come home without anything.

The next two hours I spent interviewing various members of the Paris knock-out whom my Flemish friend had mentioned, but they all made the same reply: they did not remember the figure. After the fourth statement to that effect, the unanimous denials of having seen the figure struck me, and I realized that this was the *parole*. So when the fifth and the sixth made the same reply I felt sure that a warning had gone round after my first interview, the one with the woman. I also knew that her husband was a wealthy and influential man, and that he was wont to lay down the law autocratically.

I looked at my list again and at the bottom saw the name Vandermeersch, a Fleming who, besides being a clever restorer of porcelain, also had a little antique-shop. I therefore cut out the intervening two and went straight to this man's shop on the other side of the Seine.

When I entered, his wife was seated, with a little child standing by her side. I asked the lady in good Flemish whether the *Meester* was in, and this apparently broke that chain of laconic answers that had been ordered by the Chief, for she asked me: "Are you from London?"

"No," I replied, "I am from Holland, but I was at school at the Belgian École de l'État in Hal."

"Monsieur Vandermeersch is busy in his *atelier*. Is it anything I can do?" she asked.

As I could smell unmistakable whiffs of a restorer's *atelier*, I concluded that this sanctum was at the back of the little shop, and I replied that I should like to see the master himself. She hesitated a moment, and I had just decided to give a Dutch relative's name if she should ask for one when she rose and stepped to the door behind her. A minute passed, and I began to be uneasy. Suddenly I found the child standing by my knees and playing with my watch-chain. Just then Vandermeersch came in, followed by his wife, and at the same moment the child tugged so sharply at my chain that it broke.

"Naughty," shouted the father. The child began to cry and huddled closely against me for protection. This, fortunately, broke the ice, and I said: "It's nothing, it broke in the same place a few days ago." As at the same time I stroked the little one's hand, it stopped crying and took hold of my hand. Then the father asked me in a friendly tone of voice: "Young man, what can I do for you?"

I felt that it was best not to use any further "business diplomacy," so I told him my name, and added: "I have made a long journey to see that large Chinese figure from Mons." He looked puzzled, and I began to fear the worst, but after that momentary hesitation he said: "I am very sorry, but I am not allowed to show it to any one."

Two shocks in one! Information that the figure was still unsold and that it was only just a few feet away from me! I was able to make a frontal attack now. "I have not come out of mere curiosity," I said, "but I am prepared to buy it at a much

163

higher price than it fetched at Mons and to pay cash for it before I leave your shop."

"I regret it very much, but we have agreed not to show it
to any one until next week," was his discouraging, if polite,
reply.

I argued, and even offered a £10 note for the child's
money-box—the latter an old and very general method of
friendly approach in the Low Countries—but all in vain.

"Is it perhaps under offer to someone?" I asked.

"Oh, no!" and then, after obvious hesitation, he added:
"As I told you, we have decided not to show it to any one for
one or two weeks."

"There is something wrong here," flashed through my
mind, and then I jumped at the conclusion. "It has been damaged, and you have to repair it before it can be shown again!"
I almost shouted in my excitement.

"Which one of them told you?" he gasped, incidentally
showing his understanding of his fellow members' mentality.

"No one; but I guessed it because it is not under offer and
no one can see it for a few weeks, while at the same time it is
in your *atelier*," I answered.

"Yes," he admitted, "we had a slight accident with it on the
journey; but for God's sake don't let the others know that you
know, for then they will think that I told you," he pleaded.

I promised, but then I had to find out the extent of the
damage. He persisted that it was not serious, and when I suggested that there could be no harm in my seeing it now he began to lose his temper. This would be the end of everything,
so I begged him to let me see a small fragment by which I
could judge the quality. After a glance at his wife he agreed to
this, and a moment after, I held a small piece of roughly two
inches in my hand. The centre of it had a black ground, of

the so-called and very rare *famille noire* type. This ground
was decorated with tiny green sprigs with white blossoms, but
to my intense surprise this little medallion was surrounded by
a light rose-coloured border.

I knew that the secret of this rose colour had been given to
the Chinese potters by the Jesuit Father d'Entrecolles in
1720, and that shortly after this the Chinese had adopted this
lovely enamel colour as the chief decoration of their porcelain,
instead of the rich greens that had been the leading note of
the previous sixty years. As I held this precious fragment in
my hand I realized that it was a piece of the very short transi-
tion period.

Almost since childhood I had thrilled at such discoveries,
but at this stage this little bit enabled me to judge the quality,
fix the date, and even value this sensational figure. It was as
easy as the legendary egg of Columbus.

The colours had given me the type: *famille verte*.

The presence of the rare black had given me the value.

But the presence of that slight rose border had given me
the almost impossible opportunity to fix the date to within a
matter of a couple of years, 1720 to 1722.

The upshot of all this was that I had to secure this unicum
at any price. No one could really fix the value because it was
beyond compare, in the truest sense. But now I was faced with
the problem of how to secure this treasure. An option, to be
valid, would have to be signed by all the owners; and, apart
from that obvious obstacle, I realized only too well that such
a contract could never be drawn up in a manner that would
make it worth the paper it would be written on.

I felt that I had the goodwill of Vandermeersch, and I decided to trust to his word. I told him that I was very anxious to
buy the figure and that I was willing to give more than he or

his partners might expect. I wound up with: "Can you get them to fix a price?" He reflected for a moment and said that all he could tell me was that before the figure had been damaged they had fixed the selling price at 20,000 francs (at that time £800) and that they would probably be glad to accept that price.

I would have bought at once at that price; but, although I could have trusted Vandermeersch, I knew that I also had to reckon with his partners of the Paris knock-out, a notoriously astute band. I thought it best not to disclose my intention to him before knowing definitely that the others would sell at 20,000 francs.

I suggested that he should telephone the Chief to find out what price he would accept; but Vandermeersch objected strongly because he would immediately suspect that he had shown the figure to a buyer and was trying to do a sharp deal.

I saw the point and realized that my plan would lead nowhere. In my excitement I paced a few times up and down the shop, and I came again to the conclusion that the only way open to me was to trust Vandermeersch. I told him that, as this knock-out arrangement was so complicated, I would take his word and make him a standing offer of 20,000 francs. He was visibly impressed by this offer, and after a moment's reflection he said: "Very well, I think that I can manage this; but you must see to it that your London people do not make any inquiries, for then my friends will become more difficult."

On this we parted; but when I wanted to hand him £10 for his child's money-box, he refused to accept.

The next morning I reported to my uncle, who made me very happy by saying that I had done the right thing, and, at my request, he promised me to let me know the moment the figure came to London. But this was not to be, for when a month later I again arrived in London my uncle told me that the figure had been sold to an American client before it was sent over to London, and Uncle Henry and Cousin Joe had decided to allow me £100 commission. As I knew that this unique piece would be worth at the very least £5,000, I felt a little disappointed, and as I looked at my uncle I saw a strange look in his face. But my greatest disappointment was that I had not had a chance to look at my great find.

A quarter of a century passed, and in 1913 I had to go to New York. About a week after my arrival my uncle Henry Duveen arrived, and on the following Sunday I went to his hotel to pay my respects. Both Uncle and Aunt were pleased to see me and insisted on my staying. After lunch we played a few games of dominoes, and my uncle told me that Mr. Pierpont Morgan had bought two *famille verte* pieces from Hamburger Brothers for a very high price, but that he himself doubted them.

"Is it the three-colours variety or the five-colours?" I asked.

"Five-colours; but why do you want to know?"

"Because if it is five-colours I can see it without having to handle it," I replied.

The next morning we went to the Metropolitan Museum, where Morgan kept most of his collections with the intention of leaving them to the museum. My uncle took me straight to the case in which the vases in question were exhibited, and at a glance I saw undoubted proof that they were genuine.

My uncle wanted to get back to his business, so I asked him to show me the finest piece in this vast collection. "That's the great figure," he said.

At this I could have jumped for joy. At last I was going to see the Mons figure. It was in a different part of the large room, and when my uncle took me to a large case in which there were several figures, he pointed to a magnificent figure of Kwan Yin, but, although a glorious piece, it was *famille rose* and considerably smaller than the Mons figure. Despite my disappointment, this lovely thing made me gasp with admiration. I stood there speechless for a moment, at first from the disappointment and then from the loveliness of this somewhat later masterpiece.

In the end, I said: "Marvellous!"

Then my uncle said by way of one of his jokes: "My boy, what would you give for it?"

"Anything!" I replied.

"That's exactly what I think," he said.

To counter his joke, I said: "All right, Uncle, let's have an auction, and I'll bid you up to what I think it is worth."

He entered into the comedy, and began: "Fifteen thousand pounds."

"Sixteen thousand," I countered in my best Christie's manner.

And so we went up, sometimes by a thousand, sometimes by five hundred, until at his bid of twenty-one thousand I said: "You can have it."

For a moment he stared at me, and then he asked: "Well, imp, do you seriously mean that you would have bid twenty thousand pounds at a real auction?"

"I certainly would, Uncle, for it is the finest I have ever seen except the Mons figure, for that was even finer and much bigger."

"Yes," he agreed, "but I sold that too cheaply. I only got thirteen thousand pounds for it."

This completely took me aback, but I remembered the strange look on Uncle Joel's face when he told me that my uncle Henry and cousin Joe had decided to allow me £100 for my having secured that figure. And Uncle Henry must have remembered this, too, when he saw the pained expression in my eyes. He exclaimed: "Of course, it was you who found it!" and, realizing the disclosure he had made, he added after a moment's hesitation: "But I had to take a lot of rubbish in part payment." And this after having said that he had sold it too cheaply!

I had learnt once again that, in the art-business, friends and even relations are keen opponents—and the devil take the hindmost!

Shortly after the outbreak of World War I, Henry J. Duveen bought the Morgan collection of Oriental porcelain and eighteenth-century French furniture, including the famous Fragonard Room, which the artist had painted for Mme de Pompadour, for a sum in the neighbourhood of £2,000,000. There was a great deal of comment in the American papers, and the *famille rose* figure that had been the subject of our mock auction was then valued at £30,000.

I never found out where the Mons *famille verte* figure, this unique work of the imperial porcelain works, had gone; but I hope that my description will at last bring me the solution of its mystery.

XX

THE "DON QUICHOTTE"
TAPESTRIES

M Y OWN FATHER (who died in 1877), my uncle Joel, and I experienced many coincidences and adventures concerning a rare set of French tapestries during the years from 1868 to 1902. I became involved one autumn after-noon in 1892. As I was standing on the back platform of a Hague tram-car an unsteady figure stepped on; it was a certain porter of one of the auction rooms, who had just been pro-moted to the post of valuer. He had obviously been celebrat-ing, and his breath was most convincingly proclaiming the power of "clear" gin. I had greeted the new-comer and con-gratulated him on his promotion when, to my astonishment, he replied most aggressively:

"Yes, youngster, and in spite of your crowd!"

As I knew that my stepfather had paid a special visit to the head of the auction room to recommend him, I naturally felt aggrieved, but, realizing that he was not quite accountable at the moment, I tried to reason with him. However, my state-ment about what my stepfather had done only made him more aggressive, and after some further abuse he added: "And, my boy, I know how to treat people who were decent to me, as well as how to pay out those who were against me!"

I saw that it was useless to say any more and just stared at the man, but my silence annoyed him even more than my explanation had done.

"Oh!" he shouted, "you don't believe me, do you? Then you can tell your father from me that, by his dirty trick, he missed the finest set of French tapestries in the world, which I was asked to value at one of the biggest mediæval castles in this country. I advised the Count to offer them to my good friend Van Gelder!" As he was ending this outburst he took a step towards me, but the conductor now interfered and told the ranting drunkard to behave or he would put him off the car.

Shortly after this scene I reached my destination, and when I arrived home I told my stepfather what had happened. I particularly mentioned the man's statement about the tapestries, the mediæval castle, and the Count, for I knew that these details, which the man had blurted out in his drunken fury, would make it an easy matter to discover the owner of these tapestries. There are only very few inhabited mediæval castles in Holland, and even fewer counts. In fact, the next morning I found out that the only count who lived at such a castle was Count von der Goltz, a German, who had recently inherited Slangenburg Castle, situated in Gelderland, not far from the German border.

The end of the matter was that my stepfather decided not to go behind Van Gelder's back but to buy the tapestries with him for joint-account. This was done, and finally they were sold to Uncle Joel. In the meantime, I had gone on one of my regular rounds of the English and Scots dealers, and had no further part in the transaction.

About ten years passed, and I was already a partner of J. M. Duveen & Son,[1] in charge of the Liverpool business, when one evening while staying with my uncle at his newly built house, "The Elms," young Mr. White, who had recently joined the Bond Street staff, set the whole company roaring by relating the latest prank of "Funny" Keyes, the young page-boy, who was later to achieve fame as Nelson Keyes.

"This afternoon," said White, "Keyes came running to me with such a look of horror on his face that I realized that this time he was not at one of his jokes. 'Mr. White,' he shouted, 'Mr. Joe says that the donkey has been shot. He wants you to telephone at once.' I was just running to the lift," continued White, "when the impossibility of the whole thing struck me. 'Tell me exactly what Mr. Joe did say,' I called out to the boy, who was running in front of me. He turned round, and, stuttering with excitement, he said: 'Mr. Joe is with a client, and he whispered to me: "Quick! Tell Mr. White to telephone, for the donkey's shot!"' Fortunately, I understood this time and telephoned to the basement for the 'Don Quichotte' tapestries to be taken up to the tapestry show-room."

Shortly after this joke we left the dining-room—some to dance, others to play billiards—but my uncle and I went to the library for our usual chat. The mention of the "Don Quichotte" tapestries moved me to inquire how he had become master of the tapestry market. "Funny you should ask me that now," he replied, "for it began indirectly through that very set, and although I could not buy these tapestries at that time, my seeing them led to a deal over which we did quite well, and which, in the end, led to two weddings."

[1] See Author's Note.

I was thrilled at the prospect of such a story, and I opened my note-book. My uncle smiled at the sight, and began:

"One day in December 1868 your father and I were travelling in an old-fashioned diligence through the Achterhoek [Back Corner] of Gelderland. We had been to a large country-house near Ruurloo, not far from the German border, to look at some family porcelain, but we had arrived too late; a member of the family had bought everything for a tenth of what I would have given, and the new owner would not sell. Your father was upset at having asked me to make such a long journey for nothing. But I used to take these things as they came, and I was already dozing when he shook my arm. 'Would you buy the finest kind of Beauvais tapestries?' he asked.

"I was always keen on extending into new lines, but at that moment I could not have told the difference between one kind of tapestry and another; nor did I know anything about values. All the same, I asked him for particulars. He told me that at the old Castle of Slangenburg . . ."

Here I interrupted my uncle by calling out: "Slangenburg!" but he was not the man to be lightly interrupted, and he growled: "Shut up! Am I telling this story or are you?" But sensing that I had been hurt, he added: "All right. I know how you found out about them." Then he went on with the story.

"Your father said that Frenkel, of Utrecht, had told him that there was a complete wall-covering of Beauvais tapestries with scenes from the history of Don Quichotte, from the designs of the Flemish painter Coypel. There was just a chance that the owner might sell, and Frenkel also had said that these tapestries would fetch a fortune in the Paris market. But your

173

father could not give me any idea of the value, as he had not seen them, nor had any price been mentioned.

"I decided to go. The castle was not far off our road back to Haarlem, and the driver informed us that the best thing to do was to get off at the village of Zelham, about five miles from Slangenburg, where we could hire a post-chaise from the local inn. We followed his advice. At Zelham we changed into one of those beautifully painted old shays, drawn by a racing trotter. I drove myself, and as the road was fairly good, it took us only about twenty minutes to reach the castle.

"It was a large, mediæval-looking building, and the last place in the world in which I would have looked for dainty eighteenth-century French tapestry. After explaining that we had called at the wish of Mr. Frenkel, the Utrecht *antiquaire*, we were received very courteously by Count von der Goltz, who showed us over his beautiful castle, informing us that nothing was for sale. The place was full of antique furniture and other works of art; but in the large room with the tapestries I was immediately struck by the incongruity of the very modern mahogany furniture and the glorious eighteenth-century tapestries. It was the first time I had seen a complete room of them, and even the clumsy mid-nineteenth-century mahogany monstrosities could not spoil the impression of rich and elegant beauty. The lovely scenes of Don Quichotte's adventures, depicted in eighteenth-century figures on a white background, and each panel surrounded by magnificent borders, brought on my usual fever for possession. The Count must have noticed my excitement, for he said, smilingly: 'No, my dear sir, all the money in the world would not tempt me!'

"But as you know," Uncle continued, "I did get them in the end. I sold them immediately, and a few days ago I

174

bought them back again at nearly double the price for which I sold them over ten years ago."

"What about the deal that led to the two weddings?" I reminded my uncle.

"It was dark," he continued, "when we left the castle, and just as we were turning out of the drive the horse shied at something. It was a man who said somewhat mysteriously that he wanted to tell me something important. He asked me to drive on for a few hundred yards and then wait for him. Holland was always a very safe country, so I had no objection. When he caught up with us he said that he was the manservant at the castle, and that he had heard that we wanted to buy the hangings on the salon walls. When I admitted this, he asked whether we would like to buy chairs and other furniture covered with the same sort of stuff. Of course, I told him that I would certainly like to buy those things, and after making me promise that I would give him a hundred gulden if I did buy them, he handed me a bit of paper with an address in Arnhem on it. The next morning we called at this address, a rather modest-looking house in the centre of the town. A neatly dressed old lady opened the door, and when I showed her the handwriting on the bit of paper she asked us to come in and to sit down on the seat in the hall while she called her brother. The man who came in was rather older and moved with difficulty.

" 'You have come to see the Slangenburg furniture, I suppose?' he asked, and I told him that we had been asked to go and see some furniture covered with the same sort of materials as that on the salon walls at Slangenburg. 'Then come this way, please,' he said, and showed us to the 'best room' upstairs. As we entered this room it looked more like a warehouse than a drawing-room. There was an unbroken row of furniture against the walls, and the centre of the room was stacked with settees and chairs; everything was hidden by white muslin dust-covers. The man began to remove one of the covers from a settee, but as he moved very slowly we also lent a hand. In a few minutes we had uncovered them all. There were two large and two small settees, six *bergères*, six large arm-chairs, and twelve single chairs, all richly gilt and carved in the Louis XV style. Every piece was covered with the same tapestry as the Slangenburg hangings, and it was clear that they must originally have belonged to that room. I was just on the point of saying something to that effect when the owner said that they had been at Slangenburg until about fifty years ago, when, owing to a friendly family division, the furniture had become the property of his mother. When he had to move into this small house, he said, he wanted to sell these family things to the cousin who owned the castle; but as the Count disliked their branch of the family, he sent a rude refusal.

"I never wasted time on preliminaries, so I interrupted him by asking what he would take for the suite; but he answered that he wanted to sell all the furniture that had come from Slangenburg. He made a sweep with his arm, indicating the shrouded pieces around the room, and we started unwrapping again. I don't think that I have ever seen such an unexpected sight. Every piece seemed more beautiful than the previous one. There were fourteen pieces of furniture, apart from two threefold screens to match the tapestry suite. The screens were obviously carved by the same hand that had carved the chairs and the settees. Each fold was covered with a small panel of the same tapestry. The furniture consisted of four 'commodes' [chests of drawers]: one pair was Louis XV with rich ormolu mounts, by Caffieri, and the other pair was Louis XVI, by Riesener with ormolu mounts by Gouthière.

"The next pieces that we unwrapped were a small escritoire, also by Riesener, and a chiffonier to match. There were two small occasional tables and a *bonheur-du-jour* [lady's writing- and dressing-table], all three in lacquer with ormolu by Gouthière. These last three were by Martin Carlin. There were also two small bookcases with tambour sliding doors in the shape of richly bound books. These and two large cabinets were by David Roentgen.

"Most of these pieces were signed by their makers, but at that time I knew practically nothing about French furniture, and I only found out their tremendous importance when I began to deal regularly in the finest pieces; but I was nevertheless stunned by our find. Without waiting for Henri's advice, I said to the owner: 'I think that I can do with these as well. How much do you ask for the lot?' and he replied that the local auctioneer had valued them at thirty thousand gulden [about £2,500].

"I was on the point of saying that I would take them when I remembered that I first ought to ask young Henri. I took him aside, and when I asked him what he thought about it he told me that he had never seen anything like it outside museums and palaces, but he was certain that they must be worth at least double what the man asked.

"I was just going to turn to tell him that I would accept, when Henri whispered to me to be careful, as the owner had not said that he would take thirty thousand gulden but had only mentioned that the things had been valued at that. 'If you say that you are willing to give that price, he may be sorry that he did not ask more, and back out.' I had already some experience of this way of 'playing' a keen buyer, so I said to

177

the owner that a valuation by auctioneers is for private buyers, and that we were dealers who had to sell again. I also pointed out that if the things were sold by an auctioneer he would have to pay ten per cent.

" 'Will you pay cash?' he asked after a moment's hesitation. I told him that I didn't have the money on me but that if he came to terms, and if he wouldn't mind coming to Haarlem with us that day, I would hand him the money there.

" 'I'm not used to business,' he said, 'and I did not want to take less, but we are hard pressed; so, if you think that you can't give more I will take off that ten per cent, and you can have the things for twenty-seven thousand gulden.'

"I asked him to make out a detailed account, and I paid four thousand gulden to seal the bargain. Then I set to work. Arnhem was already an important railway station, and I arranged for two special cars to be attached to the next fast train for Amsterdam. In less than two hours I had everything in two old-fashioned removal vans. The men worked for double wages, and a few minutes before our train left for Amsterdam the three of us were on it, with the furniture travelling behind us. The old gentleman had not raised the slightest objection to this unheard-of hurry; but when we got into our compartment I handed him the receipt for the load. He waved this aside, and I was rather touched by this proof of his confidence, particularly as I realized that I had swept him off his feet with this hurry.

"In those days train journeys in Holland were slow, even in so-called expresses, so we had plenty of time to chat and become friends. After some time he told us his story. It was very simple and very sad. He and his sister had become guarantors for a large sum to help a nephew. The money had been lost through misfortune and the nephew had killed himself in despair. The money had nearly all been paid off by the sale of their country estate, and they had moved into the simple house we had seen; but they still owed thirty-five thousand gulden to one man who was pressing for immediate payment. With the money he was going to receive from us he would be able to obtain terms enabling him to pay the remaining eight thousand gulden over a reasonable period. He explained that they still had a comfortable income and that they would be able to do this without hardship.

"I felt rather sorry. The old man was frank about his misfortunes, and he told me how well we had treated him. Several dealers had seen the objects, but none had offered him more than fifteen thousand gulden.

"I realized that he had not told us his story to move us to pity with a view to improving his bargain, so when after a change of trains at Amsterdam we arrived at Haarlem that evening we had become firm friends. But in Haarlem another trouble faced us. I had relied on Henri's father for the money for this unexpected deal, but he had left for Brussels. Henri and I could only raise eight thousand gulden between us. This left us still fifteen thousand gulden short, and we knew that the old gentleman had closed with us because of urgent need. I could not draw on my Hull bank, for I knew that the cheques I had already drawn for goods had overdrawn the account right up to the limit. But Henri thought of a possible way out. He took me to an old friend of his father's, a M. Prévinaire. This gentleman, a French *émigré*, was still at his weaving factory, and he received us immediately. Henri, who was obviously a favourite, did all the talking. When he had finished, M. Prévinaire said: 'So you ask me to lend twenty-five thousand gulden to a total stranger under your guarantee, which has no legal value because you are a minor?'

"It was an awkward moment, for there was no possible reply to the argument, and I was very sorry that I had come. I was just on the point of apologizing for our intrusion when M. Prévinaire, who had been looking at me rather severely, turned away from us and opened an old-fashioned money-chest. He began to count out a bundle of bank-notes, and when he had finished he handed them to Henri. 'It is most unbusinesslike,' he said almost apologetically, 'but I trust you both. You are beginners, and I like to help beginners.'

"Those were still the days of kindly spirit in business, but this act of kindness to a total stranger made an impression on me which never lost its effect. At that moment I made up my mind to be kind to beginners whenever I should have the chance."

After the usual little pause for retrospection, Uncle continued: "That night we paid the Arnhem gentleman his balance, and the next morning we sent him a banker's draft for eight thousand gulden—making thirty-five thousand gulden in all. Young Henri, with whom I had arranged a one third share of the profits, was of the same opinion as myself."

"What happened to the furniture?" I asked.

"That's rather a mixed story. We took the furniture straight to Paris, for I had no buyers in England for it and we had to realize as quickly as possible. Business was bad in Paris, and the dealers were not keen on spending large amounts. In the end I accepted an offer of two hundred thousand francs [£8,000] for the lot, much to Henri's disgust. And he was right. Soon thereafter, I knew that the furniture ought to have fetched about forty thousand pounds instead of the eight thousand that I had accepted."

"And what about the two marriages?" I asked.

"Well, the net profit worked out at just over sixteen hun-

Hawthorn Jar,
K'ang-hsi Period

Sèvres Vases
(Pair Purchased by the Author's Mother in Holland)

Gobelins Tapestry from a Boucher Design

dred pounds each to your father, Barney, and myself. I arranged with Barney that we should keep our share out of the business, and my wedding came a few weeks later. Rosetta's brother-in-law again tried to stop it, but old Barnett had by then realized that I would be able to keep his daughter properly, and he even gave her the magnificent dowry of three hundred pounds."

"But you spoke of two marriages," I reminded my uncle.

"After we had concluded the deal in Paris your father told me that he was in love with my young sister, but I told him that they were too young. He was twenty, and your mother was then only eighteen; but they were married four years later."

Uncle sat lost in his reminiscences for quite a time, but I sensed what he was thinking. After a couple of minutes he said: "Yes, it was a great tragedy that your father died so young. If he had lived those two would have gone further than I have now."

These words have remained engraved on my memory, and they are the most precious gift my uncle could ever have bestowed on me.

XXI

THE MAZZARENTI COLLECTION

SHORTLY BEFORE EASTER 1898 I received a letter from my uncle Joel inviting me to come and pass the holidays with him at Rome. I accepted gratefully, for he was the most kind and thoughtful host on these occasions. The next morning I received a telegram to the effect that the London office had been instructed to arrange all necessary details, and when two days later I called at the Duveen Galleries [1] in Old Bond Street I was handed a small Cook's *carnet* with the necessary tickets for the journey, including a deck-cabin on the steamer and a sleeping-compartment on the Train de Luxe to Rome. When at Calais I entered the restaurant-car a well-known Rome art-expert whom I shall call Edoardo was already seated and suggested that we should take our meal together. During the meal he told me that he had just bought a beautiful set of old Chinese porcelain chess-men; he said that it was *famille verte,* and he would very much appreciate it if I would give him my opinion on it. As I had never heard of such a set and was, moreover, a very ardent chess-player, I told him that I was extremely interested. Signor Edoardo offered to bring it

[1] See Author's Note.

to my compartment after our meal. Unfortunately, the set proved to be a nineteenth-century imitation made in Paris; but after the first disappointment he consoled himself. "Well, I am very fond of playing chess, so I will amuse my friends by playing with this instead of my ivory set." And this led to our playing a great deal of chess on the long journey.

Just before arrival at Rome I happened to say that I was going to pass the holidays with my uncle at the Hotel Continental. He then mentioned that he knew of a collection he was sure would interest my uncle. I asked him for particulars, but he answered that he would first have to obtain the permission of its very eminent owner. He promised, however, that as soon as he had this permission he would come to see my uncle. When I informed my uncle about this conversation he commented: "Yes, I know a great deal too much about these collections belonging to Italian dukes and princes; they have been a great source of income to the Italian dealers for centuries, and they are usually replaced as soon as they are sold."

Shortly after nine the next morning Signor Edoardo was announced and was shown up to the sitting-room. My uncle had met him before and received him very amicably. After the usual greetings our visitor went into details about the collection, but before doing so he asked my uncle to give him his word that he would not mention the matter to any one. The owner was one of the most important personages in Rome and did not wish it to become known that he was thinking of selling. My uncle said that on principle he never talked with people outside his firm about such matters, but that he would not bind himself in any way. Edoardo replied that this was sufficient for him; and he began to read a list of great masters such as I had never heard of before as being in the possession of a single collector. There were eight masterpieces by Raphael,

six Titians—and thus he went on enumerating works by almost every great artist of the Italian, French, Dutch, and
Flemish schools. There was also a great number of most important classical marble sarcophagi and statues in the list; in
short, more than sufficient masterpieces of all kinds and periods to fill a first-class museum.

I could not believe my ears, and Edoardo must have seen
my excitement. On the other hand, my uncle's face remained
quite impassive. When our visitor had finished, my uncle
asked:

"How much does the owner ask for this collection?"

For a moment the expert hesitated over his reply; and then
he answered that, so far, the owner had refused to ask a price,
but that he was a very reasonable gentleman; he did not think
that the price would cause any difficulty.

My uncle countered this with: "It is a great difficulty with
me, for I cannot be both buyer and valuer at the same time. If
you cannot tell me the amount your client will accept, I don't
want to see the things."

Signor Edoardo was obviously in a quandary. He walked
up and down the large salon a few times, and I felt quite sure
that he could not mention any price without first seeing his
client. I did not yet know the childish business tactics of the
Italians, for in less than a minute Edoardo took a totally incon-
sistent line, for he said: "I will tell you in the greatest secrecy
how much he has been offered by a great German museum
expert; but this time, Mr. Duveen, you must promise me that
you will not repeat this to any one."

Then my uncle flared up. "Edoardo, let's stop this comedy,
for I don't care what any one has offered. I buy on my own
opinion. For the last time, tell me how much the owner wants
or leave me in peace."

I was astounded at my uncle's tactlessness over such an important business matter, and the Italian's expression of indignation showed that I had reason for my misgivings; but after a few seconds this expression changed into a polite smile and, as if nothing unpleasant had happened, he said: "All right, Mr. Duveen, you will have your own way. The owner will expect two million lire [at that time £80,000] and I want ten per cent commission."

From that moment the matter went very smoothly. Arrangements for the visit to the Palazzo Mazzarenti were made for that same afternoon at three o'clock.

Signor Edoardo left, and then my uncle asked me to summon the *concierge*. As I looked surprised, he added: "My boy, the hall-porter in a Continental hotel is the most useful friend you can have. He sees to everything, from the smallest to the most important, and, what is most useful of all, he knows everything about everybody." When the man entered the room he was not clad in the usual gold-bedecked uniform but wore a perfectly tailored morning coat. I soon realized how right my uncle had been. The man knew all about old Dom Marcello Mazzarenti, and at first the details he gave seemed to me impossible in connection with such a high dignitary. According to the *concierge*, Dom Marcello owed his position and his collection to the human weaknesses of even higher dignitaries. He pandered to these weaknesses and thereby obtained everything he wanted through the knowledge of these lapses.

"Blackmail?" I interrupted.

"No! No! No! Don't use such a rude word!" exclaimed the *concierge*, and then added with a significant wink: "Only diplomacy and kindness."

When I glanced at my uncle I saw the look that I knew

only too well, and from then on I did not make any more remarks.

We had an early lunch, and after Uncle's usual half-hour's rest we proceeded to the Mazzarenti Palazzo. It was a vast building, and as we were ushered into the first large salon it looked more like a museum gallery than a reception-room. Signor Edoardo and a very smart secretary received us, and after the usual courtesies the secretary returned to his ministerial desk at the other end of the room.

"Come and look at these two marvellous Raphaels, Mr. Duveen," said our cicerone, stepping towards some very decorative pictures. I followed close behind them, and as we reached the pictures I heard my uncle ask for a better light. Edoardo shrugged his shoulders and made a gesture with his hands, which I understood to signify that there was no better light to be had. Joel Duveen was not the man to stand this sort of nonsense, so Edoardo got a surprise. "Take me to something I can see," was the riposte to the Italian's negative shrug.

For a moment Edoardo hesitated, and then he began to walk to the end of the room where the secretary was engaged in a lively conversation with two visitors. As we came near enough I heard that the conversation was being carried on in English. We went out by a door close behind the secretary's desk and entered another large room where the light was much better. Edoardo walked ahead of us towards the opposite wall, and then my uncle used the opportunity to ask me in Dutch: "Did you see those two young fellows?" I nodded, and, whispering quite close to my ear, he said: "Friends of ——," pronouncing a name that had figured a few years before in a very scandalous case. After a few more steps he added: "I don't like the atmosphere of this place."

"And I don't like the look of these pictures," I said. By this time we had arrived in front of a picture that Edoardo described as "St. George," by Giorgione. It was a dreadful daub and showed signs of very rough cleaning. Uncle looked at Edoardo and I realized that an explosion was not far off.

We passed in front of a number of pictures that Edoardo described as the works of great masters such as Titian, Botticelli, etc., and all the time I could see that my uncle was on the point of boiling over. At last, after examining a Greek statue, he said to me: "Everything *ghadish* [Hebrew for 'new,' but this word has among the Dutch art-dealers the meaning of 'imitation']." Continuing in Dutch, he said: "Practically all the great names in this lot are copies or daubs by minor painters."

Edoardo must by this time have become uneasy, for he took us away from the pictures to see a unique thirteenth-century reliquary. We walked back towards the door by which we had entered this room, and when we reached the end Edoardo turned aside a *portière* which hid a door. He opened this, and there, between two enormous church candlesticks, stood a large ark-shaped reliquary. At the same moment we heard a quite distinct conversation from the back of the recess. We could hear it word for word. The rather high-pitched voice of one of the Englishmen whom we had seen in conversation with the secretary was obviously finishing a discussion with: "You don't imagine you will be able to pass off your duds on wily old Duveen!"

Edoardo immediately intervened with: "Mr. Duveen, it is customary to uncover before a holy shrine."

"And that is exactly why I have not uncovered, Signor Edoardo, for this is a very blatant modern imitation of the 'Châsse de Sainte Geneviève' in Paris!"

At the same time he turned on his heel and walked out. The movement had been so sudden and so unexpected that I was several paces behind him when I followed. We walked past the surprised group in the reception-room, but Signor Edoardo did not follow us. He stopped by the secretary and the two Englishmen, and I quite understood why!

Now comes the most startling sequel to this story.

In the spring of 1902 I heard that Dom Marcello Mazzarenti had sold his collection to Mr. Walters, of Baltimore, one of the richest collectors in America. This gentleman had paid 5,000,000 lire (at that time £200,000), or more than double the price that had been mentioned by Signor Edoardo in 1898. My first reaction was that now the bomb would burst! And it did, with a vengeance! A few months later the scandal filled the Italian papers. This multi-millionaire had bought the collection on the advice of his own expert adviser. The most unsavoury details were given. Perhaps the worst of these was the statement that the official government adviser on export-permits for old works of art had arranged with the Italian government to retain the three finest pieces out of this collection instead of levying the export duty amounting to over £40,000. These treasures were hung in the Italian National Gallery at Rome, and then the Italian papers published that the so-called portrait of Bernini by Champaigne was a poor copy of the original in the Paris Louvre museum; that the "St. George" by Giorgione (the picture about which my uncle had expressed himself so forcibly) was a much-restored work of a very inferior sixteenth-century painter; and, last but not least, that the self-portrait of Raphael was the work of a painter who had died not long before. It is also known that, although Mr. Walters paid £200,000 sterling for the collection, Dom

Mazzarenti had received only about 300,000 lire—at that time equivalent to £120,000!

A good deal of whispering has been going on ever since, and this points to some of the experts involved in the case. It is perhaps better not to enter into details, but a few facts are illuminating.

The late Dr. George C. Williamson, expert in ordinary to John Pierpont Morgan the Elder, told me that when he made a lecturing tour through the United States he was invited, at the request of Mr. Morgan, to see the Walters collection at Baltimore, but that while on the way he was met at an intervening station by a representative of Mr. Walters with the rather strange news that the collection was not on view owing to alterations to the building. When later on the learned doctor heard that there was a great deal of commotion about this Mazzarenti collection, he realized the cause for this strange end of his journey to Baltimore.

Our conversation on this subject took place in 1935, and at the end Dr. Williamson made me a present of the catalogue of paintings in the Walters Gallery, Baltimore. As this catalogue contains only two pictures by Raphael, neither of which formed part of the Mazzarenti collection, it is clear that already before 1907 all the so-called Raphaels had been weeded out by the disillusioned collector. Obviously for the same reason, the "Three Jewels" of the Mazzarenti collection do not figure any more in the National Gallery at Rome.

This tragicomedy took place during the teething period of American collecting, and it helped at any rate to stop this kind of piracy. The multi-millionaires became much more prudent. They bought from reputable dealers, or employed them to collect for them; but then the professional expert began to assert himself. There were many of these, from the late Doctor Wilhelm von Bode downwards. Many of these experts charged fees for their opinions or their "certificates," and some even expected a percentage on the value. It cannot surprise any one that with such a fertile field to exploit some of these experts became "industrialized." Soon, work by certain masters had to be "certified" by one or more of the particular specialists in the various schools; and, humanity being what it is, what had begun as a most honourable occupation became in many cases a furious race for gain frequently degenerating into the behaviour of a pack of hungry wolves. Those experts who did not accept fees were so jealous of each other that it was often sufficient for one *deus ex machina* to pronounce a judgement to move another one of the same elevated standing to contradict it. During the last half-century the law courts had to deal with many cases resulting from these internecine wars. In my previous books I have already dealt with some of these tragicomedies, and in the events I shall have to relate there will be several more examples.

The Mazzarenti episode and other similar scandals benefited the brothers Duveen to such an extent that during the next ten years they attained the highest pinnacle of power and wealth ever reached in the art-business. The late Henry J. Duveen, who when barely out of his teens had been wrenched from an idler's life by his much older brother to be almost catapulted into a world of financial giants, had as early as the eighties of the nineteenth century become one of the leading art-dealers of the United States. He had tactfully cultivated his customers, practically all wealthy magnates. Altman, Garland, and many others already knew that they could trust him, and as these fast climbers grew he grew with them. From casual amateurs, buying because the beauty of a thing attracted them, they were becoming collectors of the Lorenzo-the-Magnificent type.

Even before this great change Henry Duveen had been approaching his elder brother's powers; and although he had not yet acquired the buying talent of his senior, he had something that Joel never learnt: a common-sense idea of finance. Joel was often carried too far in his love for something extraordinary, but Henry never lost sight of the financial aspect of business.

From 1894 onwards I used to meet Uncle Henry every time he came through Liverpool on his way to or from New York. On one of these occasions, when I saw him off on the Liverpool landing-stage, he told me that the previous New York season had ended with a profit of nearly £400,000, and as he left I said that I hoped that when he returned the next May it would have reached the half-million mark. As the steamer drew away from the stage I lifted my hand high above my head and spread out my five fingers. He laughed and waved, but when he returned from New York and saw me waiting for him he lifted his arm and repeated my signal. He had reached the half-million-pound mark!

XXII

PIERPONT MORGAN

HENRY J. DUVEEN, the younger of the two brothers, was to carry the renown and power of the House to heights unknown before in the annals of art-collecting. The formation of the incomparable Altman collection was begun in a modest way in 1882, at much the same time as Mr. Garland started to collect Chinese porcelain. This was a period when the rarest pieces could still be gathered at a fraction of the prices that had to be paid thirty years later. George Salting's red-hawthorn-on-black-ground baluster-shaped beaker, for instance, which Joel Duveen bought in my presence for £1,500 and which Henry Duveen sold to Mr. Garland, was valued at £30,000 in 1915, when after the death of John Pierpont Morgan the collection became the property of Duveen Brothers [1] for the third time.

By the time of his death Mr. Garland had spent £180,000 with Henry Duveen. Mr. Garland's son reminded him that he had promised his father that he would always take back any part or the whole of the collection at ten per cent below the prices paid for them. The transaction was concluded on that

[1] See Author's Note.

basis, and the collection became again the property of Duveen Brothers. The first I heard of this was through the first
Lord Leverhulme. I was his expert in ordinary, and he always
consulted me when fine Chinese porcelain was offered to him.
One morning his secretary rang me up in Liverpool, asking
me to travel the next morning from Birkenhead to London
with Mr. Lever (as he then was).

I agreed, and we met at the station. Mr. Lever stepped
into his reserved compartment, and as soon as we were seated
he surprised me by asking what I thought of the Garland collection. I answered that I had seen many pieces of it, but that
I had never seen the whole, and that it was said to be of even
finer quality than the Salting collection. After making me
promise to treat this as very private he told me that my uncle
Joel had offered it to him for £280,000, and asked if I
thought that it could be worth all that money. I answered that
it was impossible for me to value a collection without having
seen it. When he asked me if the pieces of a collection were
worth more because they were in a famous collection I replied, after a moment's reflection, that if they came to public
auction in the collection they would fetch considerably more
than if they were sold piecemeal. We passed much of the journey in discussing this increase of value as if I were the seller
and he the buyer.

Some days after this journey Mr. Lever came to see me in
Liverpool. He complained bitterly that he had been badly
treated by my uncle Joel. He had gone to the Bond Street
gallery to make an offer for the collection but had been informed that Henry Duveen had sold it in New York to Pierpont Morgan. I asked Mr. Lever whether he had taken an
option of the collection; but he replied that he thought that as
he was a good customer, they would have waited for his deci-

sion, and also admitted that he had not communicated with Duveen Brothers for over a week.

My uncle Joel, when I stayed with him on my next visit to London, told me that he was very annoyed with his brother for having "thrown away" the Garland collection for the paltry profit of fifteen per cent. When he concluded: "He is still a young fool. I could have sold it to Lever for at least fifty thousand pounds more," I could not restrain my amusement at the description of Uncle Henry as a "young fool."

Shortly thereafter, I met Uncle Henry on his arrival at Liverpool for his three months in Europe. Between the landing-stage and the station I learned all about the Garland deal and heard that after Mr. Morgan had bought the collection he had said: "I understand that Mr. Garland did not complete the collection." "That is so, Mr. Morgan," Uncle Henry had answered. "Then I shall be glad if you will complete it for me," had been Morgan's reply; and this meant *carte blanche*. The Garland collection remained in the Metropolitan Museum of New York, and in a few years it was raised to a pitch of magnificence that can never again be rivalled. After this first deal Mr. Morgan became friendly with Henry Duveen, and their transactions finally ran into several million pounds.

In 1902 a transaction took place that might have put an end to this lucrative business with Mr. Morgan. It was the purchase of a Gothic Flemish tapestry, the "Adoration of God the Father," which had been the property of the dukes of Burgundy and had passed through Mary of Burgundy, the only child of Charles the Bold, into the Spanish House of Hapsburg. A French officer had looted it during the Peninsular War, and it remained in this man's family at Bordeaux until Duveen Brothers bought it in the spring of 1902. Henry Duveen, who had been informed of this important find, had cabled that he wanted it kept for Mr. Morgan. My cousin Joe, who was already the all-powerful master of the London business, showed me the lovely tapestry as well as a letter from Lord Esher requesting the loan of the tapestry for the coronation of King Edward VII. He intended that it should form the background for the throne; but it was not so used after all. When Mr. Morgan came to the Bond Street gallery all the works that had been reserved for him were shown in one of the large upper show-rooms. He asked the prices but was apparently most impressed by the tapestry panel. When he had examined the various articles he asked what was the price of the whole "stack." My uncle was used to Mr. Morgan's ways and was ready with the amount, in which the tapestry panel accounted for about £65,000. When Morgan bought the "stack" he asked: "What did you pay for the tapestry, Henry?" My uncle tried to parry the question by a joke and said: "Ask me no questions, Mr. Morgan, and I'll tell you no lies."

"Ten thousand pounds?" asked Morgan; and this went on until at £60,000 my uncle said: "Now you are nearer to it; but what I paid has nothing to do with the value. I will always take it back at the price invoiced to you."

News of this transaction soon leaked out. When it came to the ears of the late Jacques Seligmann, of Paris, at that time the leading art-dealer on the continent of Europe, it led to one of the most sensational lawsuits of the period. The tapestry had been offered first to him, but he had refused to pay the price the owner asked. Soon thereafter, he heard from the intermediary who had approached him for the owner that the latter was offering the tapestry to Duveen Brothers. Seligmann then proposed to Duveen Brothers that, instead of opposing each other, they should buy the tapestry for joint-account. He also wrote that the tapestry was much too dear at the owner's price of 300,000 francs (at that time £12,000). He stipulated that the limit should be £8,000. Louis Duveen (Joel Duveen's fourth son), who was sent to view the tapestry, realized immediately that it was the finest piece of Gothic tapestry still in existence, and secured it immediately at the owner's price of £12,000. He telegraphed the news to London and also to Seligmann, who telegraphed to Duveen Brothers, renouncing the partnership and ending: I AM IN BUSINESS TO MAKE PROFITS, NOT FOR FUN.

When ultimately Seligmann heard that Pierpont Morgan had bought the tapestry for something like £100,000 he claimed that he was still a party to the transaction. The matter went to law and became a *cause célèbre*. Seligmann briefed the late Sir Edward Clarke, who kept Louis (who stammered a little when he was nervous) in the witness-box for three days of cross-examination. When Joel Duveen saw the nervous strain to which his young son was being subjected he settled out of court. Morgan heard of these proceedings but was too experienced a business man and too happy with his unique Gothic tapestry to feel aggrieved. This lawsuit was the first engagement in a determined war waged by Jacques Seligmann against Duveen Brothers.

In the summer of 1905 I had my first and only transaction with Pierpont Morgan. I had bought for £10,000 the collection of powder-blue Chinese porcelain formed by Sir William H. Bennett, K.C.V.O., the leading surgeon in London. Sir William had told me that some time before our transaction he had been approached by Mr. Pierpont Morgan to part with the finest pieces in the collection, the four 22-inch dishes. As usual, I gave the first option on the whole to Mr. Lever, whom I regarded as my best and very friendly client.

He told me that he did not care for dishes; but as I could not risk breaking up the collection I could not give him the option on the other pieces in case Mr. Morgan should insist on having the whole collection. We finally agreed that if Mr. Morgan would consent to buy only the dishes Mr. Lever would have the option on the remainder.

I wrote Mr. Morgan, offering him the dishes for £4,000. Sir William Bennett had told me that he had been offered that amount on behalf of Mr. Morgan. A few days later Uncle Henry telephoned me to bring the dishes to London, as Mr. Morgan had asked him to look at them for him. I did so, and after examining them my uncle told me that he could not advise Mr. Morgan to pay more than £3,500. I did not like this, as I knew the dishes were worth what I asked, but after thinking it over for a few seconds I realized that I would not do so badly because I knew that Mr. Lever would take the remainder of the collection. I returned to Liverpool, and the next morning as I was on the point of writing to Mr. Lever my cousin Joe rang me up from London to tell me that he wanted the remainder of the collection to be sent immediately to Bond Street. When I reminded him that I had given Mr. Lever the refusal if I sold the dishes to Mr. Morgan, he answered that Mr. Morgan might not take the dishes if he could not have the first option on the remainder. As I still hesitated, he reminded me that I had told him that Mr. Lever had said that if Mr. Morgan did not buy the whole collection he would be glad to deal with me for the remainder. This was true, and I agreed to send him the collection by passenger train that same afternoon.

A few days later I went to London again and had the usual breakfast with my uncle Joel at "The Elms." When after breakfast we went to the library he called me a fool for having sent the powder-blue collection to Bond Street; but when he added: "Joe just used it to spoil you with Mr. Lever" I would not believe it. I soon found that I was mistaken, for my uncle told me that Joe had written to Mr. Lever inviting him to see a hawthorn ginger jar that they had just bought. When Mr. Lever came Joe had taken him into his private office to see the vase. As soon as Mr. Lever had entered the room, in which my powder-blue had been left standing on the floor, he had recognized it, as he was intended to do. Then I remembered the warning my uncle had given me earlier that year of Joe's boast that he would take away my two best customers, and I feared that he might have succeeded in doing it as far as Mr. Lever was concerned. I was going straight to Bond Street to confront Joe, but my uncle begged me not to make trouble by using what he had told me out of kindness; so I agreed that I would pretend to know nothing and wait for Joe to give his version of what had happened.

When I arrived at Bond Street none of the members of the firm had arrived. Uncle Henry came in first and immediately told me that a very unpleasant thing had happened. Mr. Lever had walked into Joe's office while my powder-blue porcelain was standing there, but that they were not quite sure whether Mr. Lever had noticed it. My uncle advised me to tell Mr. Lever that I had been trying to sell it to Duveen Brothers. Although I felt certain that my uncle knew quite well that Mr. Lever had seen the collection, I was also certain that he had not been a party to the trick by which Joe was trying to ruin me. I did, however, say repeatedly that if I told Mr. Lever that I had offered the porcelain to Duveen Brothers I should lose his custom. We were still arguing the matter when Joe came in; as I now could tackle him without implicating my uncle Joel, I asked him why he had shown the porcelain to Mr. Lever. He answered that Mr. Lever had come into his office and had seen the porcelain by accident and that Mr. Lever had asked why it was there. Then I heard the worst. "I told him that you had offered it to us, but that you asked a mad price for it"; and then Joe walked out of the door to keep an urgent appointment.

Joe had not only made the transaction with Mr. Lever impossible, but he must also have succeeded in making the man who had always trusted me believe that I was a trickster. On my return to Liverpool I wrote to Mr. Lever that Duveen Brothers had now returned the collection to me after asking me to send it to them because Mr. Morgan wanted to see the whole collection as well as the four dishes; but that he had decided to buy only the dishes. At first I had been on the point of writing the whole plot to Mr. Lever, but the thought of involving my uncles decided me not to make this disclosure.

Mr. Lever's reply came by return of post. He informed me in a few curt words that he had changed his mind and was no longer interested in the powder-blue porcelain.

XXIII

THE ANTIQUE STAMPS

ONE OF THE WORST FEVERS to grip me during my young days was stamp-collecting; but it was only a school-boy craze that died out when I was sent to school in Belgium to study languages. The Belgian school-boy of that day had no use for stamps, and when I returned home, just before my sixteenth birthday, I dropped into such a whirl of exciting adventure that my fever for stamps remained dormant for some years. I still felt that indescribable mania for stamps whenever I attended some country sale, but disappointments became so monotonous that for some years I almost forgot the existence of the collection I had started. Strangely enough, it was during these few years of indifference that I communicated the fever to one who was to become one of the greatest collectors of the last half-century.

During the spring of 1893 I was staying with my uncle Henry J. Duveen at his London home, Hertford House, Finchley Road. His only child was approaching his seventh birthday, and I was wondering what I could give him to mark the anniversary. He was a very bright and advanced boy for his years who had learnt to read when he was four, and when

I presented him with a Gibbons album and a parcel of one thousand stamps my uncle was highly amused. He had reckoned, however, without the studious mind of the boy, to whom they immediately made a powerful appeal.

When I came in for dinner that evening I found father and son on the carpet of the drawing-room, trying to find the exact places in the album for the various stamps. After that, my uncle spent every spare hour during the next few days arranging the stamps.

When the "first thousand" had been framed in their little squares my uncle thought they made such a mean show that he himself decided to complete some of the sets. Every night he returned home with more missing specimens, and in about a fortnight's time the fever had gripped him so strongly that he was spending hundreds of pounds to complete the boy's collection.

"I must carry this thing on myself," he said one evening. "I've spent too much money to leave all this in the hands of the boy when I am in America." And so it continued. When he died in 1919 his collection was valued at over £300,000. The growth of this collection caused many exciting incidents, but I will confine myself to telling of a heart-breaking adventure that concerned both my uncle and myself.

Late in 1893 I settled permanently in Liverpool, where I had been placed in charge of the newly opened branch of our business, and I was kept too busy to look after anything except works of art. In the spring of 1896 the ne'er-do-well son of a local art-dealer came in and asked me if I took an interest in what he termed "antique" postage stamps.

"Antique stamps?" I exclaimed. I condescended to explain that there was no such thing as an antique postage stamp; but today I am inclined to think that there was more in the man's description than I then realized. The dealer, who evidently had a good opinion of my knowledge, explained what he meant.

"A woman over seventy told me that she has collected stamps ever since she was a little girl. I naturally thought that she had inherited them and that therefore they must be antique. They are all pasted in dozens of old-fashioned exercise books, and the lady says that each is a complete set."

"Are they all English stamps, or stamps of foreign countries as well?" I asked the young dealer, whom I will call Channer.

"I don't know one stamp from another," he admitted. "And I did not look carefully at them, though to me they all looked foreign."

"I do not buy stamps in the ordinary way of business," I explained, "but only for my own collection; however, if I like them I will give you a good commission. How much do you want?" I concluded, with a little too eager note in my voice.

My visitor scratched his head. "I don't know anything about stamps," he confessed, and dodged the question by asking me what they would be worth.

"It all depends on the state they are in," I replied a little more cautiously, "but we can easily come to an arrangement on a percentage commission. That's fair to both."

"I'll take ten per cent," he exclaimed rapidly; "but I'm very hard up, and I shall want two pounds on account." The latter part of this proposition was made with such a comic mixture of timidity and bravado that I began to suspect it was one of the many little games for which this young man already had a reputation.

"Very sorry, Joe, but commissions are not paid before a

deal has been concluded," I told him. However, he pleaded so hard, and he swore so fervently that it was "God's Truth" that I gave him the money on the strict understanding that he would arrange with the lady to show me the stamps the next day. But Joe did not show up, despite his promises. It was not until two or three days after that I met him in company with two of his cronies. I frustrated his endeavour to evade me and, following him up, came straight to the point.

"Joe, what about those stamps?" I demanded.

"Stamps?—Oh, yes, I remember! I'm going to see the old woman now," he stammered in half-dazed fashion, while his breath betrayed the cause of his bad memory. I was half tempted to accompany him, but he looked so unkempt and behaved in such a disgraceful manner that I decided to lose my chance of any find rather than be seen in his company. Then another complication arose.

"Here," exclaimed one of his disreputable friends, "I collect stamps too! You're not going past a pal to let this fellow have them?"

"Course not, you come with me!" said Joe. "Let's take the bus to the Pier Head."

The matter was now becoming serious. I was not going to argue with a drunken crowd, but I made up my mind that I was entitled to protect my interests. No sooner had I seen the three board a bus than I took a hansom cab and followed them. They took the ferry-boat to Woodside, Birkenhead, and then changed to another bus. I continued the pursuit and trailed them eventually to the entrance gate of an important-looking house in Claughton. From a safe point of vantage I saw the door slammed in the face of the drunken trio, who walked away venting their feelings in the most lurid language.

I considered the situation for a moment or two and decided on immediate action. Telling my cabby to proceed to the door of the house the three had just left, I presented my card and asked to see the lady of the house, who received me very courteously in her drawing-room. I explained the situation to her in a few words; my youth and obvious sincerity evidently made a good impression, for after the first moment of obvious surprise the old lady began to laugh so heartily that I thought her lace cap would shake off her head.

"Well, you are a very energetic young man!" she said when her mirth subsided, "and I will overlook the connection with that young scamp who dared to come to my door in such a shocking state of intoxication." With that she ordered tea and began the story of her stamps.

"I began to collect stamps many years ago when my father was still alive," she said. "He was a manager for several small sailing-ship owners and knew a great many captains. As he knew I liked stamps, he asked the various captains to bring sets of stamps from whichever foreign port they touched. He made only one stipulation: that no stamp should cost more than a shilling.

"This continued from 1846 until the end of 1861, when he retired. By that time I had filled many books with my beautiful stamps; then for many years I forgot all about them until I was recently told that they might be worth a lot of money. The idea came to me that I might be able to sell my stamps and devote the money to some of my little charities."

Tea was brought in, and with it came four little girls, to each of whom she gave a cake, after which they left. "My maid's nieces," explained my hostess. "They come every Saturday afternoon to play in my garden."

All this was very charming, but I was burning with impatience to see this remarkable collection. The ceremonious tea seemed to last for hours, but finally the old lady rose and fetched the books. Just simple-looking exercise books they appeared, tied in two parcels.

"There are sixteen of them," she explained as she deposited them on a console table.

I was now in a red-hot fever of anticipation. Sixteen years of complete series from all parts of the world! Sixteen books full! Then followed a nervous search by my hostess for the first year, a procedure that tried my nerves to breaking-point.

"Here is 1846!" she exclaimed suddenly. She handed me an exercise book on which the figures "1846" were written. When I opened it I found the first pages, marked "American," covered with all sorts of strange-looking stamps and envelopes I had never seen before.

"I don't think these are worth anything at all," observed the old lady, noticing my look of disappointment. "You see, I was told that they were only local stamps of various ports. Nor do I think there is anything in this," she added, handing me a second volume, "but I think you will find something better here," she continued, handing me two other books she took haphazardly from the pile.

I opened one marked "1860" and happened on a page marked "Hamburg." Row upon row of unused Hamburg stamps—the pet aversion of my young collecting days. In fact, these Hamburg and Papal States unused stamps were practically worthless because they were reprints from the original blocks.

"How is it," I asked, "that you have so many duplicates on the same page?"

"The captains very often brought back sets that others had already brought for me," she explained, "and I put them all in, just entering the port and date of purchase against them."

I examined the other book, marked "1851." But by now I had lost my great enthusiasm and allowed the pages to slip through my fingers. I looked here and there, only to find unused stamps. I remember glancing at some very insignificant specimens from Hawaii underneath which was written: "The first stamps made in Hawaii." A few days later this casual glance was engraved on my memory, but at that moment it contributed only to my contempt for the entire collection.

"Nothing but unused stamps," I observed at last.

"Well, you see, I thought that it would not be money wasted if I collected unused stamps," said the lady apologetically. "In fact, that is why I fastened them by a corner only."

"They are worth nothing if they are not obliterated," I remarked, proud of the technical term.

"How strange; our captains often had the greatest trouble to get unused stamps," sighed my hostess.

"Are you sure there are only unused stamps in these books?" I asked after running hastily through several more of them.

"I am positive because I only collected unused ones. But," she continued after a moment's hesitation, "there are thousands of them. Are you *sure* they are worth nothing?"

"Not unless there are some that can still be used, but as they are all foreign and colonial stamps issued prior to 1862, I do not think there is the slightest likelihood."

The lady was impressed by my obvious honesty, and, unfortunately, even more with my apparent knowledge.

"Ah, well," she said, with a gentle sigh, "I am very sorry for the trouble you have had, and also for my little charities.

I should have loved to have given them a little more this particular year."

I thanked my hostess for a very pleasant tea and left. Another great disillusionment; and the fact that Joe Channer had
treated me so badly did not help to improve matters.

It was about a week later that my uncle Henry arrived
from New York for his yearly stay in Europe. I met him,
with the tender, and we had the usual eager conversation
about family and business matters. This was before the train
could come alongside the Pier Head in Liverpool, and passengers had still to find their own way in cabs to Lime Street
Station. We had so much to talk about that the matter of
stamps did not arise until he said: "Have you thought of looking for some fine stamp collections for me?"

Then I remembered the wild-goose chase in Birkenhead.

"The only one I have seen was a lot of rubbish belonging
to an old lady. Thousands of them, but they were all old, unused stamps." This last I added to show how utterly useless
they were.

"How old?" rapped out my uncle, with more excitement
than the occasion seemed to warrant.

"From 1846 to 1861," I answered, confident that this
would quieten him. I shall never forget his change of expression. He literally gasped for a word. "What?" he almost
shrieked. I repeated my statement, sure that he had misunder-
stood me.

"Are they still to be seen?"

"Certainly," I replied, though with serious misgiving.
This conversation took place a few minutes before the train
was timed to leave, and my uncle was talking to me through
the carriage window.

"Porter!" he suddenly shouted, and did not waste so much

as another glance on me until his hand-bags had been removed from the train.

Then the storm broke. Even now I cannot think without emotion of all the kinds of fool he called me; but in spite of his vehement eloquence, he wasted no time. We were seated in a hansom when he barked: "I'm going to see that collection. Give the address to the cab-man!"

"We have to cross the river," I said diffidently.

"I don't care how far we have to go. Hurry up! Don't you know that unused stamps are by far the most valuable?"

I had never seen my uncle so excited by any of his most important deals; but I understood; this time he was the collector and not the dealer. His excitement was almost uncontrollable when I told him the extent of the collection and some of the details that I remembered.

"What year is written on that book in which you saw those 'very ugly Hawaii stamps'?" he asked, imitating my words and tone in a most unpleasant manner.

"1851," I replied.

"How many were there?"

"Three sets of three each, Uncle," I answered, proud of my memory.

"Any heads of men or women on them?"

"No, just the value, and there was something written underneath them about being the first stamps printed in Hawaii."

"My God! The rarest stamps in existence."

How right my uncle was in his opinion is shown by the fact that these three series of three would have been worth considerably over £20,000 today. After a few painful moments I explained that I had not collected since I was thirteen, but if my uncle heard me he took no notice.

"Which year is the earliest you remember among these books?" he asked, interrupting my apology.

"1846, Uncle."

"Do you remember if there were any American stamps?"

"Yes, pages full of them, but they were only various kinds of local stamps."

Before I concluded I saw unmistakable signs of a fresh storm, and I was not wrong. This time the verbal hurricane ended with: "If we miss this collection neither of us will ever have such a chance again. These local stamps of the United States are worth a fortune by themselves."

I felt unutterably miserable after these shattering blows to my self-respect. However, after some time my uncle must have felt sorry for me, and his good nature again asserted itself.

"Well, well," he said soothingly. "It's all right now. We'll get them yet."

When we arrived at the house in Claughton the old lady again received us in her drawing-room, and my uncle took the lead.

"I'm extremely sorry to intrude, madam, but I am a very passionate stamp-collector, and my nephew told me that you have a large collection of stamps you wish to sell. Would you allow me to have a look at them?"

Our hostess hesitated a moment and I sensed the coming blow. "I am so sorry," she said, "but I gave them to my maid's little nieces."

Uncle Henry shot me an agonized glance. "Do you mind giving me the address of where the stamps are? I should so much like to see them."

The lady seemed in a quandary, and again I felt that something was wrong. At last, with an apologetic smile, she said: "You see, this young man told me that they were of no value; so I gave them to the children to cut up for some kind of stamp mosaic-work. If you like to see them the children are working in my sewing-room now."

We followed her and found the children busy pasting bits of stamps on to small pots. Several small baskets stood on the table, and in these all that was left of the stamps was arranged according to their colour. The children had worked extremely hard, for all the stamps had been cut into small fragments for the mosaic work. This was the last straw. My uncle could only stare in speechless contemplation of the calamity. I was the first to speak.

"Have they all been cut up?" I asked as calmly as I could.

"Yes," answered one of the little girls proudly, "we finished the last lot yesterday."

Out of this unique collection not a single stamp was left. And it was all my fault! After staring another moment at the basket my uncle recovered himself. He thanked the lady for her kindness and excused himself for intruding. Then we left. I entered the cab trembling in apprehension of what was to come. But after a few minutes' painful silence my uncle laid his hand on my knee: "Don't worry, Jack, you could not be expected to know how things have changed. I've been too hard on you." He paused for a moment. "You see, I was so angry because this is my own hobby; not business."

"I shall never forget the lesson, Uncle!" I exclaimed.

My uncle did not refer to the matter again, and when I said good-bye to him at the train he gave me the best consolation possible. "Such is life!" he laughed as the train moved off, and, seeing my dejected looks, he added: "I won't tell any one and we'll never talk about this again."

He kept his word and, although he loved to chaff the younger generation mercilessly, he never hinted by word or sign at my stamp "Waterloo," when I innocently caused a fortune to be destroyed.

XXIV

ELEVEN REMBRANDTS

Shortly before Easter 1905 my uncle Joel tele-graphed me to come immediately to him at The Hermit-age at Monte Carlo, and that his chauffeur would be meeting me at Euston Station next morning. This telegram was ad-dressed to me at Liverpool, and, although I was used to these imperative messages, I realized that my uncle would not order me to travel at such short notice unless it were on some urgent business matter; something that he could not telegraph. I answered that I was coming, and travelled to London by the night-train. At Euston the chauffeur met me with the car— a very noisy and very fast Panhard-Levassor. A mid-winter snow-storm accompanied us through London as far as Maid-stone. In Paris one of my young cousins joined me. On the third day after leaving London in a blizzard we arrived about noon at Aix-en-Provence, where in the lovely fountain-lined avenue the trees were in full bloom and the townspeople sit-ting outside the cafés enjoying their second *déjeuner*; a con-vincing reason why people should go to the South of France for spring sunshine and colour instead of suffering snow-storms

212

Nankin Vase
(the "Embarrassing Vase")

British Museum

Famille noire Vase

Victoria and Albert Museum

"The Night Watch," by Rembrandt

(After Cleaning)

at home. After another dream-like trip, along the Corniche road by the side of the sunlit Mediterranean, we arrived at Monte Carlo about tea-time.

Uncle Joel received us with his usual happy smile, but I could see that he was worried. After tea he took me for a walk and lost no time in broaching his subject. His brother Henry and his son Joe wanted to buy the Rodolphe Kann collection without even asking his advice.

This was equivalent to telling me that the National Gallery was for sale, for the Kann collection was known to contain the finest masterpieces in pictures, tapestries, old French furniture, European and Oriental ceramics, and other treasures. The works of the Dutch, Flemish, and Italian schools were reputed to be unmatched in private collections, but to me its unique attraction was the collection of eleven Rembrandts of the master's last and greatest period.

When this reflection flashed through my mind, I exclaimed: "Marvellous!"

"Yes," grumbled my uncle, "but they wanted to conclude this business without even consulting me. Just as if I didn't count any more. They want to push me out of the active lead of the business with this great coup."

I could not believe this. I said that he was too suspicious and that Joe would never do such a thing to his own father. My uncle called me a fool for taking Joe's part; he said that at dinner the night before he had left for Egypt Joe had said that I was getting too ambitious, and that he was sure that some day I would open a business in London but that he would stop me before that. He also had said that I only had two really big customers—Mr. Lever and Sir William Bennett (the famous London surgeon). Joe had added that he could easily take these two great collectors away from me.

At first I was inclined to laugh at these threats, but my cousin Charles's frequent warnings recurred to my mind. I had never taken these seriously because of the bad feeling between the two brothers; but now that their own father also warned me I could not ignore the danger. So I said that I had not the slightest intention to open up in London, as I was perfectly happy in Liverpool, and added that if Joe should ever try to ruin me I would defend myself to the best of my ability.

My uncle stopped his walk and shook his head.

"My boy," he said, "you don't know Joe," and after this further ominous warning he returned to his subject.

He went on to explain that if he let his brother and his eldest son buy this great collection before he had even seen it they would have established a precedent that would take all power over the business out of his hands. To this he added: "I would rather dissolve the partnership and start a new firm with Charley and the other boys than become a nonentity in the firm I built up."

I saw that he was very upset by the intrigue against him. We walked a short distance without speaking. Then I asked whether he had made up his mind what to do.

"Not quite, but I want you to tell me exactly what you think. I have always been kind to you, and I want the truth."

Although I was thirty-one at that time, I had always felt like a school-boy in the presence of this great man, but now his evident distress and his expression of trust in me gave me self-confidence. I saw the whole affair in its true proportions, and without any further reflection I told him that for the sake of his own peace of mind, and in the interest of his numerous family, he ought to do everything to keep the firm united. I also pointed out that by making the Kann-collection deal impossible he would only be cutting off his nose to spite his face.

There were several snorts of disagreement while I was talking, but I wound up my arguments with: "Instead of sulking here and ruining everything, go to Paris, take the lead, and show them that yours is still the master-brain."

This had a great effect, and, as I noticed this by his changing expression, I added: "Send a telegram that you are coming to Paris to see the collection yourself!"

He stopped again, and then, roaring with laughter, he exclaimed: "You are very cheeky, but you are right!"

A telegram that he would arrive on the following Friday was sent, and we spent the next days on short excursions in the Esterel Mountains; but that evening brought an extremely unpleasant reminder of intrigue. A relative by marriage was also staying at The Hermitage, and she passed most of the time with us. Just towards the end of dinner a letter for me was brought in. I did not open it, but as soon as we had adjourned to the adjoining salon I opened the letter and saw that it was from my cousin Charles, my uncle's second son. He had opened an antique-business in New Bond Street. This, of course, had created open warfare between him and his eldest brother, Joe, which was ultimately reduced to a kind of armed peace by Charles changing the name of his firm from Charles J. Duveen into C. J. Charles; and for this concession he received £1,500 a year from Duveen Brothers.[1] His father had insisted on this, in spite of Joe's fight against this yearly *douceur*. But Charles had the same weakness as most of us: overbuying by being unable to resist a thing of beauty. The result was continual money-worries, and his letter begged me to

[1] See Author's Note.

215

talk to his father about a guarantee at the bank for an additional overdraft of 5,000 pounds.

My uncle must have watched me as I read the letter, and when I looked up he asked in Dutch: "Bad news?"

I thought it best to hand him the letter, and when he had finished it we had a fairly excited discussion in Dutch, which ended up with: "All right, I will telegraph to my bank, but you will have to take the telegram to the post-office yourself, as I don't want the *concierge* to see it."

I asked him the reason for this, and he replied that too many people were interested in his affairs.

About an hour after I had returned from the post-office the ladies retired, and my uncle and I began a game of "five hundred"—an old-fashioned Dutch card-game. We had been playing for a couple of hours when the French maid of the relative walked in and went straight to the writing-table. She picked up the waste-paper-basket and began to walk out with it. Suddenly my uncle called out: "Where are you taking that?" The girl, who had not noticed us in the corner behind a large palm, stumbled and almost fell, obviously badly frightened, and then she stuttered: "To Madame."

"Just bring it here a moment."

She brought it, and Uncle removed the many papers that had accumulated during the day. He took out a very crumpled piece of paper, Charley's letter, which the worried father had thrown into the basket during our somewhat excited discussion.

"That's all right now, miss. You can take it to your mistress," Uncle said to the girl, and when she had left the room he turned to me with: "You see how I'm being spied on? Tomorrow she would have caused more trouble by telegraphing to Joe." She did, by complaining to Joe about "the insult" his father had inflicted on her.

The next morning we all left for Paris, my uncle and aunt by train, and my young cousin and I by car; but just before leaving I begged my uncle to take me to the Kann collection. He promised on condition that I would not talk about it.

During that two days' journey to Paris I was day-dreaming about the glorious prospect of seeing these famous eleven Rembrandts. The great master had been my hero ever since my early teens at The Hague, and, encouraged by my parents, I studied his work in the Dutch museums and collections. To assist these studies I read all there was to be read about him: principally in the Royal Library at The Hague. As all these reflections about the artist had a great deal to do with my uncle's final decision about the Kann collection, and, as Rembrandt's pathetic story is worth telling, I cannot resist the temptation of paying my humble tribute to his memory by giving an outline of his tragic life.

Rembrandt Harmenszoon (son of Harmen) van Rijn, the highly educated son of a well-to-do miller near Leyden, settled in Amsterdam when he was twenty-eight years old, and in a very short time he became the foremost portrait painter of that wealthy city. Within three years he had become the most successful painter in Holland, and when he married the beautiful Saskia van Uylenborch—daughter of a wealthy Frisian family—he was already considered a good match for the charming young lady, who had the considerable dowry of forty thousand gulden. A few years after his marriage Rembrandt bought the now famous house in the Joden Breedstraat (Jew's Broad Street). His studio was frequently the meeting-place of his art-loving friends and patrons, and as he was a well-informed collector of ancient art, the house was soon filled with works of art from the Greek and Roman classics to the masterpieces of the Italian Renaissance.

In 1642, when he was at the height of his prosperous career, the quarrel over Rembrandt's most famous work, known as the "Night Watch," practically put an end to his lucrative portrait-painting of the wealthiest merchant-princes in Europe; and it is a tragedy that this picture, infinitely more valuable than pictures that Duveen Brothers at times sold for sums around £200,000, caused the great artist's ruin (see illustration).

Rembrandt had undertaken to paint this picture for the officers of the Kloveniers Doelen ("Culverins' Butts" or "Targets for Their Firearms," the historic name of one of the ancient companies of civic guards). These officers, sixteen in number, agreed to pay Rembrandt 1,600 gulden (£130) for the large work. The artist gave his best to what was to become his greatest creation; but when it was finally shown to the sixteen patrons it provoked sharp criticism. These dignitaries had expected that they would be perpetuated in the usual stately ranks; but fortunately for us the artist had thought more of the grandeur of his picture than of the traditional stiff conventions for such works. The ensuing displeasure cost Rembrandt the patronage of his wealthy and open-handed patrons, and his large income derived from portrait painting was reduced almost to nothing. His great picture was hung in a position inferior to that given to works by second-rate artists. Broad strips were cut from it, to fit it in between the works of these lesser masters. Worse still, as the years passed, the rich guild of the Kloveniers lost its wealth and influence through the gradual loss of Amsterdam's leading position in the world's commerce. Their club-house, the Kloveniers

Doelen, for centuries the social centre of the wealthiest Dutch merchants and landowners, became towards the end of the seventeenth century a common drinking place and auction rooms, with the result that the lower edge of the picture was damaged in many places. At some time between 1715 and 1720 it was removed with its companion pictures to Jacob van Kampen's great Town Hall. However, the worst period in the picture's history was during the latter end of the eighteenth century and the middle of the nineteenth. During these dark years it was several times "cleaned"—at times even scoured—by various painters and "restorers." Moreover, the coats of varnish increased as the previous coats darkened. Gradually this hid the true colours of the painting. Rembrandt's original "Culverineers' Festive Progress," in all its colourful pomp, lit up by brilliant sunlight, became the dark "Night Watch," which I remember as a beautiful but very dark picture when I saw it for the first time in 1885 at the opening of the great State Museum. Even then, under the coating of innumerable layers of dirtied varnish, it was a thing of impressive beauty.

The thickness of this armour-like coating was demonstrated by the fact that when in 1911 a starving sailor tried to revenge himself on society by damaging the picture with a cobbler's knife, he succeeded only in scratching without penetrating the many coats of varnish. The "Night Watch" remained clad in its night garb until circumstances forced energetic measures. The picture had to be hidden in safe bunkers during the 1939–45 War. This had entailed removing the canvas from its stretchers and rolling it around a wooden cylinder. When in 1945 the canvas was unrolled the picture itself had not been damaged, but various parts of Rembrandt's original canvas were being affected by the decaying of a canvas which in

1850 had been glued to the back of the original canvas as a protection.

Thorough examination by the museum experts made it clear that energetic action was required, and after consultations with the official restorer of the museum it was decided to reline and restore. Thanks to the great knowledge of the committee and the outstanding ability of the museum restorer, the many difficulties were overcome, with the result that Rembrandt's greatest work was restored to light. The many coats of varnish that had hidden the glorious colouring for centuries were removed in spite of innumerable difficulties. What had become known as the "Night Watch" turned out to be a brilliantly coloured group of richly clad people emerging from an imposing gateway, an important feature of the composition that had been invisible before the cleaning. But the greatest revelation is the magnificent colouring, which, in spite of all the ill-treatment the picture had undergone during the two centuries that it was ignorantly and vandalistically misused, shows what magnificence Rembrandt had bestowed on this work, which before its restoration had appeared a sombre "Night Watch" lit up only by its golden tone, an effect mainly produced by the discolouring of its many layers of varnish. It was a courageous decision of the authorities, but it produced this happy metamorphosis. I had heard almost universal praise of this successful cleaning, but when I had already finished the manuscript for this book I heard of some strong criticism: such as that the beautiful golden tone had been lost. In spite of my age, I decided to leave my peaceful retreat and fly to Amsterdam to see for myself.

I have had many surprises, but when I beheld the restored "Night Watch" I was speechless. I can remember no occasion that had such a startling effect on me. Several art-friends had come with me to witness this first meeting; but I was in such ecstasy that I could only beg them to leave me alone, and promised to meet them at dinner that evening.

I remained with the "Night Watch" from a quarter past ten until five in the afternoon, only interrupted for a hastily swallowed sandwich. The first quarter of an hour I was unable to judge calmly, but then I realized that, in spite of the inevitable disagreements between *cognoscenti,* the museum commission and the official restorer had been more than justified by the result. They have given us back the joyful, sunlit scene as the master had conceived it. The great but somewhat sombre "Night Watch" had again become a sunlit festive progress with an undreamt-of wealth of colour and action. Moreover, the masterful, natural grouping has come into its own again by the clearing up of the dark patches. The expression on each face is as vivid as life. The great door-way of the Kloveniers Doelen, provided by Rembrandt's artistic imagination to give meaning to this moving, turbulent crowd, had been invisible before the cleaning. The central figures of the commander and the lieutenant now form a dominant note of action and colour. To demonstrate the difference between the colouring by the master and the "golden tone" effect of the numberless dirty, decaying coats of varnish, one need only look at a photographic reproduction of the partly cleaned picture. The left half of such a photo shows two figures in the foreground with a third in the background. The two faces on the foreground have been cleaned with the exception of a small portion of the lieutenant's face, and, with the exception of this small uncleaned portion, have a natural flesh-colour; but to show the vast difference between the colouring of these two portions, the right half of the lieutenant's tunic is shown in its uncleaned state, and so is the figure in the background.

Before the cleaning this figure was a meaningless object of no importance to the composition. The difference made by the cleaning of this previously insignificant fragment is clear; the figure appears as Rembrandt painted it, as an important part of the composition, for the now clearly visible musketeer is blowing the burnt powder out of the pan of the gun that he has just discharged.

Another example of the remarkable effect of the cleaning is the change in appearance of the lower portion of the lieutenant's tunic. The thick layers of varnish and dirt had rendered the surface quite smooth, and the design under the layers had become almost invisible. The embroidery with its arms of Amsterdam is now once again—to repeat the words of an eighteenth-century restorer—"in such relief that one could grate a nutmeg on it!"

It took over a year's work to soften the hard layers of varnish sufficiently before they could be removed by very small patches at a time with brushes and cotton wool.

Rembrandt obviously wanted to express the noisy character of this seventeenth-century parade, for the figure visible between the commander and the lieutenant is pushing back the still smoking barrel of another musket.

All these figures now appear as strongly portrayed, active characters with the unusual advantage of looking perfectly natural in their positions and activities in the start of their lively sally.

It is known that Rembrandt himself had stated that he strove hard to reproduce the most natural movement in his picture, and that he succeeded is strikingly borne out by the resurrection of this too long buried masterpiece.

After concluding my notes I took half an hour's rest at the hotel and then rejoined my friends for dinner, as arranged.

Almost immediately I found myself engaged in a hexagonal argument. On being asked what I thought about the restoration I said that I considered the result almost a miracle. Soon I heard the words "but the golden tone has been lost." I pointed out that this so-called golden tone had been caused by the discolouration of the innumerable coats of varnish and the ever-accumulating dirt. My chief opponent—a very erudite collector—reminded me at the end of his argument that we never removed the green patina from an antique bronze. I replied that ninety per cent of this patina's value was due to the proof of antiquity that it was supposed to establish, but that the "Night Watch" did not require any proof. My friend generously agreed.

It is sad to think that such a miracle of beauty had a great share in Rembrandt's ruin; but an even greater misfortune overwhelmed the artist. His beautiful and gentle wife died after a short illness in that same fatal year. Her fortune had been settled on her by a pre-nuptial contract, and this contained several restrictions that she had no power to change. The result was that Rembrandt would receive the income until Titus, their only surviving child—then about five years old—should reach his majority at the then usual age of twenty-three, or until his marriage. There was another proviso to the effect that if Rembrandt remarried, the whole of the income should be paid to Titus or his guardians.

These restrictions had a fatal influence on the remainder of Rembrandt's life, but his difficulties had no effect on his art. He loved his art better than his life, and although his wealthy patrons had forsaken him for less self-opinionated artists who were willing to portray them as they wished to appear to future generations, he worked all the harder. He could not find peace of mind in his beautiful house, nor even in his studio where he missed Saskia's constant company. He walked the country around Amsterdam to portray great landscapes like the famous "Mill." [2]

In his much rarer studio work of this unhappy period it is noticed that here, too, Rembrandt had become a much more sober artist. He painted many scenes from the Bible, but instead of the almost violently expressive character of his earlier biblical subjects, such as "Samson Menacing His Father-in-Law," the atmosphere of these subjects is almost mournful. He suffers, and his inspiration is affected by his state of mind; but this involuntary expression of his own sadness raises his art to sublimity.

About 1650 he engaged Hendrickje Stoffels—a young countrywoman—to take charge of his large house and his young son, and this caused another change. From then onwards his art shows renewed energy, and the work is even better than that of his richest period of expression, which produced the ill-starred "Night Watch" and the "Anatomy Lesson." He had recovered a kind of domestic happiness, but, as life brings worries as well as happiness, he found that he could not marry Hendrickje Stoffels without making himself a beggar. Like most artists, Rembrandt loved beautiful surround-

[2] Sold by the fifth Marquess of Lansdowne to P. A. B. Widener, of Philadelphia, for the then record sum of £100,000. When late in the autumn of 1913 Mr. P. A. B. Widener showed me round his collection, I stood for a long time in front of this great picture. Suddenly the proud owner broke the silence by saying: "Yes, I know that I paid too much for this picture, but it has been such an advertisement that everything in my collection has been much increased in value." It would, however, be unjust to say that at that time the financier was only swayed by the idea of money. He wished his really great collection to be kept intact for the enjoyment of his fellow citizens, and his son "Joe" Widener worthily continued his father's example by enlarging that collection of rare treasures until it had become one of the most glorious collections in the world.

ings. He had never been a careful man with money, and he had many debts, mostly incurred to satisfy his love for collecting beautiful things. He had always been fond of good living, and a man of his artistic genius cannot easily change a luxurious mode of life for a more sober one.

In the absence of his lucrative circle of wealthy patrons the upkeep of his stately house had become a serious drain, and the income that his wife's settlement had left him—ample for a less extravagant individual—was more than swallowed up. He even increased his household expenses by taking Hendrickje's mother and aunt into his house.

In 1654 Hendrickje bore him a daughter, and it is typical that the work of this period shows that he painted with renewed energy, ever aiming higher. He used light very differently from his technique in his "Night Watch." In that great composition he had used light and shadow to enhance the colour effects, but in the work of this last period he used lights and shadows to strengthen the three-dimensional effects.

The newly found happiness did not last long, for in the same year that his little daughter was born, the Kerkeraad (church council) summoned Hendrickje Stoffels before them on the charge of living in concubinage with Rembrandt, who admitted paternity of the little Cornelia. This scandal set the ball rolling. His creditors, who, knowing his talents, had been patient until then, now came after him like a pack of wolves. The Weeskamer (orphan council) intervened to protect the interests of his fourteen-year-old son, Titus, and they ordered the house to be transferred to the boy. A few months later Rembrandt was declared insolvent, and, finally, his magnificent collection—including works by Giorgione, Titian, and other great masters of the Italian Renaissance—was sold by public auction. The whole contents of the house, including his collection, realized about 4,000 gulden (£350).

Rembrandt was forced to hide himself from his creditors, and finally took refuge in the low slums of the Jordaan, the poorest quarter of Amsterdam. The devoted Hendrickje did everything she could to help him. She even took a very small shop where she tried to sell her man's pictures for anything they would fetch; and many works must have been sold there for a matter of shillings, for Rembrandt was an indefatigable artist.

Small sketches of heads, which Rembrandt's glorious technique enabled him to paint in less than an hour, and which have fetched thousands of pounds during the last fifty years, must have been sacrificed in that little shop for half a dozen or a dozen stivers!

As the artist could not afford to pay models to sit for him, he took a delight in painting broken-down tramps and strays, who gladly accepted a morsel of food or a glass of gin, costing one halfpenny. Unfortunately, in his mental distress, Rembrandt himself had taken to the same consolation. This *klare Genever* (proof gin) worked its way into his strong constitution, and when in 1662 he lost Hendrickje, drink increasingly took the place of food. In spite of this, his work became ever greater, and his last known great work, "The Prodigal Son," once the treasured property of the czars, is by many considered the greatest work Rembrandt ever painted. He had then lost his son, Titus, who had died in 1668 at the age of twenty-eight.

I have never seen this last picture, but in his "Self-Portrait," of the Florence Uffizi, which was painted during that last phase, Rembrandt clearly demonstrates his astounding ability to represent character and soul, and confesses at the same time his sad degradation. Did he intend this little masterpiece to be a reproach to the cruel world that allowed him to perish in want and misery? If so, we can only hope that he knows that the smallest bit of his art is now a treasure almost beyond price, and that his name is honoured over the whole civilized world.

XXV

THE RODOLPHE KANN COLLECTION

ON ARRIVAL IN PARIS my uncle told me that he had already made his first inspection of the Kann collection. He had been deeply impressed by its beauty and quality, but had been puzzled by the pictures of the Dutch and Flemish schools. So far he had only dealt in pictures of the very decorative eighteenth-century French school, and was inclined to judge pictures on their decorative merits. He said: "These great Dutch masters are all right for museums, but I don't think that our customers, and particularly their wives, will like them in their rooms."

I pointed out that the wealthy collectors were thinking more and more of forming great collections with the idea of leaving them to museums, and the knowledge that their acquisition of renowned pictures was being published all over the world must give them greater satisfaction than the purchase of beautiful works to decorate their houses.

I could see that he was meditating on this matter, but I was so impatient to see the collection that I broke the silence by reminding him that he had promised to take me to it. He seemed taken aback, and I could only conclude that this promise must have come to the ears of Joe. His first words proved that I was correct.

"I'm sorry, my boy, but the others got wind of this, and they object to my showing the collection to any one. They did not mention you, but they know that I would not show it to Tom, Dick, and Harry. You must have mentioned it to someone."

I had talked to my young cousin about my Rembrandt recollections, and the chauffeur must have heard a good deal of this, as in that early Panhard model the chauffeur sat inside. When I told my uncle about this he seemed at first rather annoyed, but in the end he said: "I'll keep my promise, but we shall have to meet outside and then go to the house by fiacre."

When we met the next morning he informed me that he had arranged with his son John that in case of inquiries he would admit he had visited the collection with his father. As John and I were great friends of the same age and not unlike each other, this was a good plan. When we entered the magnificent house in the avenue d'Iéna my uncle took care to call me John several times within the hearing of the man who let us in.

Once inside the house I realized the exquisite taste of the man who had formed this great collection. Every object was a *chef-d'œuvre*, but it would take too long even to enumerate the beautiful and unique works we passed. When, however, we arrived in front of the first Rembrandt we halted. It was the portrait of Rembrandt's thirteen-year-old son, Titus.[1] I was fascinated, and I noticed that my uncle was thoroughly interested. No description can do justice to the enchanting

[1] Bought by Benjamin Altman.

beauty and character of this portrait; and as half a century has passed since I saw it, I cannot do better than repeat its description in the sumptuous catalogue that was published in 1907 for Duveen Brothers [2] by the Paris publisher Charles Sedelmeyer.

"The child is represented full-face and half length, in the fancy costume of a little Prince Charming, which sets off his youth and grace, a dark crimson doublet, cut square at the neck and held in place by shoulder-straps; a chemisette pleated at the throat; a necklace, and an open cape, trimmed with fur. Over his chestnut hair he wears a flat velvet cap, with a little feather fastened by a clasp. The face is gentle and affectionate; the large eyes express a tender sensibility; a smile hovers round the closed lips, the delicate chin retains the rounded outline of childhood."

We stood a long time in front of that bewitching portrait. I remember realizing that the father had not merely portrayed the boy, but that the character that he had been able to express in this picture had been borne out during the whole of poor Titus's all too short life. The father was already a ruined man when he painted this picture, and when later Titus succeeded to the income his mother had left him, he used every penny he could spare to save his father from the creditors who made him bankrupt. Fate, however, was inexorable, for the good son died at the age of twenty-eight, and this was the final blow to Rembrandt.

The voice of my uncle recalled me from my reverie. I heard him say: "That's what I call beauty of the highest type. Youth and charm that make you feel what the father must have felt."

[2] See Author's Note.

"I knew that you would change your mind, Uncle!" I called out almost triumphantly.

Unfortunately, the next Rembrandt we saw was the large (50" x 40") "Old Woman Cutting Her Nails"—another great work, but, although perfect from every point of view, the character that Rembrandt had so vividly expressed was most unpleasant. Before I could utter a word I heard my uncle grumble: "It's no use. I can't see beauty in ugly old women and ugly old men!"

He walked away and I had to follow, but after we had admired the glorious portrait of Giovanna Tornabuori, by Ghirlandaio,[3] I pleaded with him to give me a short time with the other Rembrandts after we had finished looking over the whole collection. In spite of his obvious dislike, he agreed. We spent a long time examining the unique treasures of this wonderful collection, but, strangely enough, the one that I remember best, apart from the Rembrandts, was a family group of an old lady and two younger people. This had been given the name of Van Dyck. This time I did the snorting, and then called out: "Never!"

"So you begin to agree with me about ugly women!" Uncle laughed.

"It isn't a question of the woman. That picture is not by Van Dyck, Uncle," I said.

"There's your cheek again! Do you know that these pictures have been judged by the greatest experts in the world, including Bode?"

"I don't care what any one said. That picture can't be a Van Dyck," and saying this I began to point out the inferior points, particularly the faulty, stiff composition.

[3] Sold by Henry Duveen to Pierpont Morgan.

As I have often said before, my uncle had the most perfect eye for beauty, and the moment he looked for weak points he began to agree that this could not be the work of such an elegant artist as Van Dyck. Anyhow, when my uncle subsequently raised the question of the "Van Dyck" it was honoured with the questionable compliment "attributed to."

When we finished our walk past the collection I reminded my uncle about his promise to give me a little more time with the Rembrandts. As he did not seem keen, I reminded him that I had made the long journey from Liverpool to please him, and that he ought not to begrudge me this little pleasure. I shall never forget the look he gave me, and I was expecting the well-deserved explosion, but before he spoke, I stuttered:

"Sorry, Uncle," and it was only just in time, for the thunder-cloud passed from his face, and, instead of the thunder-clap, I heard: "All right, my boy, I know what you mean, and I'll give you ten minutes to convert me."

But the ten minutes became nearly two hours. First I took him to the three-quarter-length portrait, then known as "The Savant." He looked at it a long time from various angles and distances. Finally he said: "Yes, that is a very fine and dignified work." Just as he turned away he asked me: "Why did you take me to this one first?"

I hesitated for a moment for fear of annoying him, but under those piercing eyes I dared not prevaricate.

"To prove that this picture of an old man is even more beautiful and certainly grander than the painting of a beautiful child, or—of a beautiful woman," I said.

The next picture we looked at was the portrait of Hendrickje Stoffels, which plainly showed that already at that time the kind-hearted Hendrickje's health had suffered from the constant worries and deprivations that were sapping her health and spirit. Uncle weighed up the character of the picture by saying:

"This shows plainly that he painted more than a portrait. He painted a soul as well."

I could have jumped for joy, but I refrained from any sign of it for fear that he might mistake it for exultation. I only said: "I knew that you would see the real greatness of Rembrandt if you would take the time to look at his work without thinking of its decorative qualities." Even then I feared that I had gone too far, but Joel Duveen was one of the few great men in his business who was always ready to admit a mistake and to turn right round without hesitation when he realized that he was wrong. His only weakness was his impatience and impulsiveness.

After leaving Hendrickje Stoffels I noticed that now my uncle carefully studied everything. He was quite a time in front of the large (52" x 66", dated 1665) "Pilate Washing His Hands," and called it magnificent. Then we arrived again at "The Old Woman Cutting Her Nails"; I was rather surprised at his stopping, and even more curious at what he was going to say now. This time he did not merely glance at the work, but he looked at it first from a distance; then he approached quite close and examined every detail. I felt that he was trying to overcome his first impression; and when he stepped back to look at it from various angles I sensed that everything depended now on the result of this careful study. I even wondered whether he would overcome a probable feeling of humiliation at confessing himself in the wrong, but he evidently had no idea of explaining anything. He merely said: "Jack, my boy, we must insist on having the whole collection, pictures included!"

I said nothing for fear that any words I could say might suggest "I told you so!" Fortunately, he was now in such a feverish hurry to see the remaining Rembrandts that he did not notice my silence.

"Christ and the Samaritan Woman," dated 1655, was examined and received the comment: "Not as great as the later ones," but when we reached the smaller works he showed his excitement again. The "Young Rabbi," who had obviously sat for the later "Bust of Christ," evoked sincere admiration. The diminutive "Head of St. Matthew," the "Bust of an Old Man," and particularly the "Head of an Aged Woman," were praised most enthusiastically as "little gems."

This intense judging of eleven Rembrandt pictures had the result of changing Duveen Brothers' plans. The senior partner overcame all hesitations of the other members of the firm, and within a very short time they arranged with Messrs. Gimpel and Wildenstein that the latter would accept a considerable amount of money in lieu of exercising their option on the pictures.

Shortly thereafter, the agents of the Kann family agreed to sell the collection to Duveen Brothers for 23,000,000 francs, at that time £920,000, or $4,600,000. I believe that Messrs. Gimpel and Wildenstein received £80,000 ($400,-000 for their option on the pictures. Unfortunately, as Rodolphe Kann had left no will, difficulties ensued which delayed official delivery to Duveen Brothers for over two years, and it was only on August 7, 1907 that the completion of the transaction was published. By that time a great deal of the collection had already been sold as secretly as possible, but, as the Duveens were all rather talkative, news of some of these sales leaked out. For instance, the most famous of the contemporary art-experts, Dr. Wilhelm von Bode—the discoverer of the notorious Leonardo da Vinci wax bust of "Flora"—knew as early as the early summer of 1905 that the great collector John Pierpont Morgan the Elder had become the owner of the magnificent Ghirlandaio portrait of Giovanna Tornabuoni, the lovely picture that my uncle and I had admired so much during that memorable visit to the collection. Bode used this knowledge in a vain attempt to retrieve a most awkward situation that had been caused by a more than tactless remark by his daughter.

Bode relates in his autobiography: "I saw at Bardini's (a prominent Florentine art-dealer) Ghirlandaio's magnificent picture 'Grandfather and Grandson,' [4] which causes an overwhelmingly pathetic impression by the contrast between the repulsively ugly old Ghirlandaio with his horrible nose and the lovely child nestling against its grandfather." According to Bode, he had taken his eldest daughter to see Morgan's collection at his house in Prince's Gate, London, and that the gallant old gentleman had insisted on showing the charming young lady personally round his treasures. Suddenly, Morgan's youngest daughter entered the vestibule with her children. A lovely boy rushed forward and jumped into Morgan's outstretched arms to kiss the beloved grandfather. At that moment Miss Bode, remembering Ghirlandaio's "Grandfather and Grandchild," whispered to her father: "Ghirlandaio, Father," but Morgan, who suffered from the same nasal disease as Ghirlandaio, heard the remark. He swung round and growled:

"What's that about Ghirlandaio, miss?"

Bode intervened with: "We were just talking about the magnificent portrait of Giovanna Tornabuoni by Ghirlandaio which you have bought out of the Kann collection lately."

[4] Louvre museum.

The purchase of the Kann collection had the expected effect on Duveen Brothers' transactions, and from that time their individual deals with clients increased from tens of thousands of pounds to hundreds of thousands of pounds.

To mention only one of these transactions, Mrs. Arabella Huntington, widow of Collis P. Huntington, the greatest American railway-builder of his time, was brought to the Duveen Paris galleries on the Place Vendôme by the Hungarian Count Baltazzi. Mrs. Huntington was reputed to be the richest woman in the world, having inherited $100,000,000 from her husband. Her house in San Francisco had been destroyed in the 1906 earthquake, and at the time of her enormous purchase from Duveen Brothers she had just received the insurance money for the treasures she had lost. She bought works of art out of the Kann collection for £250,000 in that first deal with Joe, and Baltazzi received about £10,000 for interesting the lady in the Kann collection.

XXVI

THE MAYERLING MYSTERY

THE NAME OF COUNT BALTAZZI, whom I have mentioned at the end of the preceding chapter, recalled to my mind a mystery that had puzzled me since my fifteenth year. This Hungarian count was suspected of complicity in the mysterious death of the Imperial Archduke Rudolf, only son and heir of the Austrian Emperor Francis Joseph. I was still at school in Belgium when the news spread among the older boys that the Imperial Archduke and his eighteen-year-old mistress, Baroness Marie Vetsera, who was Count Baltazzi's niece, had been found shot in their bedroom at Mayerling. In French and Flemish newspapers smuggled in by the day-boys we read all sorts of stories and theories about the tragedy, and several of the older boys, including myself, began to write blood-curdling tales on the lines of whatever version we believed. In the end everyone became tired of the constantly changing theories, but I remember that even after I had left school I held to the version of one of the French-speaking boys who "knew" that the Clericals had been responsible for the murder. At that time there were two great parties in Belgium: the Liberals, who were mainly Walloons; and their Roman Catholic opponents, the Clericals, who were mostly Flemish, and blamed the anarchists for the death.

In July of that year I returned home to enter the family business at The Hague. One of the first of our clientele whom I met was the very young Count Batthyany, then secretary to the Austrian legation at The Hague, and a member of the cadet branch of the great Hungarian family of that name. He came in with an even younger and very beautiful young lady. To me these charming young people looked like the figures in an old Dresden group. They had great taste and examined only our best pieces. We were soon discussing the various characteristics of the Meissen porcelain periods, from the Böttger era, when true porcelain was first made in Europe, to what was then the rather despised Marcolini epoch. From that day onwards Count Batthyany and his lady friend were almost daily visitors. From works of art we gradually passed on to discuss other matters, and one day I had the courage to ask the Count for the truth of what was already called the "Mayerling Mystery." I was surprised by the annoyance my question evoked, and he put me off with a curt: "These are matters that we do not discuss." The Count began to develop a great interest in Chinese porcelain, and, as this was one of my pet studies, I was able to teach him many interesting things about the various marks, types, and periods. I soon noticed that he was very interested in values, and one day I said chaffingly: "You ought to become an *antiquaire*." To my great surprise he answered: "One never knows." Not long after this he gave me another surprise by saying: "I am sorry that I could not discuss the matter of the Archduke with you the other day, but we have strict orders not to. If I did it would mean instant dismissal from the diplomatic service." A few weeks after this conversation I came into contact with the mother of the young

Baroness Vetsera. This lady, with her eldest daughter, entered
our front show-room, and from their remarks I soon knew
that they were knowledgeable lovers of old works of art. The
elder lady bought several beautiful works, among them a
lovely Dutch ebony-cabinet of the seventeenth century. She
gave her name as Baroness Vetsera; and although the name
startled me, I was able to hide my interest and promised to
have the objects packed as quickly as possible. A few days
later the Baroness came in to inquire whether her purchases
had been packed, and I was able to tell her that the smaller
things were ready and that the two large cases for the cabinet
would be finished that day. The two ladies walked round
again, and the mother had practically decided to buy a
Louis XV chimney-clock when several people entered. It was
the house party of the Baroness van Brienen van de Groote
Lindt. I noticed immediately that this leader of the Dutch
aristocracy had no friendly feelings towards the Baroness Vetsera. The whole of the party showed great interest in the two
Vetsera ladies, the Baroness van Brienen unfolding her *lor-
gnette* and closely following the bereaved lady's movements. I
felt very sorry for her, and in spite of the importance of the
Baroness van Brienen, I did not leave the Baroness Vetsera.
The Van Brienen party, probably displeased at being left to
an assistant, departed very soon; but then I had an unpleasant
surprise. The Baroness Vetsera tried to vent her annoyance
on me. Her friendly manner changed, and she began to find
fault with the cabinet she had bought, pointing out various
details that she said were in bad taste and out of style. At first
I tried to show her from illustrations that these details were in
perfect keeping with this kind of furniture, but I soon realized
that she had made up her mind not to take the things she had
bought. Finally she said that she very much regretted her pur-

239

chases and that she would not mind paying something by way of compensation. I told her that we never wanted customers to keep things they regretted having bought and that all she would have to pay was the cost of making the two big packing-cases for the cabinet; the other cases had not been made specially and would serve again. The lady paid the fifteen gulden (25 shillings) and walked out without another word.

For years I had no direct contacts with my pet mystery except for the periodical revelations of "the real truth of the Mayerling tragedy" which cropped up in the newspapers, and which always turned out to be inventions. Over twenty years went by. I had become sole owner of J. M. Duveen & Son,[1] had opened business in Liverpool and London, had married, and had opened a gallery in the rue Royale, Paris, early in 1912. One of my first visitors here was Count Batthyany. He had aged considerably and did not look very prosperous. He told me that Miss Harris, as his Viennese mistress had been known at The Hague, had treated him very badly. He had taken a good flat for her in Paris; and, as he had left the diplomatic service, he had decided to form a collection of fine old porcelain with the intention of ultimately selling it at a great profit. He had spent most of his fortune on this collection and was on the point of opening a place in the rue St-Honoré when Miss Harris picked a quarrel with him and ordered him out of "her" house. His advocate advised him that he would not be able to disprove the woman's contention that the collection was her property, and as his liaison with the woman had not only led to his having to leave the diplomatic service but also had caused a permanent break with his family, he was in a most difficult position. He was now eking out a precarious existence by selling pieces of old porcelain that

[1] See Author's Note.

were entrusted to him by collectors and dealers for sale on commission. At that time I had bought Lord Ripon's collection of old Dresden porcelain, from which I let the unfortunate Count have a few figures to sell on commission. He did fairly well out of the first pieces I entrusted to him, and we became very friendly.

One day, when we were discussing the Princess Stephanie, the widow of the Imperial Archduke Rudolf, who had remarried and become the Countess de Lonyay, I asked him whether the Archduke had been murdered or whether he had really committed suicide. He replied: "He did commit suicide; but he was driven to it."

"By whom?" I asked; but then I had gone too far.

"Mr. Duveen," he replied, "I have given my word of honour, and I cannot go into details."

About a month after this conversation a somewhat dark and sinister-looking sexagenarian walked into my show-rooms, and after looking round for a moment informed me that he was Count Baltazzi. He soon began to talk of the great transaction whereby my cousin Joe sold to Mrs. Arabella Huntington, on his introduction, £250,000 worth of works of art, and hinted that he could bring me many American millionaires during June and July, the "open season" for these wealthy buyers; but in spite of the great possibilities I did not like the man. The Count had been living on this reputation ever since his great deal with Duveen Brothers. Joe had soon become tired of this constant borrower on the promise of future deals that were never realized, for the American millionaires had soon found out that he was always trying to make money out of them by taking them to jewellers and art-dealers to see "princely" jewels and great art-treasures out of imperial and royal palaces. When a few scandals had with great trouble been suppressed after the victims had been shorn in some gambling-clubs, the Americans fought shy of the illustrious Count. What was worse, Baltazzi was himself an inveterate gambler and spent lavishly on Paris *midinettes*, and thus remained in a chronic state of penury. As far as I was concerned, I disliked him, but I could not help enjoying his anecdotes of high life in Vienna. I knew that he was suspected of complicity in the Mayerling tragedy, and I even hoped that some day he would tell me the real reason for the Imperial Archduke's suicide. One morning he came in, obviously in great distress. He told me that he had to settle a bridge debt before twelve o'clock, or he would be refused admission to one of the leading clubs in Paris. He wanted 3,000 francs (£120) and stated that he had already telegraphed to one of his relatives in Vienna; although he expected the money any minute, he could not risk being expelled from his club. At this point he broke down, and, knowing the irreparable result of such an exposure, I could understand his distress. I gave him an open cheque to bearer on the Paris branch of my London bank, and he departed.

Baltazzi never turned up with the money "from Vienna," and I realized that this swindler had successfully worked one of his tricks on me. I met him a few weeks later, and, as he could not evade me, he "explained" that his relative had been very disloyal to him, and he promised to come and see me soon! In fact, he did come soon. He wanted ten francs to pay for a taxi to take him to his apartment on the outskirts of Paris, and, to prove his honesty this time, he asked my *portier* to call a taxi for him. These little tricks were repeated several times. On the first Saturday in August 1914 he again came to me in great distress, which now I knew to be real. Mobilization of the French Army had been proclaimed, and I was returning to my hotel at Compiègne, intending to leave shortly to "take the cure" at Karlsbad. On the way out of Paris the car was held up at the Barrière, where crowds were reading the proclamation. My French chauffeur, with an apology, asked me to take the wheel because he had to join his regiment immediately. All Germans and Austrians tried to get out of France before war was officially declared. Baltazzi begged me to save his life and wanted a hundred pounds in English gold. He must have been well-informed, for by the evening no one in Paris would take any French bank-notes, not even the railways, as I found out when I wanted to take a train to Compiègne.

Baltazzi had already turned to leave after my firm refusal when he suddenly whispered in my ear: "Help me, and I will tell you the truth about Mayerling." I told him that I did not want to hear any more stories, and then he whispered: "His own father killed him!" This time I laughed in his face. He glared at me for a moment and then growled: "I am an idiot; I have thrown my pearls to the swine!"

These words were the last I heard from Baltazzi. As years passed the "Mystery of the Mayerling Tragedy" reappeared at intervals in the press; but, as usual, each "real truth of the tragedy" proved to be speculation or fabrication. The latest of these was the story, published in the summer of 1955, of the "American duel," to the effect that a furious husband had challenged the Imperial Archduke Rudolf to this form of duel, in which whoever makes the wrong draw has to shoot himself.

When I saw this "news" I wrote at once to Henry May, of Essen, one of the best-informed men in Europe. I knew that he had friendly access to the Princess Clementine Metternich-Sandor, the last survivor of the great princely family whose members had been rulers in the Austro-Hungarian Empire for generations; and I hoped that after all these years and the many revolutionary changes of the last half-century he might be able to ascertain the truth. His reply startled me. Just before my letter had arrived May had been the guest of Her Serene Highness for the week-end, and because of the "American duel" statements in the press he and his hostess had discussed the matter very fully; but although Her Highness had spoken very freely about matters that did not touch the Imperial family, she had carefully avoided discussing anything that might sound disloyal. She had given a good description of the Imperial Archduke: very good-looking and of charming manners; a brilliant extempore speaker since boyhood; rather romantic; and, like all the *jeunesse dorée* of that period, with many amorous liaisons. He was commander-in-chief of the Hungarian Army and very proud of his uniform. He had fallen under the influence of the extremely nationalistic Hungarian officers who used beautiful women to entrap those whom they wanted to embroil in their treasonable conspiracies. The Crown Prince became so dangerously ensnared that his only way out was by consenting to a *coup d'état* to establish an independent Hungary, with the Imperial Archduke Rudolf himself as the head of the government. His father was informed of the intrigue by the Austrian Army's secret service. The Emperor summoned his son to an audience; and it is known that he intended to clear up several matters with Rudolf, among them the Hungarian conspiracy and his application to Pope Leo XIII to grant him a divorce from his wife, Princess Stephanie of Coburg.

All this news was interesting, but not vitally important; but May's mention at the bottom of his letter that he hoped we might meet during his forthcoming visit to England revived my hopes. We met in Gloucester, and at lunch and during the drive to Whitchurch, where he stayed the night with me, he gave me further details. It appears that from birth Rudolf had been the victim of the disunity between the Emperor and his wife, Elisabeth of Bavaria. As an infant of five weeks he had been removed from his mother's care. Later, the notorious and open infidelities of the Emperor must have further affected the child's emotional development. What was even worse, in 1863, before he was six years old, he was given into the charge of an elderly tutor who was a notorious brute, Colonel Count Leopold Gondrecourt. The child was highly strung and the new tutor swore that he would cure him of these nervous traits; and in the process he used worse than Spartan methods, having pistols fired in the boy's bedroom at night, or forcing him to undergo military training in the snow before daylight. Finally the Empress herself intervened and threatened to leave Vienna for ever unless she was given complete control of the upbringing of her six-year-old son. The Emperor gave in, to the great benefit of the child. Young Rudolf was a quick learner and became a good linguist; he studied with great zest and soon knew how to apply what he had learnt. Before he was fifteen he had become a fluent extempore speaker, who in his public speeches dispensed with notes.

By the end of our journey I had gathered enough information on the life and character of the highly intelligent Archduke to fill a book. It was clear to me that the early removal of the infant from its mother's care, the cruel treatment of the six-year-old child by his stupid tutor, and the open enmity between his father and mother had produced an unstable personality and had turned the growing boy's mind into a fertile receptacle for agnostic nineteenth-century philosophies. Before he reached manhood Rudolf believed in nothing; he did not value life, and he laughed at the idea of a hereafter.

But the most important item was told me next morning during the drive back to Gloucester. I had asked Henry May whether he could throw any light on the exact cause of the tragedy; and after a moment's hesitation he said that there was one important report in existence which proved that a few days before his death Rudolf had had a fierce quarrel with his father. After he had spent some time in his father's study he suddenly rushed out, shouting: "If you do that, I will shoot myself"; to which his father shouted back: "If you do that, you will not be worth the bullet with which you do it." This had been heard unintentionally by the aide-de-camp on duty in the vestibule and after many years had become common knowledge. May commented that though it proved the decision to commit suicide, it did not disclose the reason for the threat; it seemed that the reason had died with the deaths of the son and the father.

Early in November 1955, while I was staying with an old pupil of mine in the Bavarian Tyrol, I heard from May that the Princess Metternich would be pleased to see me at Corvey Palace. She was anxious to show me her collection. I accepted gladly, and travelled north to meet May at the neighbouring small town of Höxter. As we approached the palace I was astounded by its size. It had been built in the ninth century for a son of Charlemagne; and the Chapel that forms part of the buildings was built for Charlemagne himself. The Princess received us in a large sitting-room, which immediately impressed me by the number of well-chosen *objets d'art*, and I soon found that this brilliantly informed lady could, in spite of her eighty-five years, more than hold her own in discussion on art and history.

After the tasteful collection had been examined, tea was served, and we settled down for a pleasant conversation, mostly about people whom we had both known in the good old days. When May led the talk round to the subject of Mayerling, the Princess began to tell us how the news had stunned Austria at the time. "I was only nineteen, but the sorrow it caused is still painfully fresh in my mind." At these words I thought that at last I was going to hear the solution of the question that had puzzled me for nearly seventy years. But I soon noticed that apart from a few details of lesser importance, the Princess avoided anything that touched on secret matters; and at the end I realized that this great lady had disclosed nothing that, as a surviving member of the intimate court circle, she might consider as a breach of loyalty.

The one vital question, of what had been the final cause of the Archduke's desperate decision, I could not ask in face of this loyalty. My expression may have betrayed some disappointment, for after a moment's silence the Princess added: "I am sorry, Mr. Duveen, but I cannot go into further details." My admiration betrayed me into saying: "A worthy descendant of the great Metternich!" I saw the sudden frown on May's face, who at that moment was standing beside the Princess's chair; but, to my relief, Her Highness's immediate reaction was a generous smile and the words in English: "Mr. Duveen, I take this as a great compliment as well as a proof of your kind understanding."

It was quite late that evening before we ended our conversation, mostly on art, music, and reminiscences of people we had known, and here again the Princess showed herself a worthy match even for that walking encyclopædia, Henry May.

We were taking leave of our hostess when she asked if I

would help her in a difficulty that had arisen over some Italian tapestries in the vestibule. Many years ago the beautiful wide borders had been removed from these tapestries to fit them into smaller spaces, and this made the edges, which until recently had been hidden under narrow mouldings, look very ragged. I said that it would be too costly to have the wide borders rewoven at one of the French State Manufactures; and even then they would not harmonize with the nearly three hundred-year-old panels. I advised her to surround them with a band of narrow dark-green tapestry that could be bought in Paris at reasonable cost. But then I remembered that the Princess had called these tapestries Italian; so I added that, unless I was very much mistaken, these tapestries were not Italian, but late seventeenth-century French, made at Beauvais under Béhagle, and therefore much more valuable than Italian ones of that period. The energetic Princess led the way, and after examination I was able to assure her that I had made no mistake. I pointed out the lovely quality of the panels, and I also told her that, with the exception of one similar set I had bought at The Hague in 1912, I had never seen early Beauvais tapestry of such fine quality.

"Oh, Mr. Duveen, how can I thank you?" I thrust down a momentary temptation and replied without hesitation that I was only too happy to leave her this souvenir of our very pleasant conversation. But as we walked to the door the Princess stopped suddenly. "Mr. Duveen, what was the next important point you wished to know about Mayerling?" "Only one point; and I do not wish Your Highness to reply if it should hurt your sense of loyalty."

"Then please tell me; and if I can answer it without doing injustice or injury to the departed, I will do so."

For a moment I hesitated; but when she continued: "Come on, Mr. Duveen! If I cannot answer your question I will tell you so." I said: "Would it be against Your Highness's principles to tell me what was the final reason for the Archduke's desperate deed?" Without the slightest hesitation came the reply: "The shame of being deprived of the uniform." These few words, like a flash of lightning, cleared up the whole mystery. They explained the last few words that father and son had shouted at each other: "If you do that, I will shoot myself"; and the retort: "If you do that, you will not be worth the bullet with which you do it." The Princess's words about the loss of uniform, meaning that Rudolf, who was lieutenant-general and commander-in-chief of the Hungarian Army, was to be stripped of all his military dignities, showed without doubt that the vital subject of his meeting with the Emperor had been his promise to lead the revolution for Hungarian independence.

Rudolf spent that night and the next day in writing farewell letters and making his last dispositions. On the second day he left for his hunting-lodge at Mayerling, where Marie Vetsera decided to share his fate, as her farewell letters prove. The next day the Archduke did not join the shooting-party that had been arranged; and during the night he carried out the compact by first shooting Marie and then shooting himself. The medical reports state that his death took place several hours after that of the young Baroness; but as these documents were notoriously concocted on Francis Joseph's orders, no reliability can be attached to them.

As for Count Baltazzi, if there was any foundation for the stories that he had anything to do with the actual affair, apart from his unsavoury character and his blood-relationship to

Marie Vetsera, it can only be that he was implicated in the intrigues by which the Hungarian nationalist officers had secured the hold over the Archduke and by which they compelled him to accept the leadership of the proposed *coup d'état*. At any rate, Baltazzi was banished for life from the Austro-Hungarian Empire.

XXVII

THE HAINAUER COLLECTION

ONE JUNE DAY in 1906 Herr Kopp came to Joe with
news. This dealer had risen from page-boy to *concierge*
of a Lucerne hotel, and had graduated from antique-dealer's
assistant to become the antique-dealer who "sold" Trajan's
Column to a wealthy American. The news he brought was
that Frau Hainauer, the widow of the greatest collector in
Germany, had placed the sale of the collection in his hands.
The lady was anxious to sell, but Bode, the Berlin Museum
director, had done everything possible to prevent the sale to
any one. He wanted to buy it for the Berlin Museum and had
even forbidden the few important Berlin dealers to offer more
than 1,250,000 marks, although he knew that the collection
was worth more than double that amount. These dealers were
afraid to thwart the all-powerful art-dictator and had promised
to help him. The lady, who knew from her husband that the
collection was worth much more, had refused to accept these
offers.

From that time Bode had kept a sharp watch and had
threatened the lady with the Kaiser's displeasure if she should
try to sell the collection to a foreign buyer. Kopp had made

251

use of Bode's absence, and approached Frau Hainauer with an offer to sell the collection for her at more than double the sum that had been offered. The two set out for Berlin less than four hours after Kopp had entered Joe's private office. During the long train journey from the Hook of Holland to Berlin, Joe carefully studied the catalogue of the Hainauer collection, compiled by Bode himself. Its treasures included European tapestries and Oriental rugs of the fifteenth and six-teenth centuries, pictures of the early Italian and Netherland-ish schools, sculptures in marble and bronze and terracotta groups and figures by the greatest masters of the early Italian Renaissance like Donatello and Rossellino, as well as glorious works by mediæval and Renaissance goldsmiths and jewellers.

Oscar Hainauer, who had made this collection, had built a large house and had decorated it with works by contempo-rary painters. His purchase of the collection of old art brought together by his fellow banker Jacques brought a complete change of attitude. Hainauer now became a collector who was satisfied by nothing less than the best. As Berlin representa-tive of the Paris Rothschilds, he frequently visited their houses, and learned and assimilated their refined taste; and he pursued his studies further in the great European museums. From this time until his too early death he bought nothing but the fin-est. He radically changed his collection and used the master-pieces he acquired in the manner he had seen in the Roths-child houses. He also profited from his friendship with Gustave Dreifus, an art-lover of consummate judgement whose collection was bought a generation later by Duveen Broth-ers [1] for over a million pounds. Among these connoisseurs he rapidly developed the taste and judgement that made him the most important collector in Germany.

[1] See Author's Note.

As early as 1879 he was already ahead of his contemporaries in his flair for picking the rarest and the best. He bought two fifteenth-century marble reliefs by Antonio Rossellino from an Italian nobleman at what other collectors, like Spitzer, regarded as a ridiculously high price. The purchase showed the accuracy of his judgement, for Spitzer, the collector-dealer, offered him more than double a few years later, but Hainauer had not bought to sell. This acquisition also established for him a criterion of beauty and authenticity which guided him as he built up his collection. Even the redoubtable Dr. Bode himself praised his "extraordinarily fine taste and keen eye."

Hainauer had made a great fortune, and in 1892 he retired from banking, intending to spend the rest of his life in forming a model museum of works of art which would be unique. He was planning a rebuilding of his vast house for this purpose when, during his stay in Paris in 1893, he felt the first pains of the malady that was to end his life within two years of his retirement, in June 1894. As he was dying, foreseeing the dangers that the ambitions of Wilhelm II might create for Germany, he told his wife that if the situation deteriorated she could sell the collection and that it was worth at least 3,000,-000 marks. As the years passed, his widow became increasingly perturbed by the threatening political atmosphere and the growing anti-semitic spirit that the Prussian aristocracy showed even at court. She discussed the position several times with Dr. Bode, who had finally made her the offer she knew was far too low; but she could not dispose of the collection elsewhere without annoying Dr. Bode and incurring the Imperial displeasure.

When Joe Duveen reached Berlin with Kopp the interview with Frau Hainauer was rather pathetic. At first she was terror-stricken. She had reflected on Kopp's offer. The prospect of Bode's ill-will and the displeasure of the Kaiser had caused her three sleepless nights; but when Joe made her an offer of 4,000,000 marks (£200,000) for the collection as described in the catalogue, she was very powerfully affected. She began to walk up and down the room. After a few minutes she asked whether she could have two days to think over this offer; but Joe insisted that he was offering more than double the sum that anyone else would pay and would not make a standing offer. If she refused, the deal would be off as soon as he left the house. He also warned her that the moment Bode heard of the offer he would use his influence with the Kaiser to make the deal impossible. "He has threatened me with this all the time," sobbed the lady. Finally she herself proposed that the deal should be completed immediately, since she could not afford to lose 2,500,000 marks to please Herr Bode.

News of the sale soon reached the ears of the Kaiser, who was furious. He summoned Bode for an explanation. At the moment the Emperor was staying at Wilhelmshöhe, and Bode had to pass through some minutes of the all-highest's displeasure for not having prevented this offence against the declared Imperial wishes. Bode explained that he himself had been tricked because the Duveens had forbidden the widow to communicate with him and had offered her three times as much as he himself had bid. He had been in London, and she had telegraphed her regrets to him only after the deal had been completed. Bode saw clearly that the Imperial displeasure was not decreasing during this explanation, and hastened to add that the Duveens had presented several important works of art from the Hainauer collection to the Berlin Museum. Even then the Kaiser's annoyance was not allayed, and he declared that he would stop the export of all works of art. The Imperial Chancellor, von Bülow, who assisted at this stormy audience, offered to issue an immediate decree prohibiting the export of works of art; but this did not suit Bode. He pointed out very diplomatically that their own museums, whose collections were still very inferior to those of the other European museums, would be the worst sufferers. They were still importing more works of art from abroad than were exported from Germany. If Germany should place an embargo on art exports the other countries would immediately do the same. The Kaiser realized that this would be the end of his dream of making the German museums "worthy of his glorious reign." The end of it was that, instead of asserting his Imperial displeasure in the manner of his hysterical "Mailed Fist" speech during the Boxer rising, he veered right round to his other Imperial manner. He bestowed one of his Orders on the head of Duveen Brothers, Henry J. Duveen, who returned this distinction to its Imperial Head during the First World War.

The Hainauer collection, although not so large as the Kann collection, contained only *chefs-d'œuvre* of the highest quality and the most exquisite beauty. From the monetary aspect the purchase of the Hainauer collection was much better than that of the Kann collection. The latter had been bought for much above the then reigning values, but the Hainauer had cost a bagatelle in comparison with the larger collection, as Uncle Henry told me shortly after its purchase. Its dispersal was easy and rapid and its contents were scattered among the great American collections, where they formed centres of distinction in the most distinguished company.

Kopp himself received the stipulated commission of eight per cent, which amounted to £16,000. He spent it that same summer by travelling around Europe with a harem of pretty *midinettes,* and at the end of that summer the £16,000 had vanished, a good part of it at the Monte Carlo roulette tables.

I myself had several meetings with this great adventurer, mostly to my disadvantage.[2] Kopp's end was miserably sordid. His princely career ended when he was arrested in Bavaria after a particularly dangerous deal. He was condemned to a long term of imprisonment, and when he came out of prison he appealed to Joe, although he had swindled him out of a considerable amount of money since the Hainauer transaction. Joe sent him £800 to enable him to start again, but it was of no use. The imprisonment had changed the handsome adventurer into a broken old man, and he died in great misery shortly after the outbreak of the First World War.

[2] For the story of his "sale" of Trajan's Column in Rome to a credulous American collector, see my *Art Treasures and Intrigue*, Chapter VI. One of his love-intrigues cost him a priceless Frederick the Great snuffbox that had been entrusted to him (James Henry Duveen: *Secrets of an Art Dealer* [New York: E. P. Dutton & Co.; 1938], Chapter X).

XXVIII

OPEN WARFARE

FOR SOME TIME after the powder-blue affair—when Joe had made Mr. Lever think I was a trickster—I did not go near Duveen Brothers,[1] but Uncle Henry insisted that I let bygones be bygones, so gradually business recommenced. One day as I was discussing a transaction with Joe in his private office he asked me whether I had bought anything important in Nankin porcelain lately. He explained that one of their old customers for blue-and-white had begun to buy again. I answered that my stepfather had sent me from Holland a very important set of five Nankin vases, but that they were at that moment under consideration by one of my customers. He asked me to let him know if my client should not buy the vases. The next morning I saw Sir William Bennett at the usual hour of breakfast, at 8:30. I noticed at once that something was wrong, and I had confirmation when he said that he was annoyed at my having mentioned to Joe Duveen that I was trying to sell a fine set of Nankin vases to him. I told Sir William exactly what had happened and particularly that I

[1] See Author's Note.

had not mentioned his name. I asked whether any of his servants could have told Joe; but the next answer brought the solution. Larkin, the Oriental specialist, had told Sir William
that he had heard from Joe Duveen that I was selling an important set of five Nankin vases to Sir William. I realized that
Joe had been in earnest when he had told his father that he
would some day take my two best clients from me. He had
mentioned Mr. Lever and Sir William Bennett to his father
when he had uttered that threat.

Mr. Lever had been the first, and now he had tried Sir
William Bennett. I was furious. I told Sir William that it was
now clear that Joe had made up his mind to ruin me and that
this underhand attempt was another of his machinations. I
made up my mind then and there that I would now open a
gallery in London, a step which my uncle Joel had advised
me to take for some time, but which I had hitherto refused for
the sake of peace in the family. I told Sir William, who agreed
that it was the right thing to do; and he also decided to purchase the Nankin vases. I went to see my uncle Joel and told
him my plans. He guaranteed an overdraft for me at the Bank
of Liverpool and asked his second son, Charles, to lend me
eight large show-cases that were not being used at the moment
so that I could make a good show with the powder-blue collection. I rented a roomy first floor in an old Georgian mansion
in Dover Street and opened my gallery. My first exhibition was a great success; but with the exception of an important pair of cylindrical vases that were sold to the late Gaspard
Farrar, the powder-blue collection remained unsold. Joe had
the few London dealers in Oriental porcelain "in his pocket,"
and whenever a piece of powder-blue came into the open
market there was no bidding by the dealers. Joe, who was
already the unchallenged master of the London art-business,

went about boasting that he would ruin me. Then, by good fortune, I bought the four black vases,[2] which I felt sure would make a great difference to me. My uncle Joel advised me to offer them at once to Pierpont Morgan, who was staying at his London house in Prince's Gate. In reply to my letter an appointment was made, and I went to see the great man, but I was unprepared for the meeting with him. I had heard of a disfigurement, but what I saw upset me so thoroughly that for a moment I could not utter a word. If I did not gasp I must have changed colour. Mr. Morgan noticed this, and his small, piercing eyes transfixed me with a malicious stare. I sensed that he noticed my feelings of pity, and for some time that seemed centuries we stood opposite each other without saying a word. I could not utter a sound, and when at last I managed to open my mouth I could produce only a raucous cough. He grunted. Then I showed the large photograph I had brought.

"This is a picture of the vases about which I wrote you, Mr. Morgan."

He snatched at the print, glanced at it and rapped out: "How much?"

"Twenty-two thousand pounds."

"Much too dear."

Turning his back on me, he walked away. It was devastatingly final, but I was never more relieved in my life to be in the open air again after that nightmare of an interview. I thought that his obvious unwillingness to consider the vases was a revenge for my pity; but later I heard that on receipt of my letter he had asked advice from Uncle Henry, and that my uncle was in the house at Prince's Gate when I arrived. The secretary who accompanied my uncle was present during his conversation with Morgan, and repeated it to me.

[2] Chapter XXX, "Benjamin Altman."

"Doctor Bushel [3] told me that these vases are very fine," Morgan had said.

"They look fine at a distance, but they are very coarse, and the young man asks a ridiculous price for them. He is mad," was my uncle's uncharitable reply. Uncharitable, because he had never seen the vases.

"Henry, can you conscientiously tell me that I don't require them for my collection?" asked Morgan.

"I give you my word that they are not good enough. You have much finer black vases."

For a long time I felt annoyed with myself for my weakness in allowing myself to be discomposed by Mr. Morgan's features; but I regained my self-respect when I heard of his meeting with Pope Pius X. A well-known Italian journalist who took Morgan to this audience tells the story. He was a trusted friend of both these great men, and, as the Pope did not know any more English than Morgan did Italian, the friend was to interpret. The sight of that incredible nose had the same effect on the Pope as it had on me, and evidently with the same reaction from Morgan. Both men were nervous and silent. Not even a word of greeting was exchanged. They both sat down by a desk.

"When the silence began to become painful," relates Signor Salvatore Cortesi, "I decided to apply extreme measures to save the situation. Taking my courage in both hands, I addressed the Pope in Italian: 'Does not Your Holiness think that it would please your visitor'—I purposely avoided mentioning names—'if you were to tell him how much you appreciate his kindness in wishing to visit you and pay you his respects in person?'

" 'Oh, yes, yes,' he exclaimed in Italian. 'Tell Mr. Mor-

[3] The great expert and author on old Chinese porcelain of that period.

gan how much I appreciate his kindness in coming to visit me and pay me his respects in person.'

"I translated the phrase to Mr. Morgan in English and he, though obviously pleased and relieved that Pius X had been the first to speak, was evidently at a loss for a reply. Again I came to the rescue of the two illustrious personages. Turning to Mr. Morgan, I suggested: 'Don't you think that you might tell the Holy Father how glad you are at making his personal acquaintance, and how much you appreciate his kindness?'

"Mr. Morgan repeated what I had said almost word for word. The ice had now been broken, and with a little more assistance to both sides the conversation took a normal course. It lasted over half an hour." [4]

But Joe had not done with me yet. During the summer of 1909 Edmund, an old Liverpool friend of mine, came to see me in my small gallery in Old Bond Street. He told me that he had made the journey specially to warn me of another plot against me. He had been staying a few days at Harrogate and had bought an engagement ring from a mutual friend, an art-dealer and jeweller, whom I shall call Tom. Joe was also staying at Harrogate and had visited Tom, who was an old friend of the family. Joe saw a small but fine collection of blue-and-white Nankin that I had sent on approval to Tom. Joe exclaimed: "Those are Jack's, I suppose." Tom admitted this, and then Joe let fly. "You be careful. He's a thief, and he'll cheat you! I hate him like poison, but I'll ruin him!"

Tom replied that he had done business with me for many years and that he had found me to be of complete integrity; but this angered Joe even more, who went on trying to stop

[4] This account of Pope Pius X's and my meetings with Pierpont Morgan was also included, in substance, in my *Art Treasures and Intrigues*, pp. 147–9.

Tom from doing business with me. After Joe had gone Tom was very upset, for he felt that Joe had meant what he said. Tom was in a quandary, for he had been an intimate friend of the family for many years and at my uncle's house was treated as a member of the family. When he had opened a jeweller's shop in Harrogate I had helped him to start an antique-business as well, by sending him quantities of beautiful things "on sale or return," and he had created a good clientele for good-class antiques.

A few days passed, and Joe's violent threats continued to worry Tom increasingly. One afternoon the late Marquess of Ripon came in for his usual afternoon chat, and as this old collector knew us all, Tom decided to ask his advice. The result was that Lord Ripon told him that it was his duty to warn me. Shortly after His Lordship's departure Edmund had come in to buy the ring, and as this was another mutual friend, Tom had asked him to warn me.

I could see no other way to stop this persecution than by taking legal proceedings. I was still hesitating about this when one of my younger cousins came in. I knew that he had been present when Joe had uttered his accusations against me, and I asked him about it. He admitted that even he had been up-set by Joe's violence, and, when I asked why he had not stopped Joe, replied: "You know what Joe is when he is in a temper."

I hesitated no longer. I took action and briefed Sir Edward Carson—later Lord Carson—and Rufus Isaacs—later Marquess of Reading. Shortly after accepting my brief Rufus Isaacs was appointed Solicitor General and had to give up all his other work; so I briefed F. E. Smith, K.C.—later Earl of Birkenhead. Joe briefed O. M. Hogg, K.C.—later Lord Hailsham.

My case was lost before it came into court. Some of my witnesses were suborned; one of them was bribed to go on a long voyage before he could be subpoenaed. One of Joe's legal representatives visited my friend Tom at Harrogate and pointed out that he was doing a very foolish thing by going against Duveen Brothers, who could "do him a great deal of good but also a great deal of harm." Tom refused to sell me, and when in court Sir Edward stigmatized this visiting of plaintiff's chief witness as grossly improper professional conduct, Mr. Hogg jumped to his feet and appealed to the Judge. The Judge ruled that for a legal representative of defendant to visit plaintiff's witness was highly improper professional conduct.

Mr. Hogg very cleverly used every opportunity to make it appear that this was merely a family quarrel with which the court should not have been troubled. This argument must have influenced the jury, for they awarded me one farthing damages. Joe had in effect won again, for I had to pay my own costs of over £5,000.

A few months later Uncle Henry was arrested on board the liner that had brought him to New York on charges, going thirty years back, of having defrauded the United States Treasury Department by undervaluing great works of art by as much as ninety per cent. And I suffered again, for Asher Wertheimer, one of the most respected Bond Street art-dealers, when asked by a reporter of a widely read newspaper who might have denounced Duveen Brothers [5] to the Customs Bureau suggested that they had not far to look because their cousin brought an action for libel against them a few months ago. The next morning that paper published this statement in all its editions, with the usual embellishments. I

[5] See Author's Note.

was now forced to take legal action again. Wertheimer took the course that my lawyer had foreseen and denied that he had made any such statement. This threw the whole of the onus on the paper, and proceedings began. But what surprised me most was that Joe let me know through a mutual friend that he felt sure that I had not done this. Such an unsolicited compliment from that source made me very uneasy. I reflected that Joe knew that I could now ruin Duveen Brothers by disclosing the real value of some very important consignments that had been imported into America and that his diplomatic move was intended to "soften" me.

Uncle Henry, having been taken ashore, had been released on bail; but the New York business premises had been occupied by the Customs Bureau, and an embargo had been placed on the whole of the valuable stock. Uncle Henry was taken seriously ill and was allowed to go to London. He sent for my mother, who had lost her husband a few months before and was now living there. He besought her to make me visit Joe, for they were anxious to have my help. I never refused my mother anything; and when she pointed out that her brother was in a very weak state I had to forget all I had suffered and went to see Joe at his house in Park Lane. As I sat down opposite him the memory of the misery that man had caused me even while I still considered him a friend at first prevented me from uttering a word. Eventually I asked: "What do you want me for?"

He explained that the owner of the newspaper was helping them very energetically in New York and that the publishers were anxious that I should drop the proceedings against them. I saw, of course, that Uncle Henry himself had not dared to ask me that, but that Joe, to whom "the end justified all and every means" was less proud.

264

I did not feel like discussion or bargaining, so I merely said that if it would help them in their trouble I would instruct my lawyer to withdraw the case.

The New York case ended by the infliction of very big fines on all the partners individually and on the firm as a whole. It cost Duveen Brothers £450,000.

Duveen Brothers decided to write off this great loss against the year's profits, which, although the New York galleries had been closed for more than six months, still showed a gain of £50,000. Unfortunately, Uncle Henry never entirely recovered from this shock. He was not the same strong, energetic man again, and he died eight years later at the comparatively early age of sixty-three.

The mystery of the betrayal was cleared up by another lawsuit. A New York barber brought an action against one of Duveen Brothers' American employees for a share in the money that the United States Customs Bureau awarded to informers in cases of this kind. The temptation had come when Joe ordered that the whole of the *real* New York business books should be sent over to New York. These had for obvious reasons never been there; but as the old import laws had been out of existence for some years he ordered the London office to send these books to New York. There they had been placed in the strong-room; but one day one of the American book-keepers, when Joe had bullied him too much, thought of a way of revenging and enriching himself. He had the key to the strong-room and could have access to those dangerous books at any time after business hours. He did not know exactly how to secure this modern kind of treasure trove, so he discussed the matter with his barber friend, who advised him. During the next few months he worked diligently during evenings and week-ends on the books and sent the results to the United States Customs Bureau, which began investigations. Finally, he received ten per cent of the money recovered by the Treasury and then refused to pay his barber friend; however, the barber won, too, and received what he merited.

XXIX

EXCAVATED TREASURE

IN 1908 I had been the victim of the Neapolitan Camorra, which blackmailed me out of a good sum of money after I had bought a very fine set of Chinese *famille rose* vases from the Marchese Imperiali. The vases were in danger of destruction, and a friend and I might have lost our lives if one section of the infamous secret society had not proved the old saying that there is honour among thieves. I have already told the details of how these unique vases and we ourselves escaped thanks to the sense of honour, amounting to chivalry, of the man who had blackmailed us.[1]

Not long after this minor naval engagement in the Bay of Naples, business took me again to Naples, and I had hardly arrived at the Hotel du Vésuve before I found myself involved in another adventure. I was just enjoying a very necessary bath after my forty-eight-hour journey when I heard someone moving in my bedroom. Italian servants are indifferent to the lesser conventions, so to prevent an untimely intrusion of a chambermaid I called out that I did not require any one at the moment. The bathroom-door opened and Don Enrico,

[1] *Secrets of an Art Dealer*, Chapter XX.

the Camorra chief who had fought so bravely to save us, walked in. He saw my annoyance, but his only apology was a childish grin. Then began a torrent of truly Neapolitan volume and incoherence. "The rarest and most important 'scavi' (excavated antiques) must be bought at once—this night. The property of a great prince who does not want the government to place them on the list of museum pieces. Worth an enormous fortune!" These were only a few of the excited statements that began in a mysterious whisper and soon grew into descriptive explosions of eloquence that must have been easily heard in the adjoining rooms and corridor.

In my helpless position in the bath I was unable to stem this torrent of words. Now and then I interrupted with shouts of *"Momento! Momento!"* but words had no effect. At last I seized the towel, and wrapping it round me by way of dressing-gown, stepped out of the bath and walked into the bedroom. My uninvited visitor followed me, and as soon as he had passed through the door I stepped back and shot the bolt before he had time to interfere. I began to dress hurriedly to the accompaniment of bangings on the door and almost anguished shouts of "Mistaire Duveen, Mistaire Duveen!" Now and then, when the banging and shouting became too hysterical, I replied: *"Aspettate!"* or *"Subito!"*

When I came out the excitable Neapolitan was almost foaming at the mouth. "Ah, Mistaire Duveen, how can you lose the valuable minutes? It is a question of life and death!" he spluttered. The question of life and death did not prevent Don Enrico from holding forth for another quarter of an hour with every possible and impossible exaggeration. However, I managed to extract sufficiently exciting facts from the unnecessary details to realize that I had to see these pieces. "The finest collection of 'secret' antique bronzes ever brought together; many more and much more important pieces than those in the 'Secret Cabinet' of the Neapolitan museum."

This meant works of art of the highest type, in spite of the too realistically erotic subjects of these bronzes. So great is the quality of these "difficult" gems of the ancient Greek and Roman masters that the frank eroticism seems to lose its repulsiveness, and nothing but an impression of art remains. Vast sums are willingly paid by the most respectable collectors for these bronzes, and this was the first time that I had a chance of buying such things. These considerations had flashed through my mind during the Camorrist's monologue, and I had nearly decided to go further into the venture when my pleasant dreams of interesting purchases were shattered by the realization of the probable illegality of the whole transaction.

So far none of my interjections and questions had been able to stop the talk, but when I said loudly that I was not interested the man's theatrical declamation suddenly subsided in a reproachfully wailed "But why, Mistaire Duveen?" I began to explain why the deal was no use to me; but as soon as he had gathered the reason for my refusal he began to roar with laughter. "I wouldn't do anything against the law, the law is with us!" He caught hold of my coat-button and said quite seriously: "If you like I'll get the mayor of Naples to deliver the things for you!" I took this for a typically Neapolitan "manner of speech"; but as not much later it was rumoured that some of the heads of the municipality were leaders of the Camorra, I do not doubt the real significance of the offer. The man convinced me in the end that there was no illegality intended, except the necessary precaution of the negotiations remaining secret to prevent jealous interference by other interested parties.

When I wanted to come to business I could not get a word

in until I had recourse to my previous tactics. I demanded in a louder voice than his own that we should go to see them at once. "Impossible, Mistaire Duveen!" It dawned on me that the "life and death" hurry was not quite so vital as had been represented. Don Enrico explained to me that we had to wait till dark and that then we would go with his own little *carozza* to the castle of the "Principe." I was to meet the carriage in Portici just past the Hotel Coppa Scopa at seven that night.

When the time arrived for my departure from the hotel I felt some misgivings about this nocturnal adventure with a man whom I knew to be a leading member of the dangerous Camorra as well as a man of violence himself. However, I came to the conclusion that it was safer to go than to refuse, for the two contradictory reasons that the Camorra was the law in Naples and that if they wanted to rob me there was no necessity for them to get me out of the town.

A little carriage was at the appointed place when I arrived, but I saw only the driver on his box. Not being sure that this was the right carriage, I was sauntering on when a slight whistle from the driver made me look, and I saw him nod to me. The carriage began to follow me slowly, and after a short distance it stopped in a curve of the street, which was not served by any lamp-posts.

"Mistaire Duveen!" whispered the coachman. It was Don Enrico himself who jumped off the box and made me put on a loose-fitting cloak with hood over my own coat. He invited me to sit next to him on the box, and we started on a trip over some of the worst roads I had experienced. I had to hold on to the metal bars at the side as well as to the seat to save myself from being thrown into the road. After some time my eyes got used to the faint light of the two oil-lamps, and I saw that the very violent bumps were caused by deep holes that broke up the road. My friend knew his road well, and he managed to zigzag round the worst places. It was a nightmare of violent bumps and dangerous lurches.

There is an end to everything, even to the bad roads around Naples of those days; and after nearly two hours of this seesawing mode of progression we stopped in front of a large stone gateway. The moon had risen, and I could see that great hinges still stood out boldly from the stone piers; but of doors or gate there was no more vestige.

We got down and my companion set up a lusty cock's crow. Owing to the constant earth tremors around Vesuvius, cocks are heard to crow at any time during the day or night in Naples; but I had also been told by a friend that at one time the members of the Camorra used the cock's crow to announce the approach of a likely purse. After half a minute the ominous signal produced nothing more terrible than a little girl who appeared from the darkness behind some trees beyond the gateway. "Hold," said Don Enrico, handing the girl the bridle straps.

"Let's go!" he whispered to me, and led the way over what had once been a wide drive but was now vegetation difficult to distinguish from the overgrown garden. After two hundred yards of this silent progress the path led under some high trees, and suddenly a dark mass of wall loomed up before us. Just before we reached it my guide led off on a much narrower and well-trodden path. This took us to a small door in the wall, which he pushed open without any ceremony. A light from an open door shone across the narrow passage in front of us, and almost as soon as I perceived this light it was darkened by someone coming towards the corridor. "It's me, Signor Principe!" called out Don Enrico.

The shadow retreated, and we entered a doorway giving

access to a small but gorgeously decorated room: lovely red velvet on the walls; curtains of the same material in front of the enormously high windows and doors; a perfect little collection of Italian Renaissance furniture, plain but appealing to any art-lover by its simple architectural beauty; a good eighteenth-century Smyrna carpet on the tiled floor. A few bronzes, set off by some pieces of good "Urbino" majolica, kept up the severe taste of the room, and a dozen wrought-iron candlesticks and wall-lights supplied a pleasantly vague light for this warm interior.

This faultless setting impressed me as only too professional. The room was too severe in style; it betrayed the dealer behind the scene. At the same time my brain was busy with the strange appearance seated at the table. The short, very stout figure rose as we entered. This man clad in a very loud silk dressing-gown was the only incongruous element in a too perfect room.

My guide's face was far from pleasant to behold; but this squat figure, with its overweighted head, enormous bushy eyebrows, and blue, unshaven chin, looked more like a dressed-up gorilla than a human being. Don Enrico presented me to "His Highness"; but apart from the title he mentioned no name. I did not believe the princely legend, but I acted up to their comedy with the appropriate courtesy.

The "Prince" began his story. "Found in 1775 in a dry well on one of our estates." This recital was enriched by much local colour and unnecessary detail, but I could not interrupt it. Finally I could think of no better hint than a look at my watch. His Highness understood, and without a change of expression on his forbidding face strode to a large *credenza* and opened the two doors. He signed to Don Enrico to take the things out.

There were fourteen bronze and two lovely terracotta groups. I examined them as they were placed on the table and saw that every one of these pieces was a peerless work of art. I had never in a long and varied experience beheld such beauty. The subjects were not such as one could exhibit, but the glorious art of these ancient artists brushed aside all idea of pornographic intent. Don Enrico had been right when he told me that they were finer than anything in the "Secret Cabinet" of the Naples museum; only two of them were anything like those I had seen before.

I had lost all thought of the two people near me while I examined these gems by the trying light of the flickering candles, until Don Enrico could not restrain his impatience and broke in on the silence with: "I told you that you would be enchanted!"

I looked up and caught the fleeting stare of reproof on the face of the "Prince." He evidently knew something about the higher methods of selling works of art. The time for action had come. "How much do you desire for the collection?" I asked the "Prince."

As a rule, an Italian when faced with such an abrupt question studies the buyer's face first, and if he asks a price at all he soars into ridiculous heights of exaggeration. This man, however, was evidently of a less childish calibre, for without the slightest hesitation he said: "Fifteen thousand pounds for the sixteen pieces, delivered free on board."

After all, here was a man after my own heart. He knew what he wanted and asked a price that suited me. "*Va bene,*" I said. The "Prince" did not move a muscle, but I could not help noticing the startled look in my companion's face at this unheard-of way of doing business. I took out my cheque-book; but as soon as the "Prince" saw this he waved his hand and

shook his head. "Cash," he said, as he made a significant gesture with his thumb and index finger. At the same time a light
smile flickered across his features for the first time. In Italy,
particularly in those days, cheques were little used. I knew
this, and his refusal of a cheque did not ruffle me in the least,
so I produced 2,000 lire (£80 at that time).

"I will pay you this on account and tomorrow I will bring
the rest," I said. He picked up the notes without looking at
them, merely saying: "I will have the collection delivered to
you at your hotel tomorrow morning at eleven." As he did
not even suggest giving me a receipt for the money I glanced
at Don Enrico, who gave me a reassuring nod.

The "Prince" bowed and walked towards the door, clearly
signifying that the matter was at an end for that evening. My
companion observed that I did rightly in not asking for anything in writing, but wanted to know why I did not offer him
half first. I replied that I did not think that he was the man to
try hard bargaining with. "You don't know our people!" observed the Camorrist with unconcealed disgust.

It was past two in the morning when we arrived at the
hotel, and my companion, who had remained silent during
the last few minutes, said: "Mistaire Duveen, what about my
ten per cent?" Obviously he had concluded that I was a fool
because I had bought for such a vast sum without bargaining.
When I observed that the deal had not yet been concluded
he retorted that he had done his part and that he would see to
it that the deal was carried out. He added, as an additional
argument, that he would take a cheque. When I told him that
there was nothing doing until the deal was concluded his childish grin betrayed his inward agreement with my caution, and
with a friendly good-night he drove off.

The next morning I went with my letter of credit to one of

the big banks and drew the money. Punctually at eleven, two gentlemen were announced and were shown into my sitting-room. The "Prince" looked very smart, and his forbidding look was not so repulsive in the sober hues of modern tailoring as it had been in the flamboyant silks of the previous evening. Don Enrico had surpassed himself. His get-up must have been intended as a compliment to his English friend, for he was dressed in a yellowish Norfolk jacket, reddish-brown riding breeches, an even more incongruous cap, and light-grey sporting stockings, set in white, pipe-clayed shoes. I must admit that I was rude enough to stare at the shoes; and when I looked up I caught the only other smile I ever saw on the face of the "Prince."

After a few preliminary words two trunks containing the collection were brought up to my sitting-room. As soon as they had been unpacked I began to take the groups, one by one, to the window in my bedroom, as the light in the sitting-room was not good.

After I had examined the third I got a shock: these three pieces, although of three different periods, had something in the modelling of certain unimportant details which seemed to point to the same artist for all three. I took a magnifying glass out of my pocket and examined every detail. Everything, including the ancient patina, was perfect: not the slightest trace of faked surfaces; in short, nothing to prove any piece wrong, only that baffling, almost imperceptible likeness in little details.

Every group represented a different scene or act, and in each one the figures, the poses, and the style of execution were totally different. Only in the nails of the hands and feet, as well as on the navels of all the figures, was there that baffling, almost imperceptible likeness. It was so minute that the man who was responsible for it had not noticed it himself; but its significance was so great to the trained observer that the artist might as well have signed these three pieces with the same name. The examination of the other pieces did not take me long; I did not have to carry them into my bedroom, for a glance at each of them was sufficient. Every one carried the same "signature."

For a moment I was in a quandary. It was clear to me that the whole of this collection had been made to pass as classical antiques by the same hand. The further fact that the patina differed in every one made the whole thing even more sinister. I stood before a very unpleasant quarrel with this unreal "Prince" who had the very real power of the Camorra behind him. Still, I could not dream of giving away £15,000 even to such a fearsome combination.

I decided to use sweet reasonableness. When I looked up from the groups I found the eyes of both my visitors fixed on me. The "Prince" was not scowling; he was just looking unconcerned; but this did not mislead me. I knew that he understood. Don Enrico's face exhibited frank astonishment, and I concluded that, at any rate, he was not so well-informed as his august companion.

I turned on a table lamp and placed two bronzes under its light. One represented a satyr teaching a young boy to play the pipes, Greek work of the third century B.C.; the other, a Roman work of the time of Augustus, portrayed the Rape of the Sabine Virgins. There was a gap of three centuries between the two pieces.

"Has Your Highness noticed the strange likeness of these small details in these two very different groups?" I asked very politely, pointing to some of the fatal characteristics.

"What do you mean, sir?" growled the "Prince."

"If you will give yourself the trouble to look at all these

pieces you will see what I mean," I replied, looking him straight in the eyes.

The scowl had come back before I spoke, but it now as-sumed such fierceness that I could no longer see his eyes; the brows had dropped over them as might those of our primeval ancestors. I felt violence in the air, and I was not mistaken, for the brute's arm shot out to the jaw of Don Enrico. It was only an open-handed smack, but this made it all the more in-sulting to a Latin.

"Idiot!" growled the "Prince," rising to his full height and broadening his shoulders.

"Bandit," hissed the Camorrist, as his right hand shot to his hip-pocket. For a moment the two stood glowering at each other, and I fully expected the ever-ready Neapolitan dagger to hurtle through the air. However, the proud bearing of the "Prince" seemed to shrink somewhat under the murderous stare of the Camorrist.

"Give those eighteen hundred lire back to Mistaire Du-veen!" Don Enrico's words sounded something like the lashes of a whip, and they had the same effect, for the "Prince" put his hand into his breast-pocket. Again I thought of lethal weapons, but the hand reappeared, holding a black-leather wallet with a large crown on it. The "Prince" placed the notes on the table, and as soon as he had done this Don Enrico hissed: "Get out!" The "Prince" bowed slightly to me and walked out of the room.

My honest Camorrist took two bank-notes from his pocket and said: "Here are the other two hundred, but His Highness will pay me my whole commission now before he gets any of his *porcheria* [filth] back again!"

Subsequently I made two discoveries. A dozen years later I met the "Prince" in a famous Florence club; he was a real prince, after all, and kept up his incognito by not remembering me. We played some very pleasant bridge, at which I lost consistently.

In 1934, when the first publication of my memoirs appeared, I was overwhelmed with correspondence from readers who owned treasures. Among them was one lady from the Midlands, who confessed to owning a rather embarrassing antique work of art, a terracotta group signed "Giustiniani." I had heard a good deal of this "Giustiniani" work, but had never seen any piece signed by this artist. He had made a speciality of working in the antique style at the beginning of the nineteenth century. The factory had been carried on by successors until the works disappeared at the beginning of the present century. I was anxious to learn, and the piece was sent down to me.

When I unpacked the small group I realized at a glance that I stood in front of another little masterpiece of faking by the same hand as the princely collection that I had nearly bought a quarter of a century before. There were the same characteristics that had saved me on that far-off morning in Naples; but this piece was at any rate honest because it proclaimed openly that Giustiniani had made it! Those that had puzzled me were unsigned. Clearly, the artist had worked for two distinct types of clients: for admirers of art for art's sake, and for art-dealing Neapolitan princes!

XXX

BENJAMIN ALTMAN

Henry J. Duveen had the same personal magnetism as his elder brother Joel, but he lacked the gift for effecting big sales at a first meeting. Joel made an immediate impression of combining great taste with absolute reliability, whereas Henry never tried to rush matters. He gradually impressed clients with his complete trustworthiness and usually made intimate friends of them. One of the best examples of this is his thirty-one-years' connection with Benjamin Altman, owner of one of New York's greatest department stores. It began one Saturday evening in 1882, when Henry Duveen was twenty-six years old and Altman forty-one. That evening my uncle happened to be the last to leave his gallery, and when he was walking towards the door he saw someone staring through the glass as if he were on the point of coming in. Henry Duveen could not very well stop; but on opening the door to go out he asked the stranger if he intended to look round.

"As a matter of fact, I was thinking of it, but I see that you are leaving and don't want to bother you." Henry told him that no one was waiting for him and that he would be very pleased to show him through the gallery.

My uncle soon noticed that his visitor knew nothing about

old art, but that he was obviously very interested. During the inspection the visitor explained by way of apology that he was a very busy man and that he never left his business until late. He very soon became interested in the descriptions of the various objects, and after nearly an hour of looking around and of friendly conversation, he said that he would like to buy some nice pieces of Chinese porcelain and that if he were treated decently he would buy from the man he could trust. "I am a very busy man and can come only on Saturday nights after the close of my business," he concluded. Henry Duveen assured him that he would meet him at any time and that whatever he sold he would always buy back at the same amount. This clinched the matter, and Mr. Altman began by buying a pair of Chinese enamelled vases at a modest figure. From then onwards the two had their weekly sessions on Saturday nights.

As time went on, the successful business man became one of the wealthiest department-store owners of New York, and with the growth of his wealth his purchases increased in importance. From articles running into hundreds of dollars the sums steadily increased through thousands into hundreds of thousands. The less important pieces were continually weeded out and replaced by the highest class of collector's pieces. Henry Duveen always took back previous purchases at the price Altman had paid. In 1893 this buying of only the very finest led to the purchase of the magnificent rock-crystal crucifix that my uncle had bought for over £6,000 at the auction of the Spitzer collection in Paris. Ultimately the transaction between the two ran into millions of dollars, and the result was one of the most exquisite collections that has ever been formed in the United States. It is generally agreed that although there are several much larger collections in the United

States, the Altman surpasses every one of these by the care that has been taken in bringing together only the finest obtainable. This was Mr. Altman's constant aim, and it was the great knowledge and perfect taste of my uncle Henry which gathered this unique private collection of true masterpieces. Because his space was limited Mr. Altman always sacrificed his previous best to make way for the better. The result was that when he died he was able to leave to the Metropolitan Museum of New York the most perfect collection of great works of art which had been assembled by one man. His helper had procured him the pick of the Rodolphe Kann and the Maurice Kann collections. Of Mr. Altman's fourteen Rembrandts the majority came from this source, as did the priceless little Vermeer that I had seen in April 1905, just before Duveen Brothers [1] bought that collection.

Apart from great examples of the Dutch school, Mr. Altman possessed masterpieces from the early Netherlandish painters; the Italian painters of the fifteenth and sixteenth centuries; magnificent portraits by Velasquez; the Holbein portrait of Margaret Wyatt; a portrait by Albrecht Dürer; unequalled Persian rugs worth more than their weight in gold; early Italian Renaissance sculptural works by Rossellino and by Mino da Fiesole; eighteenth-century statuettes by Houdon, Clodion, Falconet, and a terracotta bust by Donatello. Rembrandt's "Bathsheba in the Bath" is the most attractive picture among his fourteen works of that master. I saw that picture for the first time in 1888 when I was a boy of fifteen. Uncle Henry had taken me with him to see the Steengracht van Duivenvoorde collection at The Hague. The house was full of marvellous pictures of the Dutch school, but when we came in front of the "Bathsheba" I gasped and I heard my uncle

[1] See Author's Note.

whisper: "My God!" Ever since, this picture has remained engraved on my mind. Rembrandt painted it a few months after he had lost his idolized Saskia, and to the artist it must have appeared as a reincarnation of his beautiful young wife. The delicate flesh colours of the nude figure are just sufficiently draped to obviate any sensuous impressions. The graceful little figure, accentuated by a beautiful Persian carpet; the Negress at one side; all these further heighten the effect of the main subject. King David is watching the scene from a doorway in the background; a peacock on a marble stair and a landscape with part of the palace complete the background. Unfortunately, old varnish had rather toned down a good deal of the picture, but even this could not lessen the effect of this glorious scene.

I do not know how long we stood there; but even after we had left it we returned several times. My uncle asked whether there was any chance of the Jonkheer [2] selling that picture, but I knew that the Steengracht family were all very wealthy and were still collecting. There were three brothers, and only the eldest, Baron Steengracht van Moyland, had an only son. I advised my uncle to see our old friend Jan Teunissen, who knew everything about everybody in Holland. Mr. Teunissen said very much the same but he also pointed out that according to Dutch law the estate would ultimately go to the only son of Baron Steengracht van Moyland; and as this young man cared little for art, he would be fairly certain to sell the collection if it came into his possession. This is what happened a quarter of a century after we had seen it. The then Baron Steengracht van Moyland sent it to the Salle Georges Petit, the foremost art-auctioneers in Paris, where it was put up for auction in the early summer of 1913.

[2] Title of the younger sons of a noble family.

Of course, Henry Duveen was there. The auction created several records. The "Bathsheba," even darker than when we had seen it twenty-five years before, was the chief treasure. Henry Duveen bought it for £44,000, and when it had been knocked down to him, he whispered: "I don't think that I could have stopped bidding." The true family failing! In less than a quarter of a century that picture would have fetched three times as much, but it was then safe in the Metropolitan Museum of New York, for its owner had died about a year after he had acquired it.

I have very pleasant personal recollections of Mr. Altman. In the early summer of 1909 I travelled to Karlsbad on the advice of my cousin Charles to offer my four unique black Chinese porcelain vases to him. I was quite surprised at the simple friendliness with which he received me. After telling him the reason for my call I showed him the photographs and told him that I wanted £22,000 for the vases. He examined them closely and then asked me whether the vases were really early K'ang-hsi, with a strong emphasis on the "early." I told him that they had been brought over from Holland by William III, to whom they had been sent as a gift by the Emperor of China when he was appointed Stadholder of Holland and Zeeland in 1673, and that the vases had remained at Kensington Palace until 1837, when the Duke of Cumberland had left his London residence to occupy the throne of Hanover. Before leaving London he had presented these vases to his English mistress, from whose last descendant I had bought them.

"As K'ang-hsi only came to the throne of China in 1662, when he was eight years old, the vases must be early K'ang-hsi," observed Mr. Altman to my surprise. Here was evidently a well-read American business man, and this moved me to tell

him that the previous year I had sold these vases to Mrs. Arabella Huntington for £22,000, but that the next day she had
come back to look again at the vases and had then informed me
that she did not want them. I also told Mr. Altman that my
cousin Charles knew that his brother Joe had stopped Mrs.
Huntington from buying these vases.

"Yes," commented Mr. Altman, "he is very jealous of
any one doing business with her," and after a moment he
added: "But I am not Mrs. Huntington." We both laughed
at this, and it was then arranged that I should reserve the vases
for him until his arrival in London in a few weeks.

Mr. Altman invited me to stay to lunch, during which we
conversed on works of art in general and on Chinese porcelain
in particular. I think it was because of this talk that he asked
me whether I was likely to come to New York, and when I
replied that I hoped to go there next year, he said: "I should
like you to come and see my collection. I think that I can
show you some pieces that you will think unique."

A few weeks after this interview Mr. Altman let me know
that he had arrived in London, and that he would call the next
morning. I had the vases placed in the best daylight, and
when he arrived there was no mistaking his admiration. He
took one of the vases in his hands and examined it by letting
the light play over every inch of it. After subjecting all the
others to the same scrutiny, he said: "Look here, young man,
we may do a good deal of business in the future, so what is
the lowest price you will take for them?" I answered that we
both knew that these unique vases were cheap at £22,000
and that I was sure that he would never regret buying them.

"Very well," he said, "I'll let you know tomorrow," and I
felt that he meant to buy them. The next morning he let me
know that he had changed his mind!

I suspected Joe, but for years I did not even guess how he had been able to stop first Mrs. Huntington and then this very experienced collector from buying these glorious vases. In the case of Mrs. Huntington I had been told by a former secretary of Joe that he had used a trick that amounted to criminal conspiracy, but that he dared not tell me the details. In the end I found out. The whole matter had been very easy from Joe's point of view. When I bought the vases the owner had made the condition that I should have four copies made to take the place of the vases, which all her friends were going to miss. I took one of the vases to Paris to have this done, and tried to arrange that no other copies should be made. The firm refused this because it never accepted this condition, and as I believed that no one else could do it, I proposed that if they did make any copies these should be two inches higher than the originals. This was agreed, and I forgot all about the matter until one day a dealer in antique silver with whom I was quite friendly telephoned to me that he had something very fine to show me. I went across to his shop, and he showed me into a small room. He drew a *portière* aside and I exclaimed: "Copies of my black vases!"

"Are these really copies?" he asked.

"Of course," I replied.

The silversmith apologized and explained that he did not understand anything of antiques except his silver, but he thought that he was doing me a good turn by telephoning me. Many years later, I found what had really happened. Joe knew through one of my employees who was in his pay that I was trying to sell the vases to Mrs. Huntington. He also knew that four copies had been made for the previous owner, so he sent someone to order another four, but as the Paris works would not disclose the name of their original client, he had to make sure that they were really copies of my vases. That is why they had been planted at the silversmith's, and my first surprised exclamation had provided satisfactory proof. He also knew that I had visited Mrs. Huntington at Franzensbad and that she had asked me to show her the vases during her forthcoming stay in Paris. When the time came I arranged with a well-known firm of art-auctioneers to place a show-room at my disposal, and when the lady arrived the vases stood in a case in the middle of the room, strongly lit up, as Mrs. Huntington was very short-sighted. She was very much impressed, and when I asked £22,000 she said that she would take them on condition that they would be delivered to her at her New York home.

The next morning Mrs. Huntington telephoned me that she would like to have another look at the vases and would come that afternoon. When she did come she examined them very closely and told me that they were much coarser than she had thought. I believed that this was due to the fact that these early K'ang-hsi pieces were always much bolder in design than the later ones. I explained this, but she became very impatient and interrupted me by saying that the vases lacked artistic feeling and that she would not have them.

Five years later I opened a gallery in the rue Royale in Paris, and when Mrs. Huntington came in one day while I was in London she complained to my manager that Joe Duveen had stopped her from buying the finest black vases she had ever seen. She knew that the vases had since been sold to Mr. Widener, of Philadelphia, for £35,000, and she had been very annoyed with Joe Duveen. Only after Lord Duveen's death in May 1939 did I find out the whole story.

When Mrs. Huntington went into the Paris gallery of Duveen Brothers immediately after having seen my vases Joe told her that he knew that I was trying to sell those "coarse" black vases to her for a ridiculous sum but that he could not stand by and see her swindled. He took her to another show-room and showed her the four that I had seen at the silver-smith's place in London.

"I can sell you these for less than a thousand pounds, Mrs. Huntington, but they are not good enough for you, so be-ware!" Of course, the same deception was used with Mr. Alt-man, but I did not know how these tricks had been played on me until much too late.

Some time after the fiasco with Mr. Altman, Edgar Gorer, the London dealer in old Chinese porcelain, came in to see me and proposed that I should let him take the vases to New York, where he was going to hold an exhibition. Since all the machinations against me left me in financial difficulties, I agreed on condition that he should advance me £8,000 while he had the vases. This was agreed, on condition that I should sign a bill of exchange, payable three months after date, on the understanding that if the vases should not be sold he would continue to renew the bill until he had sold them. Gorer took the vases to New York, but when he returned a few months later he had been unable to sell them. As arranged, the bill was renewed, and when another three months had nearly passed I reminded Gorer of his promise to renew. He told me this was quite in order, but on the evening before the bill was to be presented he told me that he found that he would be unable to renew as he himself was badly in want of money. I saw the trick too late: I should be ruined if that bill were presented at my bank the next morning. As the vases were in Gorer's hands, I could not even try to sell them to someone else. Later, when Gorer had quarrelled with Joe, I heard that when the vases had arrived in New York, Joe had arranged with Gorer not to show them there and to force them out of my hands at the lowest possible price. This was easy enough, for the market for such costly pieces was very limited.

So the vases were "stored" in Duveen Brothers' cellars to make quite sure that they could not be offered by Gorer. He was only too glad to have any "friendly arrangement" with Duveen Brothers in New York, as he was a stranger on that market, and he knew their power there. Unfortunately, there is no honesty among certain people, for when Gorer had forced me to surrender the vases to him he informed Joe that he had bought the vases for Sir William Bennett, and when Joe reminded him of their arrangement Gorer pointed out that he had been forced to exceed the price that Joe had mentioned as his limit, £14,000. When in 1911, at the pleading of my mother, I had to help Joe in his firm's terrible difficulties with the American Treasury he asked me how much Gorer had paid me for the black vases, and when I told him, he exclaimed: "He was not even straight with us when we were friends!" But in spite of this case of "thieves falling out," I did not come into my own. Nor, for that matter, did Gorer, for Joe ruined him, too. Gorer was forced to take legal action for slander against him just before the First World War broke out. Early in 1915 Gorer had to go to New York for the case, and when returning in the *Lusitania* he lost his life because although he could not swim, he gave his life-belt to a sobbing woman; and when he had found another one he parted with this also to a Hungarian girl, who afterwards visited his widow to thank and condole with her.

This touch of humanity made me forget even my black vases.

XXXI

THE PASSING OF THE FOUNDER

Eᴀʀʟʏ ɪɴ 1906 the internecine quarrels between the partners came to a head. Joel J. Duveen, as founder of the
firm, still held a greater share than his younger brother, Henry.
Joel's eldest son Joseph (later Lord Duveen) had an even
smaller share, but these two junior partners now conducted
practically all the great deals, and they considered that there
should be a revision of the partnership contract. John Duveen,
Joel's third son, sided with his father, and Louis Duveen, the
fourth son, sided with the others. They could not arrive at an
agreement, and the matter went to the lawyers. The greatest
leaders of the bar were briefed, and now the quarrel became
public property. At this juncture my uncle proposed to me that
I should join the new firm that he was going to form, con-
sisting of himself, Charles, his second son, John, his third son,
and Edward, his fifth son. This partnership would have galleries in London, New York, and Paris, with a probable ex-
tension to Buenos Aires in the near future. I should have to
give up my very prosperous business in Liverpool; but I had
always looked upon my uncle as a father, and I accepted without hesitation.

A few weeks passed, and my uncle telephoned me one evening that he had to see me on a most important matter at eight the next morning. He wanted me to travel by the night-train from Liverpool to London and meet me at "Gangmoor," Charley's house, which was only a few hundred yards from "The Elms." During the journey I was perplexed to discover the reason for this mysterious discussion, held away from his own home. On arrival at "Gangmoor," I found my uncle already there. He had aged considerably during the few weeks that I had not seen him, and he had evidently been worrying. His first words confirmed my impression. He had not been sleeping well with all these worries, and now the other side had made a proposal for a settlement which worried him even more.

I was deeply moved by his evident distress, but also puzzled why he should want to see me in secret when others among the sons who had remained faithful to him were in London. When I mentioned my surprise he replied that he had already discussed the matter with them and that they were strongly against the settlement. He took a long document from his pocket and asked me to read it.

There were eight points that the other side suggested for a settlement. Five of these I considered fair, but three I thought unacceptable. Two of these clauses to which I objected were:

1. That the £300,000 that were invested in the firm in the name of his wife, and produced ten per cent interest per annum, should remain invested in the firm and should on her death be divided equally among *all* the children instead of leaving the disposal of this capital to her own discretion.

I pointed out that the sons who were in the firm were very much better off than the other children and that if their mother should wish to leave that part of her own fortune to those who were not so well off she should have the right to do so.

2. Part of the father's share in the firm should on his death not go to Ernest, the youngest son, as a junior partner.

I advised my uncle that he should reject this clause and insist that this part of the share should go to Ernest. I also pointed out that although the proposals by the other side for a diminution of his predominant share in the profits of the firm were unpleasant, he had also to consider that his own activities had become comparatively small. He objected that he had brought them all to their present position. Though I could not dispute this, I pointed out that he was now a very wealthy man and need not endanger his peace of mind and his health for the sake of increasing his fortune still further. This clinched the matter. He accepted my advice and said that he would settle if they gave in to the three minor points. Agreement was reached; but John, the third son, who was then only thirty-five, refused to remain a member of the firm. When I asked the reason he told me that he wanted peace and would never get it in that firm. He was able to retire with a handsome fortune; and although he bought very beautiful things from time to time, he never re-entered regular business.

The irony of this episode is that I became the victim of my own efforts for peace. Joe ultimately became aware of his father's intention to include me in the projected firm; and as he obtained this knowledge during the last phase, when he had gained complete mastery over his father's weakening mind, a codicil was added to the will revoking legacies to my mother, my brothers, and myself. Ten years later my uncle Henry at his death reversed the injustice of this intrigue by leaving me a handsome legacy.

By far the greatest sufferer was the father. His already delicate constitution had been worn down by this violent family quarrel in which his brother and two of his own sons had turned against him. When a year later he received the accolade from King Edward VII he was a dying man. Bright's disease, brought on by his worries, was killing him. The King, having heard of the weakness, granted a private audience for the ceremony; and when he saw the great weakness of the energetic man he had known he stopped him, with a smile and a friendly gesture, from kneeling for the accolade. The doctor who had accompanied him was in constant control and lived with his unhappy patient, whose mind was already tottering. This continuous watch aggravated the mental state of the suspicious patient and led repeatedly to distressing scenes. One day Joe, who at the time was in New York, received a cable from the doctor saying that he could not stand the strain any longer. Joe telephoned to the doctor, offering him a yearly salary of £6,000. The doctor refused to stay at any price. Joe ended the matter by saying that he would pay £6,000 if the doctor stayed "until the end." As at that time it looked as if the patient would not last longer than a few weeks, the man accepted; but although the patient's mind was growing weaker every day, the malady took a very slow course. Late in September it became necessary to protect the patient against the cold weather, and it was decided to send him to Hyères on the French Riviera. His brother Henry went to see him off at the station; but as he entered the reserved compartment Joel became furious and had to be restrained. The younger brother, who dearly loved him, hoped that this excitement would pass, and in the confusion no one noticed that the train had begun to move. Joel became more excited every second and, to prevent a fit or worse, the doctor pulled the communication cord. The train was brought to a standstill outside the station, and Henry was able to leave the train.

Joel died on November 9, 1908; he had become the greatest dealer in works of art the world had seen up to that time. He had created a gigantic business out of nothing. His capital was a dynamic energy allied with courage and a quick brain; but his greatest asset was an incomparable eye for beauty. Beginning as an almost unwanted employee in the wholesale produce-business and rising within a few months to a commanding position in it, he returned by accident to the vocation of his forebears as an importer of old works of art and brought his firm to unprecedented heights. The million-pound purchase of the Rodolphe Kann collection was the culmination of his career. From this foundation his younger brother, Henry, and his eldest son, Joseph, were able to carry the House of Duveen to towering heights that may never be reached again in the world of art-collecting.

Joel Duveen should have died a baronet, for he was offered a baronetcy in reward of his gift of the Turner Wing to the Tate Gallery; but this was prevented by his eldest son who, knowing that he himself would have no male issue, realized that this title would ultimately descend to his younger brother, Charles.

A quarter of a century after his father's death, when Sir Joseph Duveen, already a baronet, had been elevated to the peerage as Baron Duveen of Millbank, his younger brother, Edward, a director of Duveen Brothers, London, asked his eldest brother to allow his only son, Raymond, to learn the art-business in the firm so that a Duveen could carry on the family tradition. Joe, who was then president and sole owner of Duveen Brothers, London, Paris, and New York, replied: "I don't want any Duveen to come after me."

INDEX

Agnew, Messrs. (Messrs. Thos. Agnew & Son), 35, 114
Altman, Benjamin, 134, 190, 192, 229, 279–88

Baltazzi, Count, 236–7, 241–3, 249–50
Barnett, Barney, 27–33, 37, 40, 44, 45, 47–8, 114, 181
Barnett, Rosetta, *see* Duveen, Rosetta
Batthyany, Count, 238, 240–1
Behrman, S. N., 4
Bennett, Sir William, 196–7, 257–8, 288
Boas-Berg (Amsterdam dealer), 30–3, 123
Bode, Dr. Wilhelm von, 135, 190, 234–5, 251–5
Boucher, François, 66, 70, 98–100, 133, 146–7
Bushel, Dr., 260

Caffieri, Jacques, 177
Camorra, 267, 270–1
Canfield, Richard, 118–19
Caravaggio, 8
Carlhian & Beaumetz, 101
Carlin, Martin, 177
Carson, Sir Edward, 262–3
Ch'êng-Hua, 42
Ching-tê Chên, 42
Chippendale, 115–19
Clarke, Sir Andrew, 127–8
Clarke, Sir Edward, 196
cobalt blue, 41–3, 109
Cockshott, 88–90
Correggio, 8
Coureau, 92
Coypel, 173
Croiset, 141–2

Donatello, 252, 281
Dowdeswell Brothers, 134
Dreifus, Gustave, 252
Drucker, J. C. J., 91–2

i

Dumouriez and Gotschalk (provision merchants), 15–24, 26–8

Dürer, Albrecht, 281

Duveen, Annette, 84

Duveen, Betsy, 10, 12, 47–8, 51–60, 78, 96, 125–8, 181

Duveen, Catherine, 86

Duveen, Charles, 95, 107–8, 112–19, 214–15, 284, 289

Duveen, Dora, 79–80, 95

Duveen, Edward, 3–4, 121–3, 135–6, 289, 293

Duveen, Ernest, 291

Duveen, Esther, 10, 78–86, 96

Duveen, Eva (*née* van Minden): 11–13, 51

Duveen, Evaline, 84–5

Duveen, Sir Geoffrey, 5

Duveen, Henoch Joseph, 7, 9, 11

Duveen, Henri (Henri Hangjas), 10, 29–32, 40–4, 45–6, 51–2, 54, 173–81

Duveen, Henry Joseph: birth, 12; leaves home, 47; enters the business, 61–71; advice to the author, 83; characteristics, 93; marriage, 94; breaks with Joel, 95–6; makes it up, 97; in New York, 98, 103, 190–1; and Charles Duveen, 112; and Mons figure, 167–9; deals

Duveen, Henry Joseph (*continued*) with Pierpont Morgan, 111, 192–5, 259–60; stamp-collecting, 200–1, 207–11; and Kann collection, 213, 231; and Hainauer collection, 255; arrested, 263–5; and Altman, 279–83; place in firm, 289; legacy to James, 291

Duveen, James Henry (the author): writes the family history, 3–5; childhood, 10; meets Esther and enters business, 79–86; with uncles, 93; discovers Gobelins tapestries, 100; and Mr. Salting, 105–11; and Charles Duveen, 114–19; and Edward Duveen, 121–3; at uncle's illness, 125–30; and embarrassing Chinese vases, 137–44; and Mons figure, 160–9; and Don Quichotte tapestries, 170–2; and Mazzarenti collection, 182–91; and Lord Leverhulme, 193–4; and Joe's trickery in deals with Lord Leverhulme and Pierpont Morgan, 196–9, 213–14; in Liverpool, 200–11; Kann collection and Rembrandts, 212–34, 281–2; and Mayerling Mystery, 237–50; marriage and opening in Paris, 240; and Prin-

Duveen, James Henry (*continued*)
cess Metternich, 243–50; tricked again by Joe, whom he rescues, 257–65; adventure in Naples, 267–78; tricked again by Joe in deals with Altman and Mrs. Huntington, 283–8; kept out of the firm by Joe, 289–91

Duveen, Jeanette, 62

Duveen, Joel Joseph (Sir Joseph): founder of the firm, 4; early days, 9, 13–14; in the provision trade, 15–25; becomes an art-dealer, 26–36; buys hawthorn jar, 40–4; decides to set up in London, 45–50; the author's trustee, 53, 59; brings Henry into his firm, 62–70; moves to Oxford Street, 71–7; starts the author in business, 81; stops the author's engagement, 84–92; break with Henry, and reconciliation, 93–7; in New York, 98–103; and Mr. Salting, 104–8; and his sons, 122–4; illness, and visit of a swindler, 125–30; moves to Old Bond Street, 131; and Mons figure, 160–1, 166–8; and Don Quichotte tapestries, 170–81; and Mazzarenti collection, 182–91; and Lord Leverhulme and Pierpont

Duveen, Joel Joseph (*continued*)
Morgan, 193–4, 196–7; and Kann collection, 213, 228–36; advises the author, 259; trouble with Joe, 289–91; knighthood, 3, 10, 292; final illness, 4, 292–3; gives Turner Wing to Tate Gallery, 293

Duveen, John, 229, 289, 291

Duveen, Joseph, Lord (Joe): ability, 64; opposes sister's marriage, 85; characteristics, 94; quarrel with Charles, 114; his fortune, 123–4; in London, 134–6; and Pierpont Morgan, 195; trickery in deal with Lord Leverhulme, 197–9, 213–14; and Kann collection, 213, 229; and Charles Duveen, 215; spies on his father, 216; and Hainauer collection, 251–4, 256; tricks James Duveen, 257–8, 261–3; sued by James Duveen, 264–5; tricks James Duveen again, 284–8; keeps others out of the firm, 289–93; final ascendancy over father, 4

Duveen, Joseph (of Zwolle), 55, 59–60, 160–1, 170–7

Duveen, Joseph Henoch, 11

Duveen, Louis, 125–8, 196, 289

Duveen, Raymond, 293

Index

Duveen, Rosetta (*née* Barnett), 26, 47, 59, 75, 82, 84, 125–8

Edward VII, 3, 195, 292
egg-shell china, 37 ff.
Esher, Lord, 195

famille noire, 91, 164
famille rose, 37, 110, 168–9, 267
famille verte, 37, 107–10, 116, 160–9
Farquhar, Earl, 100–1
Fragonard, Jean, 133
Francis Joseph I, 237, 245, 249
Frenkel, 173–4
Fresco, Levy, 9

Garland, 106, 190, 192–4
Ghirlandaio, 231, 235
Gimpel and Wildenstein galleries, 133, 234
Giorgione, 8, 188, 225
Giustiniani, 278
Gobelins tapestry, 65–6, 68–9, 98–101, 146–7, 149
Gorer, Edgar, 287
Gouthière, Pierre, 68, 177
Greenwood, Mrs., 68
Grego, Henry, 44, 50

Hainauer collection, 251–6
Hamburger, 37–40

Hamburger, Mozes, 56–7
Handelaar, 100, 126–7
Hangjas, Anna (*née* de Misiers), 28
Hangjas, Henri, *see* Duveen, Henri
Hangjas, Jacob Levy, 9, 28–9, 38–40, 52, 54–5, 61
Hangjas, Joseph, 78
Hangjas, Levy Joseph, 7
hawthorn vases, 40–5
Hogg, O. M., 262–3
Holbein, Hans (the Younger), 281
Huntington, Mrs. Arabella, 236, 284–6
Huth, Henry, 50

Jabach, Eberhard, 8

K'ang-hsi, 42, 109, 283–8
Kann collection, 134, 213–15, 217, 228–36, 281, 293
Keyes, Nelson, 172
Koopmans brothers, 64
Kopp, Leo, 251, 253, 255–6
kylin, Chinese, 121–3

lange lyzen, 30–6, 104–5, 137–44
Largillière, Nicolas de, 133
Le Brun, Charles, 8
Leete, George, 152–5
Letts, Sydney, 117–18

iv

Lever, W. H. (Lord Lever-hulme), 142–4, 193–9
Lowengard, Armand, 5–6
Lowengard, Jules, 10, 49, 72–3, 84–6

manganese blue, 109–10
Marks, Murray, 110–11
May, Henry, 243–7
Mayerling Mystery, 237–50
Metternich-Sandor, Princess Clementine, 243, 246–9
Moens (Brussels dealer), 88
Morgan, John Pierpont, 111, 167–9, 189, 231, 235–6, 259–61

Nankin vases, 30–7, 58, 80–1, 137–44, 257–8
Neilson, Jacques, 99–101
Nichols, 33–4
"Night Watch" (Rembrandt), 218–23

Old Curiosity Shop (Dickens), 9
Orrock, James, 44, 74

Partridge, Robert, 50, 145–59
Petty, 145
Phillips, Messrs. (English dealers), 72, 88–9
Pius X, 260–1

Pompadour, Madame de, 99–100, 145–7
Prévinaire, 179–80

Rae, 33, 36
Raphael, 183, 186, 188, 189
Rembrandt, 213, 217–27, 229–34, 281–2
Ripon, Marquess of, 241, 262
Roentgen, David, 177
Rossellino, 252–3, 281
Rudolf, Archduke, 237, 241, 242–3, 245–50
Rumbold, Sir Horace, 120

Salting, George, 74, 104–11, 193
Samson copies, 40, 91
Scott, Ben, 82
Seligmann, Jacques, 195–6
Shêng-tsu, 42
Smith, F. E. (Earl of Birkenhead), 262
Steengracht collections, 281–2
Stoffels, Hendrickje, 224–6

Teunissen, Jan, 46, 88, 282
Titian, 8, 184, 225

Uylenborch, Saskia van, 217, 224, 282

Index

Van Dyck, Sir Anthony, 8, 231–2

van Esso, Ridder, 9, 11, 12, 54

van Zuylen van Nyevelt, Baron, 120

Velasquez, 281

Verrocchio, 110

Vetsera, Baroness Marie, 237, 249

Victoria and Albert Museum, 44

Vinci, Leonardo da, 135

Volant, Joseph, 160–1

Walters, Henry, 188–9

Watson, W., 95–6

Wertheimer, Asher, 91, 263

Widener, Joseph ("Joe"), 224

Widener, P. A. B., 224, 286

Wilhelm II, 253–5

Williamson, Dr. G. C., 189

Wilson, Arthur, 75–7, 87

A NOTE ON THE AUTHOR

James Henry Duveen was born in Haarlem, Holland, in 1873. He was educated in Holland and Belgium. Mr. Duveen studied for many years in the great art capitals—London, Paris, Naples, Florence, Berlin, Madrid—and pursued the exacting career of dealer in works of art from 1889 until 1923. Two volumes of his reminiscences, ART TREASURES AND INTRIGUE *(1935) and* SECRETS OF AN ART DEALER *(1938), have been published in the United States. A British subject since 1904, Mr. Duveen now lives at Whitchurch, Herefordshire.*

A NOTE ON THE TYPE

The text of this book was set on the Linotype in a face called *Eldorado*, so named by its designer, WILLIAM ADDISON DWIGGINS, as an echo of Spanish adventures in the Western World. The series of experiments that culminated in this type-face began in 1942; the designer was trying a page more "brunette" than the usual book type. "One wanted a face that should be sturdy, and yet not too mechanical. . . . Another desideratum was that the face should be narrowish, compact, and close fitted, for reasons of economy of materials." The specimen that started Dwiggins on his way was a type design used by the Spanish printer A. de Sancha at Madrid about 1774. Eldorado, however, is in no direct way a copy of that letter, though it does reflect the Madrid specimen in the anatomy of its arches, curves, and junctions. Of special interest in the lower-case letters are the stresses of color in the blunt, sturdy serifs, subtly counterbalanced by the emphatic weight of some of the terminal curves and finials. The roman capitals are relatively open, and winged with liberal serifs and an occasional festive touch.

This book was composed, printed, and bound by The Plimpton Press, Norwood, Massachusetts. Paper manufactured by S. D. Warren Company, Boston. Designed by Harry Ford.